HOW TO PREPARE A RESEARCH PROPOSAL

Guidelines for Funding and Dissertations in the Social and Behavioral Sciences

THIRD EDITION

It is hoped that this book's
suggestions will result in:
a) early recognition of good ideas
b) avoiding the loss of such ideas
because of inadequate presentations
c) more pioneering leads being funded.

HOW TO PREPARE A RESEARCH PROPOSAL

Guidelines for Funding
and Dissertations in the
Social and Behavioral Sciences

THIRD EDITION

David R. Krathwohl

Distributed by
SYRACUSE UNIVERSITY PRESS

DEDICATION

To our children: David, Ruth, Kristin,
and Jim (who left us early);
Kathy and Chris (who joined us later).

Each has added a splendid new dimension to our lives!

And how does it feel to live in nine dimensions?

Thanks to them, Absolutely Wonderful!!

Library of Congress Cataloging-in-Publication Data

Krathwohl, David R.
    How to prepare a research proposal.

    Bibliography: p.
    Includes index.
    1. Proposal writing in the social sciences.
I. Title.
HG177.K73 1988   658.1'5224   87-26768
ISBN 0-8156-8111-9
ISBN 0-8156-8112-7 (pbk.)

2

Third Edition, Copyright ©1988 David R. Krathwohl
Second Edition, ©1976, 1977
First Edition, ©1965, 1966

Distributed by
SYRACUSE UNIVERSITY PRESS
1600 Jamesville Avenue
Syracuse, New York 13244-5160
315-443-2597

Table of Contents

Section V
Suggestions and Insights
for Beginners and Doctoral Students

Appendices

List of Figures

Preface to the Third Edition

The public assumes the researcher spends the day dreaming up and trying out creative ideas. In reality, proposal development is an invisible but critical barrier over which even a good researcher may tumble. This book is intended to lower that barrier. It should increase first-trial recognition of good ideas and ensure that rejections do not result because a proposal poorly represented either the ideas, the investigator, or both. Like all communication, proposal writing is part science and part art. Classes in painting can instruct an artist in the principles of shading, contrast, and perspective, but the artist's creative use of these is critical. Thorough understanding of the condensed wisdom of past practice must be followed by imaginative application. That is the nub of excellent proposal writing. This book presents condensed wisdom from past practice.

Proposals have assumed increasing importance as agencies have tried to assure fair competition for resources. Often the proposal is the sole communication between proposer and sponsor for all but the very largest of grants. And even where supplemented by site visits, the proposal carries heavy weight as the main determiner of who is visited and what questions the visit is to answer. Therefore, skill in proposal writing is a must for those who seek resources.

Proposals are not only important for research, although that is the major emphasis of this book, they play a big role in business and nonprofit agency activity as well. Regardless of the purpose of the proposal, much of the basic logic and principles applies. Thus a substantial portion of this material is generic to proposal writing and useful to a variety of readers. In addition, Chapter 7 discusses a wide variety of proposal types and the adaptation of the basics for each type, from qualitative research to action proposals.

Funding agencies seek much the same information. Some use application forms, others outlines, and still others (especially foundations) leave the form of application to the proposer. The outline followed in this material is a general one, a composite of the organization and information required by various agencies, especially federal ones.

Organization of the Third Edition

The previous edition has been revised from stem to stern: material updated, sections strengthened and a great deal of new material added-- almost tripling the volume's size. This edition is organized in five sections: I) an introduction dealing with basic questions, II) the preparation of the proposal itself, III) a variety of aids to proposal preparation, IV) where and how to find funds (federal or foundation), and V) help for beginners and doctoral students. Three appendices contain new sources of additional information and readings, and there is a new glossary as well.

Section II, the heart of the book, divides the proposal into three parts:

the development and presentation of the problem (Chapter 3), how one intends to go about attacking it (Chapter 4), and the resources available and needed to carry out the project (Chapter 5). The section's final chapter deals with submission and negotiation. Included in the new material is a section on quantitative literature summaries (meta-analysis). The work plan section includes the wonderful new computer aids available for project planning, and its illustrative project is carried through a markedly enlarged treatment of the budgeting process in order to show the integrated nature of these two proposal parts.

But don't begin your reading with Section II. It needs to be considered with the background of Section I in mind. There is a new definition of the proposal in Chapter 1 that may cause you to think differently about the nature of a proposal. Further, the preproposal preparation material of Chapter 2 includes important new material modeling research as a chain of reasoning, a feature reflected in the proposal development chapters of Section II as well as amplified and put in perspective by a new chapter tracing the development of findings into knowledge, Chapter 11.

The variety of aids to proposal preparation in Section III includes an expanded and strengthened Chapter 7 dealing with the problems of 11 kinds of proposals, from qualitative research to action projects. The checklist for critiquing proposals that followed the table of contents in the previous edition has been given its own development in Chapter 8. Prepublication comments suggest that Chapter 9's proposal development process checklist is an extremely valuable addition. Its list of "things you may not have expected"--sources of unanticipated delays--may alone be worth the "price of admission." Chapter 10 on why proposals fail, includes new studies. The advice in Chapter 12 on writing is further developed in a section on writing in Chapter 17.

Section IV, on finding funding, is now more current and consistent with new federal procedures. New sources of information are given both in its chapters and in Appendices B and C as well.

Section V is entirely new. Although advice to beginners, the book's major users, is sprinkled throughout the book, this section reinforces some points and suggests new ones. Originally written to help the employed professional, previous editions have been found to be widely used by doctoral students. Therefore, two new chapters have been added for them.

A Note to Graduate Students and Dissertation Advisers

The last two chapters of the book are for you. Chapter 16 deals with understanding the different meaning and nature of the dissertation as viewed by students and by faculty and the consequences of these differing views. Chapter 17 traces the steps in the dissertation process from finding an adviser to choosing a committee, preparing the proposal, doing the dissertation, and passing the final oral. Suggestions and advice accompany each step. These chapters will give the greatest benefit if used early in doctoral study.

Proposal writing is of importance in a wide variety of positions, business as well as research, so practicing it before one's position is dependent on it and while faculty assistance is readily available makes just plain good sense. Chapters 3 through 5 are directly applicable to dissertation proposal development. Some students may wish to only skim the section on budget in Chapter 5, but they should not skip the section on the work plan, which helps them budget their one most valuable resource, their professional time.

Dissertations that might be eligible for small-grant programs should be considered for this possibility, which could provide for both research expenses and personal support. Time so purchased may permit more meaningful projects and a more realistic research experience. In addition, the student gains important skills not only in proposal writing but also in grant negotiating, managing, work scheduling, budgeting, possibly staff recruiting and supervision, and, most likely, publication. Somebody is winning these competitions and resources; it might as well be you.

Acknowledgments

I would like to thank the many individuals who have provided assistance for this and previous editions. Many of the students in my classes have suggested additions and corrections for which I am very grateful. In addition, I have had help in previous editions from Drs. Ted Andrews, Glenn Boerrigter, Brenda Bryant, Eric Gardner, Steve Gyuro, and Drew Lebby. I am most grateful for suggestions from William Wilson on Chapter 9 and from Paul Ilsley and his class. Mr. Wilson kindly gave permission to reprint the institutional checklist in Chapter 5. Jim Cox gave me great assistance and advice in using the MacIntosh computer for the graphics. Special thanks are due to individuals who allowed me to interview them for the chapters on doctoral studies or who contributed to them. Among those are Ralph Brockett, Vernon Hall, Gus Root, Jane Root, Ruth Norton, Burt Sisco, Sharon Senk, and Lorraine Terracina. Mrs. Dorothy Sickles kindly provided editorial assistance for the first edition. Mrs. Kristin Christlieb has been extremely helpful in editing this edition, and Ms. Linda Froio has superbly and tirelessly entered the text and innumerable changes into the word processor. I am especially grateful to Rephah Berg, who did the final editing of this edition. She did such a superb job on my 1985 book I was pleased she was willing to undertake this one. Her changes and suggestions have improved it immensely!

Despite all this wonderful help, every author wonders whether some errors remain. I hope not, but if so, please call them to my attention so they may be eliminated in reprinting for later readers. Suggestions are always welcome; write to me at:

335 Huntington Hall	David R. Krathwohl
Syracuse University	July 9, 1987
Syracuse, New York 13244-2340	

Section I
Introduction

Chapter 1 sets the target for the book by defining the nature of the proposal. Though not conventional, the definition there foreshadows many of the themes emphasized later in the description of the process of proposal preparation.

Chapter 2 poses and answers basic questions about the proposal-writing process and, along with Chapter 11, provides background and perspective on the situation in which the proposal writer works.

1.

Introduction

What is a proposal? "That's obvious," you say, "let's get on with it!" I'd agree with you, except that it always pays to have a precise idea of where one is going; it makes it so much easier to get there!

So what is a proposal? It is a document that presents the case for an idea and the action one proposes to take with respect to it. Some people think of it as a sales document. It certainly has some aspects of that; typically a sales document assumes that the proposer knows best, and the task of the proposal is to bring the reviewer around to that way of thinking. Many successful proposals are written from that point of view; and there are, no doubt, instances where one can justify such a frame of mind. But in general, I tend to think that the proposer, the reviewer, and the proposal approval system are better served by viewing the process as one of shared decisionmaking--one in which the proposer does the best possible job of enthusiastically setting forth the proposed study, and the reviewers give the proposal their fullest consideration in judging its chances of success. Viewing the process this way has several advantages:

- What you are proposing has never been done before exactly as you propose to do it, so you and the reviewer are sharing some kind of risk if it is approved. Shared decisionmaking is a much more appropriate frame of mind when professional reputations, energy, time, and resources are ventured by both sides.
- Sharing the decisionmaking takes maximum advantage of the reviewer's ability to test the worth of the idea. Sneaking the ideas past the reviewer with a successful sales pitch doesn't.
- A sales job can come unstuck on sober reflection; but a judgment, carefully formulated, is much less likely to do so. Indeed, if you later need additional resources or help, a solidly based judgment is likely to result in the reviewer's real commitment to the project--a stance conducive to getting the help you need. Further, in most instances you are building a relationship: you'll be back again.
- If, even though you have presented your ideas adequately, a reviewer turns the proposal down for substantive reasons, she[1] may have done you a favor (although it may take a bit of time to realize it). You may have been saved from venturing a substantial amount of your time and energy in a useless quest. In those instances, a successful sales job would have been to your detriment. Shared decisionmaking may save you a misstep.

Most reviewers are experienced and/or have some special qualifications for making the judgment requested. Although as gate-keepers, they may be viewed by some proposers simply as problems to be

---

[1]Because of the lack of a neutral pronoun, masculine and feminine forms will be used randomly throughout the book to avoid the awkward "he/she" and "his/her" forms.

gotten around, in reality reviewers want good ideas to succeed.   It reflects favorably on them! Keeping that fact in mind results in a more positive attitude toward the staff and reviewers. Let that attitude show through in your writing!

All of the above assumes that you presented your case in such a way that the reviewer could fully encounter it, could make what *you*   consider a fair judgment based on a perception of the idea and actions *that you intended.* Somebody (I wish I knew who) once said, "Books exist in the minds of readers. It really doesn't matter what the author intended at all." Of course it matters! It matters a great deal to you. You want what "exists in the minds of readers" to be what you intended. But the old saying is right--*it is what your writing conveys to the reader that is judged, regardless of what you intended!*

It is because the reviewer's image of the proposal and proposer is so often *not* what was intended--the case for the study is not well made *but could have been*--that books like this have value.   Adequate and appropriate presentation of an idea is a skill that can be learned. This book's intent is to help you learn it.

So we have begun to define a proposal and to explain what underlies that definition. To help you with the material that follows, however, we need a more explicit definition of a proposal that both is compatible with the one with which we began and amplifies and operationalizes it. So, what is a proposal?

Basically, a research proposal describes a plan of work to learn something of real or potential significance about an area of interest. It is a logical presentation. Its opening problem statement draws the reader into the plan: showing its significance, describing how it builds upon previous work (both substantively and methodologically), and outlining the investigation.   The whole plan of action flows from the problem statement: the activities described in the design section, their sequence illuminated graphically in the work plan, their feasibility shown by the availability of the resources in the personnel and facilities statement, and their economic efficiency demonstrated by the budget. The enthusiasm of the proposal carries the reader along; the reader is impressed with the proposal's perspective on the problem; it reassures the reader with its technical and scholarly competence; and it provides the reader with a model of the clarity of thought and writing that can be expected in the final report. The reader comes away feeling that this is an opportunity to support research that should not be missed.

I can hear you mumbling to yourself, "That is a great definition, but hardly compatible with all that talk about not being a sales job!" Not true!   First, it simply recognizes the fact that if *you* cannot be enthusiastic about your idea, it is a lot to expect others to be. Material can be written interestingly and still present the idea with integrity. It doesn't have to be boring to be good. Second, the definition points out that the proposal is an integrated chain of reasoning that makes strong logical connections between your problem statement and the coherent plan of action you are proposing to undertake. Look for the discussion of this point in the next chapter under the heading "Does the Proposal Flow Logically from Section to Section?" Third, as this modified definition makes clear, it is not only your idea and action plan that are subject to consideration but also your capability to successfully carry them through. This is particularly true if you have no previous record of success or if your success is not known to the reviewer. Your proposal is the only evidence the reviewer has of your capabilities. Realizing this is half the battle; the other half is presenting yourself adequately and appropriately. Look for later discussions of this also.

Finally, let's pull it together and add a few realities. Once more, "What is a proposal?" It is an opportunity for you to present your idea and proposed actions for consideration in a shared decision-making situation. You, with all the integrity at your command, are helping the reviewer to see how you view the situation, how the idea fills a need, how it builds on what has been done before, how it will proceed, how pitfalls will be avoided, why pitfalls not avoided are not a serious threat, what the consequences are likely to be, and what significance they are likely to have. It is not a sales job but a carefully prepared, enthusiastic, interestingly written, workmanlike presentation. Your presentation displays your ability to assemble the foregoing materials into an internally consistent chain of reasoning. It is tailored to fit the maximum length allowed and to facilitate the review process. Is that what you thought a proposal was? Well, whether it was or not, now you know where we want to go. And that makes it easier to get there.

Helping you get there is what this book is about. Most aspects of the definition receive further elaboration in Section II, "Preparing and Submitting the Proposal." Some, however, are in the next chapter's discussion of general questions to be considered before full-scale proposal development efforts are begun.

2. General Considerations in the Preparation of Proposals

This chapter, organized as a series of questions and answers, discusses considerations that should enter your thinking at an early stage. It also addresses questions in the back of your mind such as "How 'fancy' should the physical appearance be?" Finally, it alerts you to some important points to look for in the following three chapters, which discuss preparation of the full proposal.

1. *What Are the Steps in Proposal Development?*

How does a proposal develop? There are many ways, but the most successful ones usually start with an idea. An idea starts the search for funding, rather than funding motivating the search for an idea.[1] But while projects typically start with an idea, sponsors fund activities, not ideas. Admirable intentions and good ideas are a great start, but sponsors are buying what you plan to *do*. So it is your activities that determine whether your project is an effective investment of their resources.

"All right," you say to yourself, "I have an idea, and I've already thought about the activities involved. Can we get started on the proposal writing?" Possibly. Certainly what you would create at this point would go a long way toward satisfying what goes into a proposal. But think a minute. If you were describing the proposal to a professional colleague, would you describe it the same way as you would to your best nonprofessional friend? Hardly! The audience makes a big difference, and your intended sponsor is your audience. If you expend the effort to develop a proposal, you want it to communicate and be attractive to the sponsor, meet that sponsor's program and submission criteria, and be designed to maximize its chances in that program's review process. That means you must not only know how to translate your idea into appropriate activities, but you must also know your sponsor, your audience.

Therefore, before too completely formulating a proposal, you should take the time to identify potential sponsors[2]--one of the first steps in the overview of the proposal development process is shown in figure 1. That process starts with the research idea (box 1), which is tentatively translated into a set of activities (box 2), which is used to locate a sponsor (boxes 3-5). Matters to consider in determining the match between your

---

[1]Rogers et al. (1970) found a 40% success rate for those who had an idea they wanted to get funded in comparison with only 24% for those who thought up an idea when they became aware that funds were available.

[2]Students preparing dissertation proposals already know their audience: their chair and committee. The dissertation process is discussed in Chapters 16 and 17. Such students may markedly benefit from having a funding sponsor as well, so keep reading.

Figure 1. The Proposal Development Process

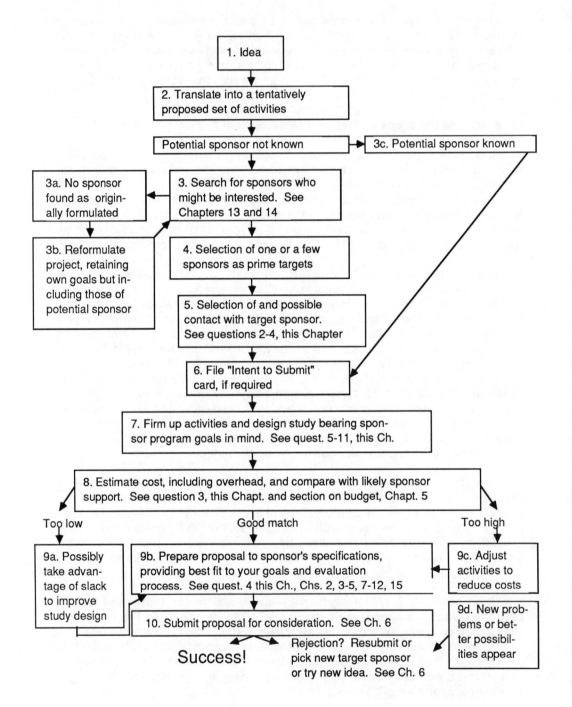

idea and the potential sponsor's funding program are given detailed consideration as the next question in this chapter. Information on how to find potential sponsors is in Section IV, "Finding Funding."

As indicated there, learn as much as possible about the program and its administration. If you are interested in a federal program, send for an application package, which will contain the basic information the program staff feels you should know. Study it well; find the best possible fit of what you wish to do with what a sponsor desires. The better this match, the greater your chances of obtaining funding.

If there is any doubt that your project is appropriate for the agency under consideration, the staff should be contacted (box 5). In fact, even if your project clearly falls within program guidelines, an inquiry may be in order. Don't expect a funding commitment, just a reaction that suggests whether it may be worthwhile to invest time in a full proposal. Your inquiry may also excite the interest of staff in your proposal, always a good sign (more detail on this in the third question in this chapter). Preparing a brief two- to four-page description of the project to test the reaction of potential sponsors is a good idea. Leave the description somewhat open so that sponsors may have the fun of helping you with the design if they wish. Further, if the project does not already fit their goals, they can then mold it to theirs as well as yours.

But what if no good match exists? You may need to decide whether to scale down the project to accommodate your limited resources or to adjust what you want to do so that it fits some sponsor's program (boxes 3a and 3b). Maybe you will have to investigate the phenomenon in an applied rather than a laboratory setting, or you may have to use certain kinds of subjects, such as handicapped children. If these changes still allow you to achieve enough of what you want to do, however, the adjustment is worth it. So be flexible about your project, but keep an eye fixed on where you want to go and how this choice of sponsor might take you there.

Once you have located a sponsor worthy of the investment, begin preparation of a proposal that will be attractive to that person or agency (box 5). Firm up your ideas and think through your proposal in detail (box 7). If you are applying for a federal program with deadlines, you may be requested to file an "intent to submit" form (box 6). (See p. 117.) This enables the sponsor to know how many reviewers to have ready and what kind of secretarial staff will be needed to handle the flood of applications. The "intent to submit" form is usually a simple postcard stating a tentative title as well as your name and address. Occasionally sponsors will send additional information to those filing such a card, so it is a good idea to complete one even if it is not required.

Researchers who already have an appropriate sponsor in mind (box 3c) can short-cut this process and move immediately to box 6.

Before beginning to fully develop your ideas, cost them out, not in detail but accurately enough that you know your request is within the realm of possibility for your sponsor (box 8). You usually will not want to exceed the sponsor's typical range of project funding--especially if this is your first project. If the price tag is too big (box 9c), see where you can cut and still retain the integrity of the design. If you have been so cost-conscious in the development of the project that the total is well within the sponsor's limits (box 9a), you may wish to take advantage of possible additional resources to strengthen the design. Knowing the typical range of project funding, keep your aspirations realistic but also try to allow for the resources needed to build the strongest possible proposal.

In most institutions, only about two-thirds of the funds given by the sponsor is available to the researcher for project expenses; one's organization retains the rest as overhead. Be sure to ascertain whether this is true of your institution and take this into account in estimating your budget. Experienced researchers need only be reminded of this fact of life. Researchers unfamiliar with project budgeting may find it useful to skip ahead and read "Preparing for Budget Development" (p. 89).

Preparation of the full proposal (box 9b) may accompany your development of the design of the study; or, more often, it is undertaken after you have satisfactorily thought it through. Particularly as you are still developing your ideas, but even after they are presumably fully developed, you may discover problems or find new and better ways of doing the study which will lead to new adjustments starting at box 7. At some point (usually the program deadline; or, without a deadline, on reaching a reasonable level of satisfaction) one calls a halt to the process and submits the proposal for consideration (box 10).

2. *Is the Proposal within the Scope of the Funder's Program?*

Sponsors cannot support every area of research if they hope to have an impact, and for most sponsors, that is their *raison d'être*. Similarly, government agencies are expected to have an impact on the areas of concern described by the laws establishing their programs. Both Congress (through its hearings) and the current administration interpret these laws and modify their focus. Philanthropic foundations similarly are bounded, initially, by their founder's intent. Later, administrators and trustees set the goals interpreting the founder's wishes in such a way as to have the greatest impact on their area of special concern or interest.

Boundaries around program scope. Because a funding agency typically concentrates its resources in one or a few areas, the proposal *must be perceived as within those boundaries to receive consideration.* Most of the large philanthropic foundations will supply an annual report, which lists recently funded projects. The list tells you what has, in practice, been emphasized, regardless of the foundation's stated goals. In some instances, personal communication by letter or phone will reveal additional areas, perhaps new ones or ones in which the foundation gave no grants because it received no proposals worthy of funding.

Most government agencies have application packets. These usually include a reprint from the *Federal Register* of the regulations describing program goals, the authorizing legislation, and sometimes a list of the previously funded projects. Again, personal communication about your project may be helpful. If you must save phone expense, call federal offices when the staff are not likely to be in, as during the lunch hour; they will return your call on the federal telephone system.

Successful federally funded proposals are in the public domain under the Freedom of Information Act, so that one can either ask to see them, if visiting the agency's office, or request copies at a reasonable fee. Do not follow these as ideal models but as illustrations and sample interpretations of program guidelines.

When agencies have more than one program, find which one is appropriate. An action-oriented proposal might fail to be supported under an applied research program but be quite appropriate in a demonstration or development program. Agencies may reroute a proposal sent to the wrong program, but the larger the agency and/or the more pressed the personnel, the rarer such service. *Learning program goals and finding the right program is your responsibility.*

Boundaries around the nature of applicants. Frequently there are qualifications regarding who can apply and be funded. Sometimes these are geographical, as when an industrial foundation restricts grants to the cities in which it has plants, or a federal program seeks proposals from regions or clientele unfunded in previous competitions. Often these restrictions are organizational, perhaps limited to nonprofit organizations or to universities that apply in conjunction with a school district (be careful to work out who controls what budget items in the latter relationship). Foundations usually give grants only to nonprofit organizations, not individuals. An individual researcher not so affiliated will have difficulty even getting considered. Such individuals should consult Margolin's excellent book (1983) specifically designed to help individuals get grants on their own.

Boundaries around project cost. Lists of past projects suggest typical sponsor funding for projects. That doesn't mean they won't exceed those amounts for the right proposal, but it gives you some idea of the size that may pass without special scrutiny. For federal programs, staff can tell you the size of current appropriations and whether these are increasing, decreasing, or stable. If they are decreasing, although standards are not supposed to change with the vicissitudes of funding, there is some tendency to be more discriminating. Further, in an effort to stretch fewer dollars, the average size of awards may be reduced. In such circumstances you may wish to be extra careful in preparing your proposal and budget to fit the constraints. Learn how much of current appropriations is available to start new projects; frequently a substantial portion is already committed to previously approved projects--in a decreasing appropriation situation, sometimes all.

Boundaries resulting from institutional requirements. Certain sponsor requirements may not be acceptable to your institution. For example, some sponsors may require that your institution share costs beyond what it is willing or able to do. They may require that your institution be willing to continue the project beyond the end of sponsor support. Some sponsors, especially defense establishment agencies, may require that the work be classified as "secret" or otherwise restrict its dissemination; many universities will not accept research with such restrictions. Each sponsor makes its own unique demands, and its requirements should be checked for their fit to your particular situation.

3. *Have Funding Agency Staff Been Appropriately Used in Project Formulation?*

Put yourself in the role of an agency staff member who is trying to make a difference, to have some impact with the available funds. Now, consider that many agencies expect staff to wait for projects to come to them. That could be frustrating, couldn't it? Therefore, staff seek, among the opportunities that come to them, persons and projects that will maximize program success, attaining self-fulfillment when their choices succeed. Discovering you, helping you formulate your project and carry it through, and especially enjoying acclaim for your work must satisfy these needs. Your success indirectly reflects on them; thus, your relations to them can be very important. This is especially true of a foundation, but it holds to a considerable extent in government as well. When you approach staff about your project, remember to show them how their helping you will be of the greatest help to them and their program.

Competing programs occasionally vie with one another for the best and most prestigious "stable" of researchers who routinely turn to them for funding. Being associated with successful projects and with prominent researchers and research institutions both impresses Congress and helps programs obtain increased funds in good times and protects them against cuts in hard ones.

If you are accustomed to direct action, you can understand why the passive role of merely reacting to submitted proposals may be frustrating. Partly as a matter of self-fulfillment, partly to find projects that achieve their sponsor's goals, program staff move toward an active role: seeking out, rather than waiting for, proposals; approaching researchers with ideas rather than waiting for them to come in; and seizing the opportunity to mold proposals in desired directions when visitors try out their pet ideas.

Whether the staff takes a proactive stance depends on the agency. Staff roles appropriate for one may be inappropriate for another; agencies differ markedly in this respect. Foundation staff more typically play proactive roles than government staff. In some instances, foundation trustees routinely approve staff recommendations, so that foundation staff actively become the program definers. Philanthropic foundations run the range from those that commit all their resources to staff-initiated projects to those that react solely to what is received. Most funding agencies, both governmental and private, fall somewhere between.

In the federal government, the naturally proactive tendencies of a competent professional staff tend to be unleashed in cycles. Administrations just voted into power exhort staff to play an active role in shaping programs into new images. Staff members work with proposers to shape proposals to the agency's new central mission. When these projects are successful in getting funded, staff are often accused by those not funded of helping friends or giving favors. Investigations follow appeals to members of Congress. Even when no wrongdoing is uncovered, the investigations tend to inhibit staff activity. For protection, staff may relegate some or even all of the decision making to panels and consultants and limit themselves to paper shuffling. But this, too, is unsatisfactory. Not only are staff restless, but judging panels rarely have a sharp conception of the overall program; the focus becomes blurred. Both administration and Congress demand staff action to focus program funding and the cycle begins again. Although such cycles appear less frequent than in the past, their nature is worth remembering; and it is always useful to know where a staff is in a cycle.

The government's efforts to have its cake and eat it too--avoid charges of favoritism but have the staff develop sharply defined and targeted programs--have dampened the cycle. To avoid charges of favoritism, government agencies have 1) developed elaborate procedures to make public all the rules of each competition, 2) established central proposal-receiving centers to ensure deadline compliance, and 3) developed detailed regulations controlling the "request for proposal" (RFP) process to purchase services or products.

The federal RFP process provides a means for a proactive staff to sharply define specific projects and, through these projects, a focused program. The process includes a formal set of rules governing staff roles and provisions for staff to define, as completely as they wish, the proposal they would like to fund. Staff then request proposals bidding for the opportunity to carry out the RFP and select the best. Conducted according to the rules, this procedure provides a proactive stance for staff and fairness for bidders. But it also means that the staff writes the research proposal and bidders are reduced to the role of implementing a project that was mostly designed by someone else. That can make the best and most creative researchers unhappy, and they tend to ignore an RFP that is too prescriptive. This, in turn, forces staff to at least a middle ground of specification if they want such researchers to bid on the contract. But RFPs were intended to be confined to procuring a product or completing a specified activity, such as evaluating a particular program, rather than used to carry out a research project.

It is difficult to generalize about the openness of staff to new ideas. The maturity of both program and staff may affect openness. Newer programs and staff tend to be more expansive, to be willing to try things that have an off chance of working. Mature staff tend to use past experience to categorize new proposals as likely or unlikely to succeed.

They are more wary of offbeat possibilities, having been humbled by failures. Thus they may close off avenues that are still viable. But, apropos of the difficulty of generalizing, some new staff who want success quickly may confine early efforts to "sure bets." Secure, mature staff may be willing to take a chance that new staff may feel is too risky. Don't prejudge staff on the basis of experience; feel them out or talk to those who have had experience with them.

Try out your idea with the staff even if you have little doubt about its appropriateness. A phone call or, even better, a personal visit can elicit not only information but often staff interest in the project. This can be crucial with foundations. It may be equally critical with government agencies, however, depending on the role of staff there. This point is discussed further in answer to the next question on evaluation procedure.

One can more readily establish rapport if one knows something about the staff members before approaching them. Many belong to professional associations--e.g., the American Psychological Association, American Sociological Association--and are listed in membership directories that are expanded every three to five years to include recent biographical information. Background on staff may also be found in *Who's Who* or similar registries. When you attend professional meetings or conventions, gather information from colleagues about their experiences. Such information not only provides a basis for striking up a relationship with staff, it shows staff you respect them, you are motivated to succeed, you've done your homework--all signs of a good prospect. Approach staff prepared!

The above is intended to just begin this topic. There is more in "Finding Funding," Section IV.

4. Have You Considered the Implications of the Procedure by Which the Proposal Will Be Evaluated?

It pays to learn all you can about the review procedure. Knowledge of the review procedure will reveal what parts of the proposal are given the most use or the most careful scrutiny and thus will suggest what sections ought to be carefully detailed and precisely worded. Sometimes knowledge of the members of the group that will review the proposal suggests particular concerns and signals key proposal sections. The composition of the review committee can sometimes be learned by requesting this information from the reviewing agency, but usually no attempt is made to disseminate it widely. Most often, a list of names of reviewers is furnished from among which panels of reviewers of individual projects will be selected.

Knowledge of the review process sometimes brings to light the fact that the panel or group of field readers who must give initial approval to a project includes one or more nonspecialists. They are useful in preventing what has been called the "specialist veto," prejudices of experts that result more from history or tradition than from reason. "We have had too many studies using multiple regression to predict achievement." "Perhaps so, but take another look at this one; doesn't it have some aspects that merit funding?" Sometimes a panel includes a nonresearcher to give the practitioner's point of view.

Having a nonspecialist among the readers means that the proposal must be written so as to communicate to that person as well as the specialists. One must avoid or explain jargon. One must not assume prior acquaintance with the problem, its importance, previous work, the value of certain instruments or procedures, and so on. Writing "down," if carried too far, may make the proposal boring for the specialists. However, writing jargon-free prose is a worthy goal for almost any document. Do your best to find the right balance.

Similarly, it is common practice to include at least one reader with special competence in the research design and methodology of the field. Therefore, *the proposal should include sufficient detail for these areas to be judged.*

Typically, a committee, council, or administrator reviews a panel's recommendation or the field readers' consensus. These persons will usually be less specialized and have different backgrounds than those giving initial approval. Because they usually oversee a large number of projects, they are likely to read only the project abstract or a staff memorandum often derived from that abstract. This points both to the importance of the abstract and to the necessity that it be jargon-free so as to communicate to nonspecialists.

Some agencies remove budgets and other identifying information before proposal evaluation. The intent is to focus attention on the problem and the research approach, disregarding personalities, salaries, size of overhead, budget total, or other potentially provocative items. Similarly, requests for proposals (RFPs) sometimes ask for separate technical, business, and/or administrative proposals. If this procedure will be used in the competition you are entering, consider whether removal of identifying information or budget might remove materials important to fair consideration of the proposal and, if so, put that information in the body of the proposal.

Staff member roles. Staff roles in the judgment and selection process differ from program to program depending on tradition, legislation, and whether they are in a government bureau or a philanthropic foundation. Certain roles are fairly typical, however.

Staff members may fulfill the following roles, arranged in order of increasing influence on the funding decision:

1. Serve as secretary to a panel whose members have multiyear staggered terms; the panel has the responsibility for approval or disapproval of proposals.
2. Same as (1), but the panel makes recommendations for review by

the staff members.

3. Select reviewers to whom the proposal is sent and accept their decision.

4. Same as (3), but the reviewers' recommendations are subject to approval by the staff member.

5. Personally make a decision for or against approval and then participate with other staff in the review of proposals, making recommendations to a supervisor (e.g., a cabinet-level officer or director named by legislation or a foundation executive) and/or a board that finalizes the decision.

6. Personally make the decision for approval, which is subject to review by a supervisor.

7. Same as (6), but the decision, if reviewed by a supervisor or board, is routinely approved.

Any of these staff decisions, depending on legislation and/or operating procedure, may be subject to concurrence by a board, council, or advisory body, e.g., the board of trustees of a foundation or the National Advisory Council of the National Institutes of Health. Although this scrutiny is often routine, some of these bodies take an active role; and occasionally, somnolent ones erupt into action, though rarely without rumblings foretelling, like earthquakes, a pending upheaval.

Staff roles 1-4 are typical of federal procedures and are usually combined with approval by an advising body and/or a top-level executive (director or cabinet-level executive). Role 5 is used in some agencies, for initial screening, when it is requested that a proposal be further developed for panel consideration. It is also typical of large foundation procedures. Role 6 is more typical of medium-size foundations with several staff members; role 7 is common in small foundations with a single, often part-time, staff member who may be a lawyer or, if still living, the founder herself.

The proposal writer will obviously want to know where a given staff member stands in the list above--especially whether she is responsible to reviewers merely for the clerical aspects of the proposal process or whether she takes an active role in selecting and advising reviewers, summarizing their comments, or otherwise shaping the ultimate decision. And the proposal writer will want to know whether the staff's decision is routinely approved or actively reviewed.

Suggestions and advice from staff members need to be viewed in relation to those persons' role in the decision-making process. The more voice they have in the decision, the more seriously you must view their comments as affecting your chances of success. The less voice they have, the more you must learn about the rest of the decision-making structure.

Past criticism that the panel system favors members of a field's "inner circle" has resulted in staff roles 4-7. Since a staff member usually knows which reviewers are "easy markers" and which are highly critical, the third role on the list also gives the staff considerable voice in the decision. Even when they play a largely functionary role, as in role 1, they may have insights that are very helpful, since they know which reviewer's comments are most influential. Consultation with staff is generally helpful. In fact, Rogers et al. (1970) found that the success rate of writers who discussed their proposal with staff was a third higher than that of those who did not.

One of the best ways to learn how judges in a particular program evaluate proposals is to talk with those who have been reviewers. Surprisingly, often they are one's colleagues or persons who can be easily contacted at a professional convention. Failing this, one can sometimes find those who have been reviewers in similar programs. Such people will paint a more graphic and current picture than can possibly be portrayed here. Names of past reviewers for federal programs are usually available from program staff.

An even better way is to become a reviewer oneself. Staff are continually having to replenish their reviewer list. Inquire about this possibility, especially if your research record has begun to be established. If they have all the reviewers they need at the moment, ask whether they will put your vita on file for future openings.

Cavin (1984) is an excellent reference for learning the variety of external review processes. Those used by five federal programs are described in detail: Fund for Improvement of Postsecondary Education; Office of Special Education and Rehabilitation Services, Department of Education; Office of Postsecondary Education, Department of Education; National Science Foundation; and National Endowment for the Humanities. It also contains a useful bibliography on the peer review process.

Criteria used in evaluating proposals. In an effort to avoid charges of favoritism, each federal program announcement (these are published in the *Federal Register*) includes the criteria by which proposals will be judged. Criteria and their weightings are also given in each request for proposal (RFP). The relative values of the criteria are indicated by distributing 100 points among them or by a percentage (e.g., design 40%, personnel 20%, budget 20%). This information tells you what needs to be given special care in proposal preparation and/or emphasized in the text. Be sure to obtain these criteria and heed their implications. (See Chapter 13 for further details.)

The author has been involved in judging proposals where the published criteria were poorly conceived. Presumably this is currently less frequent, but staff positions turn over, and institutional memories are short, so it still occasionally occurs. Where you think this may have happened, accepting the criteria at face value may be poor strategy. It depends on the part the government lawyers are called on to play. If the lawyers are consulted, they will force staff and reviewers to use the announced criteria as best they can under the circumstances. Failing that, they must hold a new competition. Since everyone wants to avoid starting over, what usually happens is that the old criteria get special definitions that permit them to be used. Where you think this might occur, try to anticipate how the criteria might be subtly adjusted and change your writing accordingly.

How the variability among competing proposals affects final rankings. The weighting in the federal program announcement indicates the importance of a criterion and determines the maximum score that can be assigned for satisfying it. But what counts in competitions is the size of that score relative to the scores of competitors (the variability of scores among competitors). That determines the ranking for funding. With requests for proposals (RFPs) where there is only one winner, being ranked first is all that counts. Even in grant competitions, funds frequently do not stretch to include all the proposals that are approved for funding; the highest possible ranking becomes the goal.

Since ranking is so critical, one must understand that in addition to the weightings given the criteria, the variability of scores on the various criteria determines the ranks. Consider a simplified example in which there are only two criteria, procedure and budget. Procedure counts 90 points out of the total of 100 and budget only 10. Now suppose that projects in this competition are given scores on budget that range from a low of 1 to a high of 10; there is considerable variability in the ratings. The procedure section, because of its importance, counts 90 points, however. It was very completely prescribed in the federal program announcement, not an unusual situation with RFP's. Therefore, all proposals were very much the same in this section, so the scores range only from 87 to 90, very little variability. Consider what happens when these two scores are added together. Even though the procedure score is 9 times the budget score in size, being at the top of the procedure score, a 3 point advantage at most, will help very little. *The budget score, with its range from 1 to 10, will almost completely determine the top few ranks* because its variability is so much greater than that of the procedure score. Criteria on which competitors score alike contribute little to the rankings even when they have a heavy weighting relative to other criteria.

Conversely, sections of the proposal where criterion scores vary greatly from proposal to proposal can contribute strongly to the rankings. Note, however, that the example above was rigged to show how even a relatively unimportant criterion can overpower an important one. By the terms of that competition, the variability of budget was constrained to 10 points while procedure could have ranged over 90 points. Clearly, had there been even modest variability on reviewers' ratings of procedure, it would have mightily overpowered budget. So one has to look at both weighting and extent of possible variability; *the most critical factors are those that are heavily weighted AND have great variability.*

Thus, if it is possible to predict on which criteria proposals will differ most widely in scoring, especially if these are heavily weighted criteria, it is obvious where to focus attention in proposal preparation. Be sure, however, that your other sections will at least meet the competition in satisfying the criteria applying to them.

5. *Does the Proposal Flow Logically from Section to Section?*

One of the most helpful points to remember is that the end goal of research that produces or validates a generalization is the development of a carefully constructed chain of reasoning. Some quantitative and experimental research operationally proceeds as the straightforward construction of a logical, deductive chain, but most proposal outlines seem to assume that *all* research is done this way. This is not true--not even of all quantitative research or of the best research. Further, most qualitative and exploratory research projects derive their generalizations inductively. *But research reports of both quantitative and qualitative research presenting findings supportive of a generalization do so deductively as a chain of reasoning.* Figure 2 portrays a prototypical chain of reasoning representing how a research study is usually reported. The research quest begins with an area of interest. This interest prompts one to examine the literature to determine what is already known about that area. Out of that examination, one builds forward from the past literature, profiting from past mistakes and strengths and presenting the strongest possible conceptualization of the problem.

If this permits one to make a prediction, then, in the next link, that prediction is presented as a hypothesis. If the prior evidence will not permit this, then a question describing the focus of attention is formulated so that one knows where to look and perhaps what to look for. If prior research permits, one might have a model that suggests the interrelation of the variables.

The question, hypothesis, or model forms the basis for the design of the study. In a very real sense a hypothesis or prediction translates into the structure of the study's research design. That translation involves six aspects: 1) subjects, 2) situation, 3) observations or measures, 4) treatment or experimental variable (independent variable or process for nonexperimental research), 5) the basis of comparison by which one knows that the treatment or experimental variable had some effect (or in nonexperimental research, how things changed as activity continued), and 6) the procedural plan, which determines what observations are made, when, where, and of whom, and if there is a treatment, how, where, when, and to whom it is administered.

For example, consider the hypothesis, as did Rowe (1974), that increasing the amount of time that the teacher typically waits before calling on a student (one second on average before training, three to five seconds on average after training) would improve the nature of classroom discourse. The "subjects" were the teachers and students in the classrooms where this was demonstrated. The "situation" was the classroom; in this instance, as in many, the choice of the "subjects" determined the "situation." The "treatment" was the teacher's increase in "wait-time." To attain delayed "wait-time" without embarrassment or discomfort, the teachers were trained to be sure the "treatment" was administered as intended. "Observations" included measures of effect such as recordings of classroom discourse to determine who talked and what kind of teacher-pupil interchange took place. There were also measures of the teacher's wait-time to ensure that it actually increased. To provide a "basis of comparison," measures of both wait-time and classroom discourse prior to teacher training were gathered to compare with posttraining observations. Finally, as the "procedure," a plan was developed indicating when and where the training would take place and of whom the observations would be made.

In the following links of the chain, the design is implemented, data are gathered and analyzed, and conclusions are drawn regarding the support (or lack of it) for the hypothesis. This, in turn, links to the beginning of the next study as someone uses these findings to build his study's chain of reasoning, linking his problem to past research, and so on.

These relationships must be reflected in the preparation of the proposal. The problem statement should be built so that the project objectives flow from it and seem both important and desirable. The statement of objectives and method of attack should build upon and move beyond the review of past research, showing how it will add to accomplishments, remedy past failures, and so forth. The objectives should translate into hypotheses, questions, or models. These, in turn, will suggest the population and sample and the rest of the research design. The data gathered will determine what analysis, statistical or other, is appropriate; and this will determine the kinds of conclusions and implications that might flow from the study.

Four useful characteristics of the chain analogy. The chain analogy is useful because many aspects of a metal chain are applicable to research chains of reasoning as well (Krathwohl, 1985). For example, a metal chain is *only as strong as its weakest link*; so, for that matter, is a proposal's chain of reasoning. If one of the links in the chain is weak--for example, if training is omitted from the proposal so the teachers do not increase their wait-time--then one can hardly attribute any change to the treatment. Like a metal chain, *the argument is only as strong as the weakest part of it.*

A second feature of the analogy and a corollary of the first is that each link in the chain should have the same strength. It would make little sense to have one link in a metal chain as thick as a ship's anchor chain and others as thin as sewing thread. Similarly, in planning a project, for the most efficient use of one's resources, *each of the links should be the same strength as the others.* Why spend resources refining measures of treatment effect to great sensitivity when resources to ensure that the treatment itself is administered as it should be are not allocated? One should allocate resources to the various links in the chain of reasoning so

Figure 2. The chain of reasoning in the
presentation of a study (from Krathwohl, 1985)

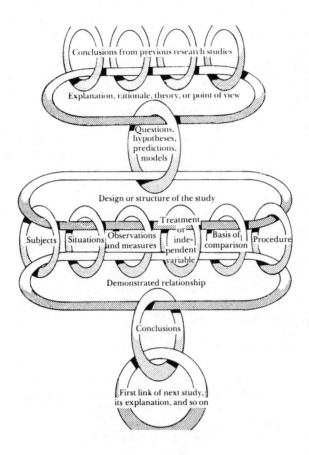

that each level in the chain can appropriately support the argument.

A third aspect is that just as a chain picks up the load at the beginning
and successively transfers it to each link, thereby determining the nature
of each successive link in terms of the load it has to carry, the same
occurs in the chain of reasoning. Each link in the chain determines the
nature of the next link. This aspect became apparent as the chain was
initially described above: past research leads to the present explanation,
that explanation to a hypothesis, question, or model, which is translated
into the design, and so on.

A final feature of a metal chain is that at any point in the chain where
several horizontal links across the chain's breadth connect the links above
and below them, each of the horizontal links shares the load. In the
research chain of reasoning, this occurs at the design level where the six
facets of design together link the design as a whole to the demonstration
of the relationship (see figure 2). *Where links share the load, one of them*

may be made stronger in order to compensate for weakness in another. In the same way, one of the facets of design may be strengthened to compensate for another facet that is weak. For instance, assume the wait-time effect, even with training, is so small it is hard to notice the change--a thin, weak "basis of comparison" link. One may compensate by strengthening any of several of the other design links. For example, one could strengthen the "subjects" link by increasing the size of the sample so the study is more sensitive or choosing a sample, such as especially bright students, who are likely to be particularly responsive to the treatment. Alternatively, one could strengthen the "observations and measures" link by using tests or observations especially designed to catch the small changes that are expected to occur. Thus various design trade-offs can be made to achieve the strongest overall chain, each of these horizontally interdependent links compensating for another.

All research studies presenting the case for a generalization are chains of reasoning. A strong proposal intended to demonstrate or validate such a generalization reflects this chain by the plan of its structure, by its internal logical consistency, and by the appropriate development of each section. Each section reflects the previous material and carries it a step further in a consistent way. Ends are not dropped, objectives slighted, data collected but not included in the analysis plan, and the like. Resources are properly allocated to strengthen weak aspects, and design trade-offs appropriately made.

Flaws in design, structure, and consistency are often most easily seen either by those unfamiliar with the proposal or by you after the ardor for your own words has cooled. *Even the most experienced proposal writer benefits from a critical review by others.* Often a nonspecialist brings a coldly analytical perspective that is most helpful. At a minimum, if time allows, put the proposal aside to gain a fresh perspective on it before sending it to the sponsor. You'll be surprised at what you see!

6. *Can the Project Be Adequately Presented in the Format Prescribed for the Program?*

The format prescribed for most research programs is designed around an experimental research approach. Exploratory studies to "see what happens," surveys, and historical and philosophical investigations, among others, are not easily presented within this framework. Is there an alternative? Most programs do not insist that their outline be followed. Only the abstract cover sheet, and often the budget, must be entered on their special forms. Be sure to check for such requirements.

You deviate from following a recommended format at your own risk. Typically, the risk is mainly that of the reaction of the readers to the differing format. But readers conscientiously attempt to judge proposals fairly. If your need to deviate from the prescribed form is legitimate, not sheer iconoclasm, they will usually be sympathetic. Thus it is better to take the risk than to force a proposal into an inappropriate form. Discard dysfunctional aspects of the outline, and adopt a form that best presents the kind of study proposed.

Increasingly, Congress and program staff have shown impatience with the slow accretion of knowledge through the experimental approach. This approach results in a strong program of definitive studies but does little to encourage exploration of pioneering leads. They have indicated they welcome proposals using new approaches and have been funding them. In this writer's opinion, such changes are long overdue. The experimental method excels for certain purposes, but we need to utilize the range of approaches available to discover new knowledge. Chapter 7 deals with some of the points needing special attention in preparing proposals using nonexperimental approaches.

7. *Is There Enough Detail?*

Proposal writing is a fine balance. The researcher should *describe the study in sufficient detail that the reviewer will be convinced both that the problem is worth investigation and that the writer has the ability to handle it.* I' is not necessary, however, to give so much detail that every single possibility is explored and all flexibility is eliminated from the plan. Half the excitement of doing research is in exploration. A researcher worth her salt will want her fun. Except for proposals built around very concrete or trivial problems, *only rarely can all details be anticipated; and reviewers know this.* The secret of success is to find the appropriate balance.

The balance between expected detail and ambiguity shifts toward detail as the nature of the project involves less exploration and more known territory. It shifts toward detail for projects that, using familiar techniques, engineer a new curriculum or tool. It shifts still more toward detail for demonstration or dissemination projects. Such projects usually can be planned much more tightly with respect to both activities and schedule. If you find it difficult to detail what will be done, state who will be consulted and when. Alternatively, describe the options open for choice and how decisions will be made.

Some federal proposals have length limitations; observe them! It helps if one understands that limitations are usually established to prevent excesses and to keep the reviewer's reading load in proper bounds. The limits on federal programs are likely to be strictly enforced if stated in the program announcement. This is to keep the competition fair to all comers. Check with staff about how hard and fast the limit really is.

When deciding how to keep within the prescribed length, *it is usually better to include important information than to omit it; put it in the appendix if that is not counted as part of the proposal length, but be reasonable about how much you include.* This permits the reviewer to have on hand such information as she may need to make a just decision but does not force her to read it if she feels she has enough information in the text. If the proposal is long, use colored paper or tabs to set off the appendix. (Colored paper is probably better than tabs, which are often lost or bent in mailing.)

Omission of critical information can be decisive for one-time-only grant competitions or requests for proposals (RFPs); there is no second chance. Omissions delay a project in grant programs with regular competition cycles. Omissions can also result in misperceptions that carry over to the resubmission. So decide what information is important and find a way to include it.

Even without a page limit, it is desirable to use appendixes to provide auxiliary information and to avoid crowding detail into the main body of the proposal. Doing so permits you to keep the focus of readers where you want it without undue distractions.

Foundation proposals, as noted in Chapter 14, are a breed apart from government proposals. Be concerned about adequate detail only after the response to the initial approach has been encouraging. Foundations prefer to receive a brief description of the project in the initial contact. They will usually tell you what they wish included when they request a detailed follow-up proposal. If they don't tell you, ask.

8. *Is the Hasty Reader Signaled to the Critically Important Parts of the Proposal?*

Ideally, each writer expects that his proposal will be given as much time as necessary to adequately comprehend and evaluate it; so, for that matter, does each reviewer. In reality, the reading load of a reviewer varies, as does the reviewer's time to read; thus there are times when reading is done under pressure. It is always safest to assume that it is your proposal that might have to be reviewed under time pressures. The outline or application form helps the reviewer know what to look for and where to look for it. Carefully following it is one assistance that can be given her. Use tabs or colored paper to indicate the organization of the proposal and make sections accessible.

More important than a fancy duplication job, lots of tabs, a fancy binding or other indications of affluence is the way the material is written, arranged, and presented. The initial emphasis should be on legibility, lucidity, and clarity of presentation. Then, make the proposal look as though it wanted to be read! Use white space to lighten the text and to surround points that you want to stand out. Avoid solid, massive blocks that repel rather than invite reading.

Good writing, like good acting, uses nonverbal gestures. Use punctuation, underlining, spacing, paragraphing, diagrams, flowcharts, tables, and other devices to command the reader's eye. Signal upcoming content with topic sentences at the beginning of paragraphs. Try skimming your proposal, reading it very rapidly, jumping from topic sentence to topic sentence, to see whether it conveys what you intend.

The reader should be able to easily find essential substance within certain parts of the outline. For example, set forth a succinct statement of the purpose of the research in an obvious place in the problem section. Similarly, listing the objectives in order of importance is useful in the objectives section.

Be careful, however, to avoid the opposite extreme, jazzing the copy with jargon or with more gesture than sense. Remember, research is essentially a scholarly activity.

9. *Where Should Precious Proposal Preparation Time Be Concentrated?*

We have already noted as part of question 4 in this chapter the critical importance of the statement of review criteria that is published in federal competition announcements. These criteria, their weighting, and where competitive proposals may be expected to vary widely suggest which parts of the proposal are most important and therefore deserving of extra attention.

A second factor to consider is any special circumstances that may affect this proposal, such as the new researcher's need to indicate competence, the solid integration required in a complex project, or the strong justification required by projects that do not look important. But in addition to unusual circumstances, a good general rule is to anticipate the special concerns of the average reviewer.

Observation and experience suggest that there are typical reading patterns. Given sufficient time, most reviewers read the sections of the proposal sequentially, letting the writer lead them through it. If severely pressed for time (or when reading in a group, where no reviewer wants to be the one who holds up everyone else), reviewers tend to adopt a pattern that a few highly energetic reviewers use regularly. They skip through the proposal, not necessarily in sequence, reading here, skimming there. Like the listener who interrupts the storyteller to tell what is coming, they anticipate what ought to be ahead of them and look for it, actively managing their approach to the proposal. The predictable part of their sequence seems to depend on the nearly universal importance of certain sections. The unpredictable part depends on the questions raised in the reader's mind as the reviewing progresses.

A typical review sequence might look like this:

1. Read and digest the abstract.
2. Skim enough of the the problem statement to get a feel for it.
3. Skim the literature review to find the unique features of this study and check the scholarly ability of the author.
4. If the objectives are not in the abstract, skim the first objectives.
5. Turn to the work plan and skim the bar chart, flow chart, or PERT diagram to get a more detailed grasp of the overall plan.
6. If an unknown researcher, check the vita of the principal investigator to see whether the necessary competence seems

present.

7. Check the budget total to be sure it is in line with what ought to be expected.

From here on, it's unpredictable, for during the process described above, questions have been forming that need answering.

- Does the problem seem inconsequential? Read the problem statement.
- Has something like this been done before? Check the review of literature.
- Work plan not clear or containing possible flaws? Check the procedure section. (Sooner or later, for one reason or another, this section will most likely be read in detail!)
- Price out of line? Analyze budget and compare with work plan and procedure statement.

Does knowing this pattern help? Perhaps, for it suggests which sections tend to be read by all and which probably get special attention by both "skip and skim" and regular readers.[3] Be sure to pay particular attention to the *summary or abstract; the first parts of the problem statement or introduction; the first part of the literature review (or if clearly marked, the part that points to the unique features of the study); the work plan; vita of the principal investigator; the budget's grand total, especially its large items;* and *the procedure description, especially sampling, treatment, and control sections.* The work plan does more than indicate the time schedule; it is used as a way of grasping the entire project.

When sections or paragraphs are skimmed, the first few words or sentences are the most important. As suggested earlier, try skimming the project using the first sentence each paragraph and see whether those sentences give the proper sense of the project.

10. How Can You Make the Sponsor Want to Support Your Project?

As noted earlier, although it may not seem like it when you go hat in hand as a supplicant seeking funds, sponsors are as dependent on you as you are on them. So, prior to that day in your future when you will have attained sufficient reputation and prestige that they want *you* "in their stable," how do you get a sponsor to want to support you? You know better than anyone what the possibilities of your project are; therefore you are in the best position to creatively demonstrate how your project

---

[3]The "skip and skim" procedure requires an alert mind and extra mental energy. The reviewer's attitude is "I'm going to master this proposal rather than letting it take me through it." It is more likely used under great time pressure, or when the reviewer is fresh. As tiredness sets in, the reviewer typically drops back to reading the proposal straight through.

relates to the sponsor's goals. To help you spot possible ways your project may benefit the sponsor, here are some suggestions:

- If yours is a problem of concern to the sponsor and you are likely to be able to contribute to the solution, this is the most obvious approach to take.
- You may be able to reach an audience that the sponsor might not otherwise contact.
- Sponsoring you or your institution may in some way redress a previous imbalance in funding of a region, class of institutions, kind of researcher, class of persons, and so forth.
- Your project may have important side effects such as supporting an organization that the agency wants to support; pleasing someone in a key position who has been critical of the program; or gathering additional data on an instrument, treatment, or research method of interest.
- Your project may have some implications of personal interest to particular members of the staff, to the agency because of past projects supported, or to a particular member of a foundation's board of trustees. (Work the implications into the flow of the materials so they make logical sense, then let the targeted member discover the material herself.)
- Because of personnel available to you, you may be able to do the project more competently than others. This may include the help of a prestigious senior researcher whose work would be a credit to the agency. Point out that the agency will get the benefit of his research skills as he consults with you or otherwise provides assistance.
- Perhaps you have access to special equipment that gives you an advantage. It need not be at your own institution; you need only give evidence of your access to it.
- Perhaps your institution is willing to partially subsidize your project; this will multiply the power of the sponsor's funds.
- There may be special public relations value in supporting your project. This might result from a conference, symposium, or publication that is a part of your project; the involvement of a national organization; or your special relationship to a professional organization.

These only begin the list. The point is that there are many possibilities. But they will not automatically appear in the proposal. You must think of them and build them naturally and logically into the proposal so that the sponsor discovers them and draws the conclusion you intend.

Give consideration to how you include this information. If you are a member of a class of persons that has been underfunded in the past, one way is to work clues into an appropriate place that allows that inference. Some persons feel strongly the importance of stating the issue directly, pointing out the underfunding problem, thereby making the sponsor consider his possible guilt. Use your own judgment; it can backfire if the sponsor feels this is an inappropriate accusation of him or his agency and becomes resentful because it appears that you are trying to justify the funding of your proposal on this basis rather than on its merits.

But let us put all these suggestions in perspective. Typically, the points we have been considering in this section are "frosting on the cake"; they are rarely basic reasons for funding a proposal. First, one must have a sound and appealing proposal! Then, as reviewers consider several meritorious proposals, if one of these additional considerations tips the scales in your favor, that is the payoff for carefully thinking through all the aspects of proposal building.

11. *Have You a Work Plan for the Preparation of the Proposal? Have You Planned for Unscheduled Delays in Proposal Development?*

Although the creative process can't be scheduled, some parts of the proposal writing can be. A work plan for proposal development just like the one developed in the proposal itself is a tremendous help, especially if you are trying to meet a deadline. Page 73 describes project work plans. Without such a plan, there is a tendency to work right up to deadline on the interesting proposal parts without leaving adequate time for the less interesting parts, for the extras one hadn't counted on, and for emergencies. See Chapter 9 as well, which contains a list of items likely to delay a complex project. Although some steps will not apply to simple projects, most will.

Section II

The Preparation and Submission
of the Proposal

This section is the most important in the book. So far we have been talking about the initial concerns and generalities of proposal preparation. Now we come to the actual preparation of the proposal. This section consists of four chapters. The proposal development process is divided into its three logical parts, each given a chapter: Chapter 3 describes the statement of the problem, Chapter 4 shows the translation of that problem into the activities of the proposal, and Chapter 5 describes the resources, those available and those needed to turn the activities of the previous part into reality. It also describes other items requiring attention up through duplication of the copy.

More specifically, Chapter 3 considers the first three sections of the proposal, in which the problem is introduced, its relation to previous literature and theory is developed, and it is sharpened into objectives.

Chapter 4 deals with the procedure section, the translation of the problem and objectives into the actual activities that constitute the research process: population (or sample), design, instrumentation, analysis, work plan, and end product.

Chapter 5 describes those sections that support the procedure section and enable it to be carried out: the personnel, facilities, budget, assurances, and clearances. It also includes the proposal wrap-up: abstract, title, final review, and duplication.

Chapter 6 describes the steps in submission and follows the proposal through the review, notification, and negotiation stages. It discusses what to do if not funded; *winners are often simply losers who wouldn't quit!*

This material deals with proposals for research, especially federally supported, but most of it is generic to proposals of any kind, regardless of type or sponsor. Application to one's specific problem is usually not difficult. To aid in making these applications and also to emphasize the characteristics unique to different kinds of proposals, Chapter 7 deals with proposals for a variety of kinds of research as well as nonresearch requests. Foundation proposals, however, generally much simpler and considerably shorter, are discussed in Chapter 14.

3. Proposal Development: 1. The Problem

The first task of the proposal writer is to describe his problem in terms so enticing as to make the reviewer or sponsor eager to give consideration to the rest of the proposal. This task falls to the first part of the proposal, the three sections described in this chapter, but especially to the first of these, the introduction or problem statement. That section typically develops understanding of the problem by showing its significance in relation to the large, important problems already of concern to the reviewer or sponsor and by showing the problem in the perspective of the field in which it is embedded.

This is followed by a section on related research, which further develops problem understanding and appreciation by showing specifically how the problem is solidly grounded in the previous work of the field and how this project will take a significant step beyond what has already been done.

This makes it possible in the third section, the objectives, for the problem to be restated in a more precise and detailed fashion with greater understanding. And from that problem statement are teased the objectives of the project in such a way that their translation into project activities, the topic of the next chapter, is natural and easy.

1. PROBLEM STATEMENT

First impressions are important! The sentences with which you open suggest to the reader whether this proposal is going to be creative and interesting or just routine. Come back after you have a complete draft and rework your opening so that it invites the reviewer to read further.

Show problem importance. The opening statement should convince the reviewer that the project is important. For example:

> Japanese adaptations of the United States's social-psychological discoveries have been an important factor in their industrial success, just as our failure to build on that knowledge base has compounded our difficulty in competing with them. This project intends to find modifications of their use of this knowledge that will be effective in our culture. The reason we think this is possible is . . .

or:

> A universal problem at every governmental level is ensuring that funds given to enhance a program are actually used to improve it rather than merely taking the place of funds already maintaining the program. Accountants are extremely resourceful at moving funds around to defeat such provisions.

This project will search for ways in which democratic governmental units, both in the United States and abroad, have succeeded in ensuring that such funds are used as intended.

Show the problem in the perspective of the larger field in which it is embedded--management practices as a part of our lagging in international economic competition, accounting procedures as a facet of making government intervention effective.

Which specifics to stress depends on the emphasis of the program to which you are applying and the sponsor you are seeking to please. Basic, applied, and developmental research programs call for accentuating different problem aspects.

Another way to emphasize the importance of your project for a particular program is to build on the criteria for the program, showing how your problem fits the program's priorities and contributes to their advancement. Work this into the problem statement as early as it fits.

Writers tend to emphasize positive outcomes, assuming the project will be successful. Sometimes there are equally important outcomes even if the project is unsuccessful; don't forget these.

State problem generality. Important as you are, programs are expected to contribute to the betterment of humankind rather than just yours or your institution's; therefore *indicate the generality of the problem and the generalizability of the research*. A good way of doing this is to point to the project's contribution to theory and knowledge of the phenomenon. Indicate how the project builds on previous theory or contributes to new theory. Relate it to the large, important problems of the field. If you can, describe the value of some concrete applications of the knowledge as well as the potential importance of these applications.

Funding agencies want to go down in history as having justified their existence. They want to make as great an impact on their targets of concern as funds permit. They can do this by concentrating their funds on a program of narrow scope, and some do so. But they can also justify their existence by funding projects that are generalizable, that have implications above and beyond the local scene. An exception to this is the project funded to solve problems unique to a particular region or area. Even here, however, there is often generality to a larger area. Another exception is demonstration research intended to produce results under normal, local conditions. These demonstrations may be placed around the country, but here again, the real payoff depends on the extent to which the model has generalizability to similar local situations.

Note, however, that a generalizable project does not necessarily require a national sample. The sample's characteristics must be known, however, in order to show how and to whom the findings can be transferred. The situation in which the research is carried out must have enough known characteristics in common with other situations that transfer locations can be found. As noted earlier, if the project can be associated with a theoretical position, its generality is significantly increased.

Limit the problem. Probably the most common error in writing the problem section is *to paint the picture in too grandiose or too general terms.* Frequently, the problem is so broad the investigator could not possibly solve it even if he were given all the agency's funds, much less a part of them. He need not be ashamed to reduce the scope of what is intended. A seasoned researcher knows he cannot solve all the world's ills and limits the problem.

Learning to focus a study is a skill. Novices often believe that only by encompassing large pieces of a problem can they avoid triviality. Doctoral dissertation proposals are often rejected three or four times as the project is successively reduced in scope; yet it is only by focusing on the manageable, on the critically important aspects of problems, that progress can be made. In competition, other characteristics being equal, a focused proposal will beat the broad one every time, while a too narrowly conceived project will lose because it is inconsequential![1] One secret to funding is finding the intermediate range.

Other suggestions. Don't dwell on the obvious. The writer recently read a proposal that used its first eight pages to convince the reviewer that research in the field was necessary. If the reviewer were not already aware of this, she would not have been asked to be a reviewer or should not have agreed to be if asked. Assume interest in research in the area.

Find the balance between completeness and brevity. Some researchers are too brief, taking too much for granted concerning the reviewer's knowledge of the topic (e.g., knowledge of the job market for technicians in a technician employment survey). Conversely, one may make this section extra long on the assumption that if one sells the reviewer on the importance of the project, little attention will be paid to the remainder of the proposal. Possibly this may be more justified in writing to philanthropic foundations, but government reviewers generally give considerable weight to procedure as well. In this section, as in several others, find the balance point between completeness and brevity; adjust the length of this section to correspond to the way the rest of the proposal is developed.

Give the reader perspective on the whole proposal. Include a two- or three-sentence sketch of the approach you are planning to use. If done briefly, also point out the merit of this approach. Foreshadowing what is to come can be used throughout the proposal to good effect, serving to integrate it. In this and other sections that tend to be lengthy and

---

[1]Proposal length does not seem to expand proportionately to the complexity and breadth of a problem. Therefore, it follows that one can do a much better job of describing the project with a limited problem.

unbroken by headings or subsections, it is especially important to help the reviewer find a succinct statement that summarizes the points being made. Underlining and paragraphing are especially useful.

Set the frame of reference. The problem section establishes the frame of reference and set of expectations that the reviewer will carry throughout the proposal; be sure it is the correct one. Unfamiliar terms or words used in unusual ways may cause problems. If they cannot be avoided, work their definitions into the presentation early and prominently so that the reader learns them.

2. RELATED RESEARCH

This section builds further understanding of the problem by showing that it is solidly anchored in past work yet moving beyond that work in important ways. It is an excellent place for you to give an indication of your scholarly competence. *Writing this section well is a sign of professional maturity; it indicates one's grasp of the field, one's methodological sophistication in critiquing others' research, and the breadth and depth of one's reading.*

No project starts de novo. The extent to which the researcher builds the project upon what has already been done shows command of the current state of the field and the extent to which the proposed project moves the field ahead in some significant manner. Some section of the proposal should, therefore, deal with how the project contributes to this forward movement. The section on related research provides such an opportunity.

In writing this section one should survey a select group of studies that provide a foundation for the proposed project, *discuss these studies in detail sufficient to aid the nonspecialist in understanding their relevance, describe how they contribute to this study, and indicate how this study moves beyond them.* Obviously the review should encompass the most recent literature in *both* content and method; an outdated review hardly adds to the impression of scholarliness. Similarly, dependence on secondary sources such as other literature reviews may be appropriate, but the scholar will usually want to *check some of the original literature* herself. Work in your original findings from the basic literature to indicate this.

In discussing studies, *point out their technical flaws* and show how these pitfalls will be avoided. State whether the findings of the studies were correctly interpreted by the authors and how they should be viewed to fit the study proposed.

If there is a *theoretical base* for the study, *be sure to discuss it.* Science is a systematically accumulated body of knowledge. Theories interrelate individual findings and permit greater generalization. This section is an excellent place to convey your grasp of how theory is currently being developed and tested in your area and to critique the solidity of the structure being erected.

The citation index is an especially valuable tool in literature reviews because it organizes scientific and technical articles by the sources that they cite in common. Starting with some of the pioneering or recently important papers in your topic of interest, you can find who has built on these to create new work in the same area. The *Science Citation Index* thoroughly covers the current literature in over 100 fields of science and technology. The *Social Science Citation Index* covers the social and behavioral sciences literature thoroughly and broadly from 1960 on. In 1977, an *Arts and Humanities Citation Index* began as well. Among the three of them, the journal literature is well covered. Since current articles refer to past work, the significant past literature rapidly becomes well mapped as one notes those references that are frequently cited.

Be highly selective in this section, citing only those studies that form the base from which the study is building. More is not necessarily better. Don't give up and say that the literature is too large to summarize easily; this is another point in the proposal where you must find the balance point between the extremes of being too broad and too narrow.

Summarize the pertinent information that is needed to understand the study's contribution to the work being proposed. Do not expect reviewers to go to the library to look up references. They may do so, but not if they are faced with a sizable number of proposals to read, a deadline to meet, and no time released from regular duties to read them. If reviewers are brought together in a central place to read proposals, a library is rarely accessible.

Become aware of literature from disciplines other than your own that bears on your problem. Even in targeted programs, persons from other fields and disciplines may be competing with you and perhaps even judging your proposal. Proposals lacking reference to relevant work from other disciplines may be at a strong competitive disadvantage. This may apply to research techniques as well. Reviewing research in related disciplines using bibliographic sources that extend broadly, such as *Social Science Citation Index,* and discussing one's proposal with colleagues from other disciplines may buy important protection. Use of colleagues in other disciplines is particularly important because it alerts you to the jargon these fields use to discuss your problem. This knowledge can help you use their journal indexes much more successfully.

If possible, *include studies currently underway* that are likely to overlap your project. Knowing what is currently being investigated in one's field is another sign of competence. Show how this project differs from such studies and/or meshes with them in a constructive way. The Science Information Exchange[2] of the Smithsonian Institution in Washington, D.C., maintains a record of projects currently funded through branches of the government as well as through the larger foundations. An amazingly large list of topics is regularly searched every 90 days or less;

and these searches, called Research Information Packages, will often do the job of a custom computer search, another available option, and are considerably less expensive. A free list of Research Information Packages is available.

There is a very easy way to find what one should read to stay abreast of developments in one's field, especially if it is spread across a variety of journals. Published by The Institute for Scientific Information (ISI), Inc. every week, *Current Contents: Social and Behavioral Sciences* reprints and indexes the most recent tables of contents from the major journals in the behavioral sciences. In addition, convention papers and proceedings ae now indexed quarterly in their *Index to Social Science and Humanities Proceedings.*

Sometimes your library may not have a journal article that is needed for your research. You can obtain any article that is in any of ISI's citation indexes (*Current Contents, Social Science Citation Index,* and so on.) by writing to *The Genuine Article,* ISI, 325 Chestnut St., Philadelphia, Pa. 19106. There is a significant fee. Orders are usually mailed within 24 hours if the request is made on their hotline. Registered users of FAXPAX can get delivery in thirty minutes. Call 800-523-1850, x1405 for complete information.

Don't make the common error of including too many references and doing too little with them. Proposals are often submitted with lengthy bibliographies on the research topic rather than selected references that relate directly to the proposal. Such a comprehensive list does little to convince the reviewer that the researcher has anything other than the ability to use an index or has a good graduate assistant available. This is especially true if many references are merely cited, not discussed. It is what you do with the references that is the basis for judging this section. The skill shown in selection, the technical competence used in evaluating contributions, and, above all, the originality displayed in realistically and constructively synthesizing conceptual bases of past and proposed work in relation to the proposed problem are what will impress readers.

Too often this section is an afterthought. After the "fresh, new idea" has been developed into a project, one may go to the library to complete the sole remaining section on related research. Such a practice makes it difficult to reconcile past research with the "new" project. If these studies are taken into account during the planning stage, the project is much stronger.

Being human, researchers naturally want their ideas to be their own, to claim them as original, unrelated to what others have done. However, research programs cannot go on "rediscovering America" to satisfy the egos of individual investigators. All too often reviewers encounter the

[2]Smithsonian Science Information Exchange, Inc., Room 300, 1730 M St., NW, Washington, D.C. 20036.

statement that this is a "new idea" and that "nothing has been written" that bears on the problem. This is a red flag! Reviewers know that few projects start from scratch, and they know how often the "wheel has been reinvented" by someone who did not do the proper background research. So your reviewer will not want to be guilty of approving still another false claim of originality. She feels challenged to search for relevant studies. If she finds some, she is inclined to question the scholarship and technical competence of the investigator. Therefore, *if you state that "no research bearing on the problem" exists, cite the closest research you found and show how it falls short.* Also indicate under what headings and in which references checks were made.

If you are researching an area where a lot of prior work has been done and if you have the skills, consider doing a quantitative literature summary. If you don't have the statistical skills, this may be more than you'll want to take on, although some of the methods, such as tabulating pro and con studies, are relatively simple. Even if you lack statistical skills, most of the next section will be reasonably intelligible if you skip the sections that are too technical, like the definition of effect sizes.

Quantitative literature summaries. Traditionally, literature reviews analyze the positive or negative support that relevant studies provide for a proposition. But to draw an overall conclusion, the authors of such reviews find it difficult to know which studies to weight most heavily--the largest, the best experimental design, the most representative sample, the most valid and reliable instruments? Rarely do the same studies incorporate all these criteria, so there are difficult trade-offs to consider. Further, studies often were designed with insufficient sensitivity to yield a statistically significant result, but the results are in the expected direction. Should these be counted as positive evidence or, as the statistical purist might suggest, as merely chance aberrations? By convention, they cannot be counted as confirming studies, even when they are numerous. A researcher encountering a series of such near misses might intuitively consider them more than a chance happening. But there is little one can do other than note the occurrence under the rules of the game for traditional reviews. Most traditional reviews conclude with some kind of equivocal generalization and then call for more studies. This contributes to the impression that the social and behavioral sciences have a weak knowledge base.

There has to be a way not only of taking into account a series of near misses but also of summarizing the ponderous weight of a series of conflicting studies. Indeed, there is an available technique--Karl Pearson long ago suggested the use of chi square for this purpose--but it has rarely been used. In 1976 Glass published the article "Primary, Secondary and Meta-Analysis," which provided an example of a quantitative summary, or "meta-analysis" as Glass called it (Smith and Glass, 1977, an evaluation of the effectiveness of psychotherapy, later published in book length in Smith, Glass, and Miller, 1980). Since then the traditional literature review has begun to share center stage with quantitative literature summaries. These not only provide answers for some of the problems noted above but go beyond them to provide new ways of understanding the effectiveness of a treatment and to expand our repertoire of methods of compiling data across sets of studies.

For example, Smith, Glass, and Miller's study of psychotherapy systematically assembled the results of over 400 studies selected from a pool of over 1200 and found that despite the pro and con picture presented by looking at individual studies one at a time, viewed across the set as a whole, psychotherapy clearly did make a difference. On the average--regardless of the type of psychotherapy, and across all measuring instruments--treated subjects were about one standard deviation better off than untreated controls. Their method of combining the studies provided a measure of average effect size.

Other comments on how to combine findings were published soon after, Rosenthal (1978) and Light (1979), for example. The logic and statistics of quantitative research summaries have since been extensively explored (Glass, McGaw, and Smith 1981; Light and Pillemer, 1984; Hedges and Olkin, 1985; Rosenthal 1984), and the exploration continues.

As these books point out, there are a variety of ways of doing quantitative summaries:

- Counting the positive, neutral, and negative results and comparing these with what would be expected by chance.
- Combining the results of individual studies into a single test of significance.
- Developing something resembling a standard score estimate of the average strength of treatment across all studies. This is called the "treatment effect size" or just "effect size."

The last method uses the standard deviation of the control group (or, lacking one, the combined variances of experimental groups) to estimate the standard deviation of the population. The treatment effect is the difference between experimental and control group means divided by the control group standard deviation. It yields something like a standard score which describes the size of the treatment effect in standard deviation units. Treatment effect estimates from individual studies are averaged across comparable studies for an overall index. Mullen and Rosenthal (1985) describe computer programs for doing meta-analysis. Further, the set of effect sizes from individual studies can be tested for variability in excess of chance (Hunter, Schmidt, and Jackson, 1982). Such variability indicates that moderator variables are likely at work. To identify them, one seeks studies with common aspects such as method variables (field versus laboratory studies or self-report versus observation), within- versus between-group comparisons, or characteristics unique to what is being studied. Meta-analyses identifying moderator variables often provide new insights invisible in single-study analyses. Crano (1986) very nicely illustrates a method factor using Eisenberg and Lennon's meta-analysis (1983) where self-reported empathy is apparently not the same as observed empathic behavior.

Quantitative summaries are not without their critics. The critics argue that combining studies of questionable quality and comparability is a dubious procedure; they suggest that the computer acronym GIGO (garbage in, garbage out) applies to combinations of studies as well. Glass, McGaw, and Smith (1981) contend, nevertheless, that even relatively poor studies can be usefully combined. The errors of the various studies may tend to cancel one another, especially when a large number of studies are combined. In some meta-analyses, however, several measures of a treatment effect (e.g., in a study of psychotherapy, measures of self-concept, of anxiety, and of stress) are used to estimate effect-size. When these multiple estimates of effect size from the same sample are included in the combined effect-size estimate, the flaws of that single study have extra leverage. Therefore, the assumption that the individual study statistics are independent is violated, so errors do not balance themselves out but are reinforced. One needs to watch for this. Some meta-analyses have found that a combined estimate based on a selected group of the best studies produces a higher effect size than one based on the whole body of studies. But this has not always proved true.

Effect-size corrections have been developed for small-sample studies (Hedges and Olkin, 1985) and for restricted or unreliable variables (Hunter, Schmidt, and Jackson, 1982). The former is so small as to rarely be of potential significance and the latter must be used with care by someone who understands the situation. Hauser-Cram (1983) has suggested a number of cautions to observe in synthesizing research studies.

Summaries based solely on published research tend to overestimate treatment effect size, since the published literature is biased toward positive results (Glass, McGaw, and Smith, 1981). Effect sizes from the published literature are usually somewhat higher than those from unpublished studies such as dissertations and/or the lengthy reports of government projects. Rosenthal (1979, 1984) provides a formula for estimating the extent to which a meta-analysis finding is resistant to the "file drawer effect." This is the weakening effect on the relationship if the unpublished studies, either filed and never submitted for publication or submitted and rejected, are taken into account. Effect sizes large enough to require a ridiculous number of "filed" studies to negate the result (sometimes called a fail-safe number) are considered to be real effects, not just the creation of editorial selection.

Light and Pillemer (1984) emphasize a critical feature of quantitative research summaries: the decision of what studies to combine and how to combine them. The system used for classifying studies into homogeneous groups is important in determining how much a meta-analysis illuminates the interrelations of variables as well as what variables affect treatment and how. Providing a classification system adequate for the variables being studied is critical to the acceptability of the summary. For example, a study of whole versus part learning of psychomotor skills must clearly delineate the different possible styles of part learning: W,P,W; $(P_1),(P_1+P_2),(P_1+P_2+P_3)$, and so on; P_1,W,P_2,W, and so on; as well as their combination with the variations in massed versus distributed practice, with which they are confounded in the literature.

Cooper and Rosenthal's (1980) study reveals the importance of quantitative summaries by showing that a quantitative literature review was more likely to demonstrate positive support for a proposition than a traditional judgmental summary. The researchers gave the same set of seven studies of a hypothesis to 41 judges randomly assigned to meta-analytic and traditional procedures.   Judges were asked to determine whether the studies upheld the proposition. Cooper and Rosenthal had chosen studies they believed supported the proposition. Whereas 73% of the traditional reviewers found "probably or definitely" no support for the proposition, only 32% of the meta-analytic reviewers so judged.   In commenting on this study, Glass, McGaw, and Smith (1981) note that "the entire set of studies occupied . . . fewer than 56 journal pages. One can imagine how much more pronounced would be the difference between these two approaches with bodies of literature typical of the size that are increasingly being addressed with meta-analytic techniques" (p. 17).

If one may generalize from that study, reviews based on meta-analytic data are more likely than traditional ones to conclude that a relation exists.   Further, both Rosenthal (1984) and Glass, McGaw, and Smith (1981) show how meta-analytic procedures contribute to understanding phenomena in ways that traditional reviews are likely to miss.   For instance, the latter plotted studies of class size against achievement translated into effect sizes. The plot shows that achievement increases very slightly from large class sizes to sizes in the low teens and then accelerates as they get below ten. Thus, meta-analysis allows one to better describe the nature of the relationship.

Examining subsets of studies can reveal the comparative strength of treatments or variables, such as the effects of different kinds of psychotherapy (Glass, McGaw, and Smith, 1981). Meta-analytic studies also will show where findings are relatively strong and where more research is needed; they can suggest when it is time to move on to new questions.

Combining a meta-analytic study with traditional judgmental qualifications about the nature of the studies is useful if the set of studies is not too massive.   Traditional reviews can take into account the individual circumstances and problems of particular studies in a way the quantitative ones don't. Further, when doing a meta-analytic study, it is often well to show the results several ways, such as 1) allowing each study to contribute only one effect size to the combined average and allowing multiple estimates from the same sample, 2) computing effect size with and without corrections for restriction in range, and 3) estimating effect sizes from the good studies separately from the poorly designed and executed studies. Doing so provides good evidence not only that you are on top of the literature but also that you really do understand how to write technically and judgmentally sound literature reviews--clearly things you wish to demonstrate in this section of the proposal.

Should I include a quantitative literature summary? The first question to ask yourself is whether there are enough comparable studies to supply the raw data for such a summary. This requires a pilot study of the literature to provide an estimate. If the pool of available studies is modest, such a summary is not difficult. Glass, McGaw, and Smith (1981) and Rosenthal (1984) provide relatively simple guides. Reading Hedges and Olkin (1985) requires more statistical sophistication.

If the pool of studies is very large, the summary could become a project in and of itself, requiring an extensive and intensive study of the literature. When that is beyond what you are willing to pursue for the proposal alone, such a summary may quite properly be included in the proposal as a first stage of the study itself. Give some estimate of the size of the pool of studies to show why the magnitude of the task is beyond reasonable proposal development effort.

Leaving the literature summary to be done as part of the study leaves open, of course, the effect of its results on the study as proposed. Presumably the proposal was based on the most likely outcome of the literature search. Under these circumstances, including a discussion of the likelihood of alternative results and how they would affect the direction of the study serves notice to reviewers that you have given this matter consideration. Note, however, that if, in this exploration, the implications of alternative results of the literature summary diverge widely from the assumptions on which your proposal is based, and if the likelihood of such results is a reasonable possibility, then it should be obvious that funding the study as proposed is problematic, to say the least. In this situation, you might suggest supplementary study designs which correspond to the reasonable alternative literature study outcomes and which, presumably, depending on the literature review outcome, could be done under the same grant. Alternatively, seek funding only for the summary of the literature stage, using its outcome to determine the direction of a follow-up proposal.

3. OBJECTIVES

So far in the problem statement, you have described the problem in general terms, shown its importance for the sponsor's program, and set it in a larger context. In the related research section, you described what previous work has been done and alluded to how you are going to build on it: going beyond previous accomplishments, opening new territory, redoing a study a new and better way, possibly replicating a study to show the generality of its findings, and so forth. The objectives section, which then follows, further shows the study emerging from the background of previous thinking and theory, restating the problem in specific, clear, and succinct terms. This problem statement may be translated into project goals and then sharpened into specific objectives, or it may be directly operationalized into objectives.

The reviewer likes to see *objectives that are specific, concrete, and achievable.* Therefore, list them, no more than *a sentence or two apiece, in approximate order of their importance or potential contribution.* Follow each major objective with its specific subobjectives. Alternatively, you can convey the flow of the project by listing the objectives in expected chronological order of achievement; this is especially helpful in a proposal that is developed in several phases.

The importance of the objectives section is that *as the next link in the chain of reasoning, it forms a basis for judging the remainder of the proposal.* It sets the stage for showing how one intends to solve or contribute to the solution of the problem set out in the first sections. Because this section comes early in the proposal, the writer, still in an expansive "I'm going to show the world!" frame of mind, may claim more in this section than it is found possible to undertake once the procedure and budget are completed in detail. One of the first things to do when the proposal is completed is to reread it *to make sure that the objectives neatly flow from the problem statement and that the procedure section adequately encompasses all the objectives.*

The most frequent error made in writing the objectives is to make them a set of vague generalities rather than clear-cut criteria against which the rest of the project can be judged.

A second error is not setting them forth clearly in priority order, but imbedding them, usually by implication rather than explicit statement, in a running description of the project. The reviewer must then tease them out as best she can, trying to infer what the writer implied and placing such emphasis on different ones as can be "guesstimated" from the contextual clues. Obviously, the reviewer's accuracy in finding the objectives and in estimating each one's importance is critical in judging the project. Rather than run the risk of misinterpretation, most writers will fare better by making the objectives obvious and explicit.

The third common error, as already noted, is to include objectives that are not developed in the procedure section. Every objective should be appropriately followed up in successive sections, if the proposal is to be an integrated chain of reasoning.

You may find it helpful to phrase your objectives as hypotheses that are to be tested or as questions that your research hopes to answer. Hypotheses should be related to a theoretical base if at all possible. If the theoretical base was not introduced in the previous sections, state it succinctly (showing how the objectives are derived from it), refine it, and extend it; carefully building the bridge from theory to study so that the relation is clear. For instance, a study of the effects of a vocational education program would be strengthened if the choices that the student must make in the program were related to the developing theory that describes why and how students go through stages of vocational choice.

Hypotheses as objectives must be stated in such a way that they are *testable*, that they can be translated into the research operations that will give evidence of their truth or falsity. The topic may be chosen because it is judged to be important, but the objectives should not themselves be stated as value judgments (e.g., "All sixth-grade boys should learn to play a musical instrument").   Research can indicate the extent of popular support for such a value statement (e.g., "Seventy-five percent of our town believe that all sixth grade boys . . ."); or it can indicate the consequences of an action (e.g., "If all sixth-grade boys play musical instruments, they will attend more concerts outside school"); but humans must judge how much value to attach to these consequences or to the extent of popular support.

Directional hypotheses should be used wherever there is a *basis for prediction.*   There will be a basis for predicted outcomes and findings if the study has a theoretical underpinning.   State hypotheses as succinct predictions of the expected outcomes and findings rather than in the null form.   For instance, say: "Students who receive the experimental treatment will have more differentiated interests than those who do not," rather than "There will be no difference in interest patterns between the experimental and control groups."   The latter statement is an important part of the logic of the statistical test, but it does not belong in the objectives section and leaves an amateurish impression with experienced researchers.

Questions, rather than hypotheses, are most appropriate where the research is exploratory or where the study is a survey seeking certain facts.   The specificity of the questions shows how carefully the problem has been thought through.   For example, consider a study of the effects of female teachers on male students. It will not give a very clear impression that the researcher has a grasp of his problem if he merely lists the question "What is the effect of the female teacher on male students?" But if the researcher poses the question "Which of these is the dominant effect of female teachers on male students?"   and then follows with a listing of the possible dominant effects and explanations, it is clear that he has thought through the possible alternatives and is prepared to investigate at least these particular ones.   Where such specific questions might be expected, and you prefer to look at the phenomenon with a fresh eye rather than try to possibly bias your search with prior expectations, be sure to explain this.

4.
Proposal Development:
2. The Procedure Section

The procedure section is concerned with translating the problem section developed in the previous chapter into project activities. *This is usually the most carefully read section of the whole proposal* because these are the activities the sponsor is really approving and/or buying. Up to this point, the researcher may have told in glowing terms and appealing generalities what she hopes to do and what this will mean to her field. The section on procedure brings this down to earth in operational terms. Frequently proposals that sound as though they will revolutionize a field appear much more mundane in the procedure section; the techniques proposed for attacking the problem may fall far short of what is claimed.

Discussion of the procedure section is in two parts. Part I discusses general considerations to take into account in developing and describing procedures. Part II is a detailed discussion of each of the parts that make up the procedure section: population and sample, design (including a discussion of common errors), instrumentation and data collection, analysis, work plan (charts showing the sequence of events and the time required for their completion), and expected end-product and dissemination plans.

PART I: GENERAL CONSIDERATIONS

Adapt the Format or Outline to Your Study

Although the format specified for some sections of the proposal easily accommodates a variety of methods, this tends to be less true of the procedure section. The format specified for "procedure" typically calls for the information required by a quantitative study or experiment; this ensures that the sponsor has requested details relevant to such a study. Rejected applicants who used to complain they didn't know such information was wanted no longer have an excuse. With this history in mind, you may feel more comfortable in adapting the outline. *Modify the procedure section outline or format to best fit your study.*

For example, if the study is a sample survey, elaborate on the sampling section. If it is a case study, collapse the sections on sample, design, and data collection into a single description of how and where data will be gathered. Suppose the study is one examining the educational and medical records of late-19th-century Italian immigrants to determine how they differed from nonimmigrants. Adjust the specified format to fit what is planned. Describe where one is going to study the records, what one expects to find there, how one gets access, what information will be gathered and how, and what analyses will be performed. Further discussion of how to adapt this section and the rest of the proposal for methods other than the experimental approach is found in Chapter 7; 11 different types of proposals are covered there.

The Procedure Flows Out of the Objectives

Since a project is basically a chain of reasoning, the "procedure" link in the chain is logically derived from the previous links, especially the objectives and hypotheses. In a quantitative study to validate a hypothesis, the procedure is a direct translation of the concepts in the hypothesis into the choice of 1) subjects, 2) situation, 3) measures and observations, 4) experimental variable (if any), 5) the basis on which the change due to an experimental treatment will be sensed (e.g., pre/post comparison, comparison with another group), and 6) the experimental procedures, the schedule of the various activities involved in administering the experimental treatment and in measuring and observing its effect.

For example, consider this hypothesis: Up to some reasonable point, the more time black students spend studying Afro-American history, the stronger their self-concept. This hypothesis suggests that increasing levels of study of black history will result in gains in self-concept up to some point. Decisions will have to be made about how to interpret the term "black students" in terms of age and grade; whether such variables as socioeconomic class or urban/rural background are important; whether just any black history curriculum will do or whether it needs to be one that stresses blacks' accomplishments. One must find a measure of self-concept that is valid for black students at the age chosen; a measure for college students would not work for elementary pupils. A design must be constructed to determine whether the variables change together as hypothesized. For example, in one design, comparable groups who have studied Afro-American history for different lengths of time would be identified. Alternatively, a longitudinal design might be developed which follows the changes in a group with increased study of Afro-American history. These are examples of the variety of interpretations that result when a hypothesis is translated into operational terms. Note that for many of the decisions--age and grade or comparable groups versus longitudinal designs, for example--there are alternative "translations" among which one must choose.

Some terms in a hypothesis immediately translate into design features. Here are some examples:

- Retention vs. immediate recall--requires multiple posttests. (Note that even here there are alternatives. The same group can be tested several times. Or to eliminate the effect of retesting, use different groups--one tested immediately, the other for retention.)
- Cumulative effect--requires multiple posttests. (Again these could all be of the same group or of different groups, each tested after a different length of treatment.)
- Anticipatory effect--multiple pretesting.
- Enhancing or interactive effect of a variable with treatment-- separate treatment groups with and without the presence of the interactive variable conditions.

Operationalizing Terms May Result in New Conceptualizations

As the terms are operationalized, one often comes to understand the study differently than when it was initially conceptualized. Terms take on new meaning, and often the initial conceptualization has to be sharpened and modified as the problem becomes better understood. Suppose that one starts out to study the relation of per pupil expenditures in a public school district to achievement. In operationally defining per pupil expenditures one finds, however, that different districts include different costs. In an effort to get comparable data across districts, one finds that the study is changing. There isn't that much variability in routine costs across districts. The study changes and begins to focus on the amount of discretionary money available to the school's principal to improve instruction. One now has to go back and change the whole front end of the proposal to fit the new conceptualization of the study.

Some researchers argue that one really comes to understand the problem only when undertaking operationalization of the study. However, operationalization may never be completely satisfactory when one is dealing with constructs that can't be concretized in a way that satisfies everyone. This point is worth remembering if you are dissatisfied with what is happening to your study and the redevelopment of the procedure section seems never-ending. Perhaps a compromise operationalization is your problem. If it is, you'll have to call an arbitrary halt to the process. Do so at the earliest point that you personally (and, in your estimate, your potential sponsor as well) can stand behind the procedural plan.

Sometimes, when the hypotheses of a study are given operational translations, it becomes immediately apparent that the problem is too large or too complex. This is particularly likely to be true of the first attempts of doctoral students, who, in an effort to "do something significant," attempt too much. This calls for refocusing and delimiting the problem so that it is feasible.

Sometimes, even after the problem has been refocused, certain requirements may still be too great. Consider whether these may be handled by alternative design choices. For example, if there are too few cases to establish both a control and an experimental group, the subjects may be used as their own control, with pre- and posttests.

Development of the procedures and design of a study is an iterative process. The researcher sets the pieces in place and then finds that one must be changed, setting off an entire cycle of changes. The treatment becomes unmanageable, so it must be cut down. That requires the size of the sample to be increased in order to detect a weaker treatment. That results in having to use subjects with characteristics which interact with the treatment and which therefore must be controlled. And so it goes. Often one must go all the way back to the beginning and plan the procedure and design on a different basis. Many cycles may take place before a satisfactory solution is reached.

Carefully Develop the Key Sections for Your Research Method

A typical program proposal guideline calls for the following subsections to be included: 1) population and sample, 2) design, 3) data and instrumentation, 4) analysis, 5) work plan, and 6) expected end product. Successful use of a particular method often depends on certain aspects of procedure which should therefore be given special attention in proposal development. Some examples: for a sample survey, develop carefully the population and sample and the instrumentation sections; for an experimental study, the design section; for a study using new analytic techniques, the analysis section; for a longitudinal study, population and sample, data and instrumentation, and work plan. See Chapter 7 for more on this point.

The design part of the procedure section is especially critical for experimental studies and deserves special mention because it is also one of the more carefully read sections for most studies. Within any research method, there are a variety of ways to proceed. Choice of any one usually involves emphasizing something at the expense of something else. *Choice of design is still an art.* It requires assessing the seriousness of the gains and losses involved in various design alternatives. These gains and losses and their seriousness is rarely known accurately; good estimates come from knowing one's field and having worked with it long enough to have learned which options yield gains, which losses, and the frequency and seriousness of these gains and losses.

Making good choices is also a matter of knowing one's audiences and being able to adequately anticipate and meet their concerns. Currently, for instance, one would not want to use analysis of covariance to correct for possible differences between groups on a pretest without acknowledging Cronbach's (1982) and ensuing discussions of the problems in this procedure.

Because choice of design is still an art, reasonable persons may differ about the best design for a given problem. Your choice of design may not be that of everyone on the reviewing panel. To minimize the impact of such differences of opinion, help the panel members to follow your line of reasoning so that they, too, may find your design an appropriate choice. To do this, make clear both your design choices and your reasons for so choosing. This last point will be covered extensively in the material that follows.

Restrain Procedure and Design to Realistic Limits

Even as the procedure section is first being considered, one must make tentative decisions on the practical level of resource limits, take into account ethical considerations, and consider what access and cooperation one can expect from other institutions. Further, one must realistically appraise whether the time available for proposal development is sufficient to get the idea into satisfactory operational form.

These estimates are important for making methodological decisions: the possible number of subjects, location of study settings, and so on. Indeed, the limits may rule out certain methods that take too long, such as a longitudinal study. The most desirable and cooperative institutions may be too far distant. Some of the limits are easy to estimate, others more difficult; but some reasonable determination must be made for all of them if development of procedures is to proceed realistically. Further, limits initially set have to be reexamined and adjusted as the plan develops.

Resource limits.   As soon as one begins to translate the study into operational terms, the question immediately arises, "How big shall I make it?"   Although it need not be answered precisely at the outset, some working limits must be set. If this is to be a funded project, one must estimate what is reasonable for this kind of project, given the sponsor's past actions.   (You may find help in reading "Preparing for Budget Development," in the next chapter.) If resources are confined to one's own or the institution's, these limits must be estimated.

If it has not been done earlier, making some kind of budget estimate at this point in the development process can still save substantial time. Adjustments are easier now than they will be later when the writing is in place. Substantial cuts can most easily be made in what is typically the largest budget item in social and behavioral science research--one's professional personnel costs. Shortening the time required for the project is a key way to cut these. Further, if there are "down" periods when there is little activity, sometimes personnel can be put on another budget or account. But be careful about cutting costs for analysis, since analysis frequently consumes more time than expected, especially if the data don't turn out as expected. The section on budget in the next chapter discusses these problems in detail.

In a few instances, one's expected budget may come in well under the sponsor's typical grant size. It is possible one will then seek ways to improve the design of the study using additional resources.

Ethical limits.   There are ethical limits that must be considered in developing the procedure section. The Committee on the Protection of Human Subjects or the comparable committee in your institution is concerned with the ethical implications of your research plan.   Its approval is required to ensure that you will do no physical or mental harm to your subjects nor subject them to unwarranted mental stress. Where you plan to do so, the committee has the task of deciding whether whatever discomfort the subjects undergo is outweighed by the value of the knowledge that presumably will be gained. As noted in the next chapter's section on assurances and clearances, if you use human or animal subjects, you will be required to show that your proposal has the appropriate committee's approval.   This can be a time-consuming roadblock if the committee sees problems you didn't.

Institutional limits.   When other institutions or agencies are involved, their perspective must be considered to ensure that requests made to them are reasonable. Most institutions have not only limited funds but limited availability of subjects, facilities, equipment, and personnel as well. Institutions tend to resist changes in their routines that interfere with "business as usual." It is important to ensure that the sites one expects to use are amenable to one's plans.

Time limits on Proposal Development. Sometimes, the short time available for proposal development forces one to use sites one would prefer not to use, to subcontract for services that might be better handled other ways, or to inadequately involve personnel vital to the study in proposal development, for example. It is important to delineate those things that can be done satisfactorily in the time available for proposal development from those that are unwise to attempt or, perhaps, cannot be done even if tried.

One must also consider the trade-offs involved in rushing to meet the immediate deadline or, if there is one, waiting for a later one when some of these problems could be more successfully resolved. A several-month delay in proposal submission might pay handsome dividends in more cooperative site conditions as the staff of other institutions and agencies are given a chance to contribute to the proposal and feel it is partly theirs. Considering that this may make for better and more convenient conditions over the period of the study, the delay may be worthwhile. But considerations such as the vagaries of Congressional funding, the window of opportunity when certain kinds of proposals are sought, or the availability of one's own or a key person's time may be overriding.

One thing is sure, however: trying to do too much in the available proposal development period usually results in a proposal that shows it.

PART II: PROCEDURE--DEVELOPING ITS SUBSECTIONS

Begin the write-up of the procedure section with a one-paragraph summary or overview of the procedure to be used. Then take up the subsections of procedure. Typical are those discussed in the material that follows: 1) population and sample, 2) design, 3) data and instrumentation, 4) analysis, 5) work plan, and 6) expected endproduct. The following discussion covers some of the common, and most serious, errors.

Population and Sample

The description of population and sample gives a good clue to the generality of the findings. The characteristics of the population define the group to whom the study's results may be expected to transfer. Obviously this generality should be consistent with the generality claimed in the problem statement and objectives sections.

The problem of sample size is too complicated to cover in detail, but it is a crucial consideration. Sample size is an important factor in determining whether you get statistically significant results. How many subjects are enough to estimate a characteristic for a whole population from a sample of it? The answer depends on several factors:

1. How precisely is the population value to be estimated? The population value usually estimated is the difference between whatever groups are being contrasted (e.g., the experimental and control groups). Put another way, this question asks "How small is the difference to be sensed?" Other things being equal, the greater the precision required and the smaller the difference to be sensed, the larger the sample required.
2. How different are individuals with respect to the characteristic being estimated; how much variability is there? If everybody is about the same, other things being equal, you can estimate from a few cases. But if people differ greatly, more cases will be needed.
3. How much certainty is required of the estimate? This is another way of asking whether you want to use the 1% level of significance, 5% level, 10% level, and so on. At the 5% level, one's confidence that the population value is bracketed by the confidence interval is expressed by odds of 19 to 1. Again, other things being equal, the greater the certainty required, the larger the sample required.

Where does the information come from to determine sample size? For questions 1 and 2 above, from one's own pilot studies, from other researchers' use of the same instruments with comparable subjects, or, failing these, from "guesstimates" made on the best basis one can command. With such estimates and a judgmental decision on question 3, any good statistics book (e.g., Hays, 1981) will show how to work backward to a sample size that will ensure that if an event of interest occurs, the odds heavily favor that it will show up as statistically significant.

Increasingly, in studies where statistically significant results are the hoped-for outcome, sponsors expect to find "power analyses." Indeed, a few program guidelines now call for them. Such analyses require the information noted above and provide a rationale for choice of sample size. Those not familiar with the procedure may want to consult Cohen (1977).

Even if not required, giving a good rationale for the sample size is more impressive to the sponsor than picking an arbitrary number or using a convenience sample. Sponsors prefer to support a study large enough to sense a difference. If, because of insufficient sample size, "the results are in the predicted direction, but there is no significant difference," one suspects that the hypothesis should have been supported. Yet, unless one can combine the results with other comparable research, there is no recourse but to run the study again with a larger sample. That is hardly good news to the sponsor! The overhead and fixed costs of a study make it much less expensive to do the study properly the first time than to replicate it. If the funding agency cannot support the study at the level required, either adjust the levels of certainty, if that makes any sense, or seek supporting funds from more than one agency.

Occasionally reviewers are sent proposals for studies using the total population, which, though large, is presumably manageable. In some of these instances, it may be preferable to sample and work more carefully with fewer cases rather than use the same resources trying to cover the entire population. For instance, tracking down survey nonrespondents in a sample may be more important than using the same resources to canvass an entire population but with no follow-up of nonrespondents. Indeed, if an adequate sample can be taken, as much information can usually be gained at considerably less expense. However, when dealing with those who do not understand or accept sampling (this is not infrequent in applied research intended to convince lay policy makers), there is no substitute for a census! The more desirable end of this trade-off is determined by the sophistication of one's intended audience and the purposes of the study.

Especially for survey research, the sampling plan should be worked through carefully. This is often a good place to employ a consultant if sampling theory is not your strength. Be sure to include information about the nature of the plan; and if stratified, area, or cluster sampling is used, describe the nature of the strata, areas, or clusters along with a rationale for your choice.

Random sampling is a basic assumption of all inferential statistics, the kind that infer that there is a statistically significant difference. Indeed, it is from the variability in the randomly chosen units of a sample or from one sample to another that one estimates the boundaries of the variability that could be due to chance. It is when this variability is exceeded that we say we have a "statistically significant difference." When using inferential statistics, make random sampling a part of your study if at all feasible.

In many instances, random sampling is not feasible; one uses the whole of a school class or similarly preformed groups. Since the selection factors that enter into the make-up of such groups vary widely and since the effects of such selection factors depend upon the nature of the particular experiment, it seems unlikely that they can be estimated and the results adjusted. If random sampling or other means of assuring a representative sample is impractical, *as much information about the sample as possible must be provided,* so that the reviewer can make his own judgment of the potential generalizability of the findings. The writer can help the reviewer by giving some indication of her best estimate of the potential generality of the findings and the reasoning on which this judgment is based.

When a complex design such as a factorial, Latin square, or nesting is used, reviewers will be interested in the available cases for each of the variables to be analyzed. Give this number as well as the minimum cell size for the design.

Design

The term "design" appears in most proposal guidelines at the point where sponsors wish a description of the structure of the study: the way the groups will be organized; if there is a treatment, when and how it will be administered; when observations will be made of the effect; and the like. Even more than the previous section on sampling, the usual sponsor proposal outline for this section is oriented toward validating rather than exploratory research. Once again, a reminder: *adapt the section to your study, not your study to fit the sponsor's outline*.

The design structure is the main protection against alternative explanations of the phenomenon. The design makes these implausible. If its structure is not adequate to ensure the integrity of the study's chain of reasoning against alternative explanations, the study is a wasted effort! The importance of this section justifies some repetition and considerable expansion of the previous discussion of these matters.

For the study validating a hypothesis, the design shows how the situation will be structured so that data can be gathered with the least contamination by factors providing alternative explanations; or if such factors have an effect, it is built into the comparison--as when control and experimental groups are equally contaminated. This means that it is necessary to *discuss which variables to control and how to control them*. For example, in a study of the effect of two different curricula, the researcher would want to control for any initial differences in the groups that might be reflected in their after-treatment performance. In this situation, the researcher might be expected to control such potentially contaminating factors as the beginning level of competence or achievement, general academic ability, and motivation.

Certain design configurations provide a lot of protection, others less. For example, the learning observed with an experimental curriculum in a single experimental group might be explained by the nature of the persons initially selected, those who stayed through the length of the study, normal growth patterns, or a variety of other factors. However, when one randomly assigns a pool of subjects to control and experimental groups, many alternative possible causal factors are eliminated because they would be expected to affect both groups equally, so that any differences between the groups could not be due to these factors. *When comparing groups one expects to be initially equivalent, one buys a lot of protection by random assignment to groups.* On the average, random assignment to groups equalizes everything from intelligence to size of belly button.

The sensitivity of a study to significant differences is greater if one can eliminate a factor rather than contaminate both treatment and experimental groups. For example, suppose that a test of letter recognition were part of the evaluation of an experimental kindergarten program. If that test were conducted by the university researcher, some children might be uncomfortable and not do as well as if their regular kindergarten teacher had given the test. By having the university researcher test both experimental and control groups, such an effect should be as much represented in the control group as in the experimental. But this introduces another factor, the child's reaction to the test administrator. It adds to the variability of the test scores. That additional variability might be enough to mask the experimental effect of the curriculum, thus causing it to be judged ineffective when it actually was effective. Eliminating that variability by having the classroom teacher give the test would make for a more sensitive test of the experimental effect. *Eliminate a factor to control it, if possible; if not, be sure that it equally affects the control and experimental groups.*

Consider another example and a slightly different solution. Suppose that in order to measure gains, one plans to give both a pretest and a posttest to an experimental group. Taking the pretest may result in higher posttest scores; the subjects may be more at ease knowing what to expect on the posttest or may have reconsidered their answers and be ready with correct ones. One way of eliminating this alternative explanation of the effect might be to create a control group and give a pretest to both groups. But students will react differently to the pretest, some benefiting greatly, others less so; and this variability overlays that of the treatment effect. Again, this reduces the sensitivity of the study, making it more difficult to discern the treatment effect. A better solution is to eliminate the pretest and have experimental and control groups that are given a posttest only. But this presupposes that random assignment created two groups that were equivalent at the beginning. One may be uncomfortable with this assumption. In that case, create four comparable groups by random assignment of subjects, a control and experimental group that undergo both pre- and posttesting and a control and experimental group that take a posttest only. Additionally one may stratify or block on a relevant variable. For example, divide the sample into fifths on the basis of a test of learning ability and randomly assign to experimental and control groups within the fifths. The pretest groups provide an indication of the comparability of groups created by random assignment as well as the change from their initial level; the posttest-- only groups show the effect of the treatment, unaffected by pretesting.

This design, called the Solomon four-group design, is just an indication of the possible design choices; there are many more. A number of such arrangements of groups and measures into designs have been analyzed for their strengths and weaknesses with respect to the alternative explana- tions commonly found in behavioral science studies. (See, for instance, Campbell and Stanley, 1963, and Cook and Campbell, 1979.) Such references are extremely valuable aids in picking a configuration that eliminates plausible explanations for the phenomenon under study.

Having determined the possible alternative explanations that must be considered, the researcher must decide what to do about each. To do this, she will ask such questions as:

- How likely is the contamination to occur?
- Is it likely to have the expected effect?

- What does it cost to eliminate it?
- Is the time, money, or other required resources available?
- How important are my intended sponsor and audience likely to think the alternative explanations are? Will they see these as "long shots" or real possibilities?
- If all cannot be eliminated, how shall they be prioritized in their claim on resources?
- Some can be eliminated for one cost, others for additional cost. Given the other claims on resources, what is preferable?
- Which design best eliminates the top-priority alternative explanations I have decided the study requires protection against?

The final decision must depend on the particular circumstances of each study, but a general principle is to find the design configuration that provides the best possible use of available resources at the same time that it 1) gives priority to the most serious alternative causes of the effect, taking into account their likelihood, and 2) eliminates contaminating influences where that is possible and builds them into the comparisons where it is not.

Control or adjust for as many variables as are important and as can feasibly be accommodated. This is one of the areas which are completely subject to the good judgment of the investigator and for which no set of foolproof rules can be provided. *Every study is a compromise between what it is realistically possible to control and those variables that would be nice to control in the most perfect of all possible worlds.*

It is possible to so tightly control a situation, using very complex designs to eliminate all kinds of alternative explanations, that one can do the study only in a laboratory-like situation. This markedly reduces the generality of the findings. Such a consideration is obviously more of a worry in an applied or developmental study than in one dealing with basic research. But even in the basic research the need for generality may force consideration of other design choices.

Unfortunately, not all judges will weigh the desirability of controlling possible contaminating factors the same way. Their "most acceptable compromise" may differ from the proposer's. Indicate your awareness that particular variables require control. Articulate how you compromised between taking care of all variables requiring control and the realistic limits of what can be controlled. Further, show that the variables chosen can be realistically controlled without sacrificing the integrity of the study.

Once again, this is a place to demonstrate your mastery of the problem. Nobody knows better than you the multiple sources of contamination that might affect the study. *Convincingly indicate the nature and basis of the particular compromise being proposed and the reasons for accepting it. State clearly the reasons for choosing to control the variables selected and for ignoring certain others. Show how the study is as precise as practically possible.*

Avoid expediency as a reason for failing to control an important factor if reasonable expense and effort would do so. For less critical variables, experienced reviewers will recognize the reality of expediency as a good and sufficient basis. In some instances, where desirable control of a variable could be provided only at considerable extra cost, prepare a budget option that would provide control of this factor if the reviewers agree it is warranted.

Although there is no formula for an acceptable design, you should be warned about some of the common errors that have kept proposals from being accepted.

Lack of control group. This would appear to be an obvious flaw, yet it is encountered repeatedly in situations where an enthusiastic investigator wishes to demonstrate the virtues of a new program (e.g., remedial reading, after-school enrichment, new counseling method). The researcher assumes that if gains can be shown between pre- and posttesting, the point is made. Without a control group, however, how can one be sure it was the treatment and not some other effect--natural maturation, "spontaneous recovery," or merely the fact that the subjects were singled out for attention? As pointed out below in the discussion of regression effect, a deviant low group will typically gain on retest even *without any treatment.*

Hawthorne and reactive effects. The effect of special attention noted above is difficult to separate from the effect of an experimental variable where that variable also creates a special situation. Both children and adults typically show reactive effects (usually positive) to such attention. In the Hawthorne plant of the Western Electric Company (from which the effect takes its name) production increased even though working conditions such as illumination were poorer, because the workers felt "special" in being singled out for study. Where the treatment or measurement of effect obtrusively stands out from the normal sequence of events, it may be difficult to attain results that have generality, since they may be due to the special circumstances, the experimental variable, or both--one doesn't know which.

This reactivity of subjects is reduced when things proceed as naturally as possible. Thus, having the usual classroom teacher, social worker, or other professional administer a special treatment, instead of the researcher, may markedly reduce or eliminate reactivity. Further, that person may be the best one to decide how and when to introduce the treatment into the situation. Webb et al. (1966) devote a whole book to the topic of unobtrusive measurement as a way to reduce reactive behavior.

Researcher expectancy effects. Another equally contaminating influence is the expectation of the researcher. Researchers or their assistants may inadvertently tip the scales in favor of an experimental treatment in a variety of ways. For example, they may unconsciously give nonverbal cues to the subjects. They may decide in favor of the experimental treatment in situations that are sufficiently ambiguous to be judged either way. When errors are made, they may unintentionally favor the experimental treatment. When you err in totaling your bank deposit, why is the error more often in your favor than the bank's?

Subjects, aware they are part of a study, typically seek to please the researcher by giving the responses they think are wanted. The Hawthorne effect is sometimes an example of a research expectancy effect. If subjects expect further help from the research, or it they merely tend to be "nice"--i.e., compliant--even without any expectation of gain to themselves they may respond as they think the researcher wishes, even to their own detriment.

Rosenthal (1969) and Rosenthal and Rubin (1980) have studied this problem and summarized 345 studies of interpersonal expectancy effects, ranging from reaction time studies to learning and animal studies. For instance, experimenters were told they were running especially able mice; teachers, that certain children could be expected to show remarkable gains based on test results. In actuality, mice and children were randomly chosen, yet they showed expectancy effects. Only 2 of 9 reaction time studies were influenced by expectancy effects, but 11 of 15 animal studies were. Learning studies, person perception studies, and laboratory interviews all showed them. It appears that the unintended impact of expectancy effect may be as large as the intended effect of many treatments.

Use of "double blind" procedures, where neither observer nor subject knows which is the real treatment or which subjects received it, eliminates expectancy effect. One uses treatments that appear identical, or at least similar, but codes subjects so some uninvolved party can tell them apart after treatment. Subjects in both groups therefore believe they may be receiving the treatment--they are kept "blind." All persons involved in contact with subjects, whether in administering the treatment or observing its potential effect, are also kept blind. The control treatment is often called a placebo or placebo treatment after the inert pill that is used to mimic an experimental drug.

In some instances, the treatment can be given and observations made without subjects' awareness. An experiment on food coloring as the cause of aberrant behavior, for instance, might use foods made to look alike with or without the small amount of coloring normally included. Observations of the subjects' behavior made behind one-way mirrors could be concealed from subjects. Neither observer nor subjects would know when food coloring was present or absent.

Double-blind procedures cannot be used when 1) one's knowledge of treatment is part of the treatment itself, 2) it is obvious which treatment is to be favored from merely observing the treatment or being exposed to it, 3) the treatment can be readily identified from side effects, or 4) withholding a more favorable treatment would have ethical consequences.

Objections to the double-blind technique, besides cumbersomeness, are that the use of therapeutic knowledge is sacrificed to methodological precision and that one's sensitivity is reduced because one is dealing with unknowns. These conditions can be demoralizing to both professionals and subjects. But such objections can often be met by having an independent team assess results who are kept "blind" even though those who administer the treatment are not (Guy, Gross, and Dennis, 1967).

Regression effect. This is a subtle but very serious error that may be committed whenever one selects the top or bottom individuals from a group for special treatment or study. For example, a group of the poorest on a reading test is selected, given remedial treatment, and retested for gain. By regression effect alone, the average score on the second measurement will be higher than on the first, *even if the treatment is utterly ineffective!*

Regression effect occurs when there is a less than perfect correlation (there nearly always is!) between two measures, one of which is used to select a particular group of high or low performers for experimental treatment and the other of which is used to measure the effect of the experimental treatment on that group.

A somewhat oversimplified explanation makes use of the fact that all test scores are subject to error of measurement.[1] Thus, given a group of scores on one testing, we are reasonably sure that on retest, because of that error, some will go up and some will go down. Suppose that we split off a group of low scorers who we think need remediation; everybody, let us say, who scores below 20. We know that near the borderline of the split, some of that group on retest will score higher than 20. Perhaps their true score is higher than 20, and they were misclassified on the first testing. Conversely, some on the upper side of the split will score lower than 20 and perhaps should have been in the remedial group.

Before the group was split, these effects would counterbalance each other, and the retest scores over the entire group would look the same as the initial test. But when an extreme group is split off, the counter-balancing downward-moving cases are removed along with the middle and top section. Thus, their counterbalancing effect is missing, and when the mean of the retest scores of the extreme lower segment is computed, it moves slightly higher (see figure 3). The result is that on retest, even with no treatment, a low group's mean will move up and, conversely, the mean of a high extreme group will come down. In general, the movement on retest of a group split off from either extreme is toward the mean of the total group.

---

[1] We use this as an example of one cause of a less than perfect correlation between two measurements. The effect would occur in any situation where there is a less than perfect correlation. The lower the correlation, the greater the regression effect.

Figure 3. Regression effect on retest.

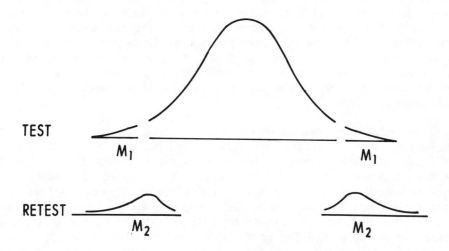

In one recent study, not recognizing that the regression effect would appear in any separate low group, the researcher noted that even the control group seemed to have improved. He concluded that his treatment had spread into the control group and was benefiting the whole school. Actually it was nothing but regression effect that was affecting both experimental and control groups.

Regression effect makes experimental treatments falsely look good because the regression effect alone raises the means just as the treatment is supposed to do. Conversely, regression effect can make an experimental treatment of a high group look ineffective or even negative. Regression effect lowers the mean of a high group, whereas the experimental effect is normally expected to raise it. Depending on the relative strength of these two opposite forces, the average score will go up, go down, or stay the same. In any event, the *apparent* treatment effect will be less than the actual effect because only the difference between regression and actual treatment effect will be reflected in the observed mean. A very weak or ineffective treatment may be overcome by regression effect and the mean score will drop. A treatment equal to regression effect will appear as ineffective, since the mean score will appear unchanged.

Regression effect can be estimated by using a control group comparable to the experimental group. Regression effect will appear in the control group's scores as well as in those of the experimental group so that the difference between the groups is devoid of regression effect.

Over- and underachievers. If there is such a thing as regression effect, one can sense there might also be a problem if two related tests (perhaps an aptitude and an achievement test) were used to select over- and underachievers without taking regression into account. Indeed, current thinking on the subject is that using the raw difference score between the two tests is very poor procedure. Using the aptitude test to predict achievement and then obtaining the discrepancy between predicted and actual achievement, or some similar procedure, appears to be the best currently available way of handling this problem (see Horst, Tallmadge and Wood, 1975).

Cross-validation. We would not model a dress to precisely fit a ten-year-old girl and then claim the dress fit all ten-year-old girls. This is analogous to what occurs when investigators complete a multiple correlation study using a single group. The procedure results in a prediction equation in which the variables are given weights that most precisely predict for the particular group on which the equation was determined. But we are rarely interested in predicting for that group; instead we want to use the prediction equation with other comparable groups. Only if the investigator applies that same formula to another such group (or uses a formula to estimate the shrinkage) can we know whether the weights will predict a comparable group's performance or how limited they are to the original group.

This process, known as cross-validation, should be used for all procedures developing prediction weights that fit a particular group. When sample size is limited, it may prove desirable to split the available cases in half, using one half to establish the weights and the other half to check their generality. Where studies employ multiple correlation or regression, discriminant function analysis, multiple discriminant function analysis, or canonical correlation, consider the possible necessity for cross-validation.

Pretest effects. Pretests have two potentially contaminating effects. One is that the pretest may result in higher scores on the posttest if individuals rethink their answers, discuss the test with others, or become more comfortable with the testing situation. The other is that individuals may be cued to the desired experimental effect by the pretest and benefit more from the treatment than they would otherwise. This is called pretest-treatment interaction. This is especially a problem with experimental curricula where the pretest sensitizes students to those aspects of the instruction that will be on the posttest. They are more likely to attend to those parts and will be more motivated to try to learn them. They will, of course, do better on the posttest than if they had not been pretested. Use of the Solomon four-group design (p. 60) can avoid this problem.

* * * * *

The discussion above by no means covers all the flaws in design but may help you to sense some of the problems. Let me again refer you to excellent sources of information on this topic: Campbell and Stanley (1963) and Cook and Campbell (1979).

At some point, one will want to *determine whether the design is adequately efficient:* whether multiple uses may be made of subjects; fewer data collection points established; more data collected at each visit, measurement, or observation; more efficient scheduling of personnel; and so on. The development of the work plan, discussed later, is especially helpful in showing where economies can be made, since it provides for scheduling of personnel, probably the major expense of most funded projects (and the major resource to allocate for doctoral studies). Considerable savings in resources can result from designing a study to simultaneously validate a group of hypotheses or from combining several studies to use the same subjects when this does not overload either subjects or staff.

Instrumentation and Data Collection

In the section on instrumentation and data collection, the measures and observations used in gathering data should be detailed and their appropriateness for the task convincingly described. In the course of describing methods of data collection, provisions for handling sources of undesirable variation should be explained.

Instrumentation for some variables--time or distance measures, for instance--presents little problem. But most studies in the behavioral sciences involve constructs we cannot directly sense that must be translated into behaviors that can be sensed in order for us to know that they are present. There is no way to directly sense intelligence, for instance, but we judge people's intelligence by their behavior--often by their behavior with respect to a standard set of problems, an intelligence test. This permits us to readily compare their behavior with that of others on a common scale. Psychological, sociological, and economic constructs such as anxiety, socioeconomic class, or marginal utility require interpretation into characteristics that can be sensed and measured. The instrumentation section is where that translation is described and the case made for its adequacy.

This is another section in which the expansive rhetoric of the problem description may be reduced to mundane terms when the reviewer sees what the problem has become in measurement terms. If the realities of measurement are modest, keep the early rhetoric modest too.

Often the translation process helps to sharpen one's understanding of the study's constructs as one is forced to choose among alternative instruments that represent different operational definitions. Thus the term "anxiety" in a hypothesis may be undefined except by implication in the explanation. But when one comes to choosing a measure of anxiety, one will find many possibilities, which range from different self-report instruments of one's "state" of anxiety to those assessing anxiety as a trait and to physiological measures; these delineate different "kinds" of anxiety. The chosen instrument must be consistent with the problem definition and explanation. If these do not provide sufficient guidance to choose among the possibilities, they probably need further refining themselves.

Where it is impossible to find measures congruent with the problem definition and explanation, describe the problem and justify, as well as possible, the measure that comes closest. Omitting the latter discussion is likely to be sufficient reason for disapproval.

Be particularly sure that all the terms critical to the translation of the hypotheses and questions included in the objectives section are provided for in the measures section. Variables mentioned earlier and then dropped without being developed further here contribute to a negative impression.

Validity, reliability, and objectivity may be well established for commonly used instruments. However, empirical evidence should be cited for new or experimental tests. If it is not available, make provisions in the proposal for establishing that the test has appropriate characteristics, if possible, before the experimental data are collected. Here as elsewhere, do not assume that the reviewer will rush to the library to look up missing reliability and validity information. If there is any doubt that the reviewer is likely to know it, supply it.

Validity. In addition to appearing to be congruent with the construct definition, other evidence of validity is important. "Face validity" means that the test looks as though it measured what we want to measure. This is very important when the study's acceptance and use is determined by policy makers, parents and others with little or no professional background. For achievement tests, "content validity" provides a comparison of the test items with specifications of what subject matter content and skills the test is supposed to cover. It provides further assurance that the test is measuring the proper things. Predictive and concurrent validity show that the test correlates with an already accepted measure of the variable. Construct validity shows that the instrument behaves as one would predict a valid measure should. For example, it correlates with measures it ought to be related to and does not correlate with those it should not. Evidence of validity is usually given in the test manual; cite evidence for those kinds of validity needed for the problem posed.

Reliability. If you are strengthening your case for the acceptability of a measure by providing evidence of validity, you may further bolster it with evidence of reliability. Just as there are different kinds of validity, there are different kinds of reliability: stability reliability--the test scores are stable over time; internal consistency reliability (homogeneity)--the various test items measure the same characteristic so the scores are interpretable; and equivalence reliability--different test forms are comparable. Which kinds of reliability are required depends on the design. For example, test results compared over a substantial period of time require stability reliability and internal consistency reliability. If the retest used a different form of the same test, equivalence reliability would be required as well. Again, such evidence is usually given in the test manual.

Objectivity. Observation scales, in particular, require that all observers use them the same way so that they agree when rating the same phenomenon; this is objectivity. Observers often train by rating a videotape of the same kind of events as they will be observing; training continues until all observers respond to events the same way. Describe any planned training and what level of agreement among observers will be sought. Remember that a correlation coefficient will show agreement on relative but not exact position on the score scale; it does not detect that one person is a tougher grader than another, for instance. Use the intraclass correlation to show exact correspondence of judgment.

Sources of instruments. At one time the sole source of information about tests was Oscar Buros's *Mental Measurements Yearbook*, published at irregular intervals since 1938. They are still being published but are now being prepared by the Buros Institute at the University of Nebraska, which has taken over the task (Mitchell, 1985). In addition, however, there are now a number of compilations of instruments. The ERIC Center at Educational Testing Service publishes a very useful bibliography of these sources, which should be used to try to find a suitable instrument. (The currently available bibliography is by Thomas Backer, 1977.) Constructing and validating new instruments is both difficult and expensive; don't "reinvent the wheel."

If no instrument can be found and you propose to construct one, give sample items in an appendix. This is especially important when measurement is expected to be difficult. Frequently the statement is made that if funds are granted, instruments will be forthcoming to measure variables for which nobody has yet successfully developed instruments--funds or no funds. Unless the author can *give some clue to why she can succeed where others have failed,* the proposal is likely to be rejected. In these instances, it may be more appropriate to request funds only for the instrument development phase of a study rather than integrating such development into a large study. Such instrument development, when successfully completed, makes it much easier to secure financing of succeeding stages of the research that might otherwise have foundered. An instrument development study should show how the test will be developed and lay out a test plan. Such plans will be found in many measurement books (e.g., Cronbach, 1984, or, for achievement tests, Ebel and Frisbie, 1986).

Instrument clearance. Be aware that *in a federally funded project, any instrument that will be administered to ten or more persons must receive clearance before it is used.* Be sure to check with program staff to determine how much time is adequate for this step in the work plan, particularly if new instruments are used. (Two months is currently not an unrealistic allowance.) Also find out what kind of information is currently being required. Originally, this requirement was established by Congress to ease the load on questionnaire respondents by reducing duplicate requests and eliminating unnecessary ones. In the recent past it has involved examination of the psychometric properties of instruments as well, thereby making it harder to qualify new and experimental instruments. In addition, scrutiny of the instrument resulted in questions about design in a recent case. The regulations are variously interpreted by different administrations. It is important to check on the current situation when applying to federal programs if instrument clearance is likely to be involved. Find out who is currently assigned the responsibility of giving clearance, how long it generally takes, what goes through routinely and what does not, and whether the surveillance is extending beyond the instrument.

Established versus new instruments. The clearance option raises the more general question of the trade-off between the use of established instruments and new ones. Established instruments may not be quite as close to the desired operational definition as new or experimental ones but usually are better validated and accepted. One can probably more readily obtain clearance with established instruments (although this should be checked, as approval practice seems to vary). More important, scores from familiar instruments will be more easily and widely understood by one's audience. However, more valid research can often be done with new instruments. Which to choose will probably be determined by such factors as whether a delay caused by clearance can be expected and would be critical to the project, how important it is that the results be widely accepted, how different the two instruments are, how well each fits the project, how well each is currently accepted, and whether adequate data are available or can be obtained to document the validity of a new instrument to one's audience's satisfaction.

Problems in data collection. The social-psychological aspects of studies are all too often ignored. Use of middle-class, white interviewers in a lower-class black or Puerto Rican community is an example. Active opposition by teachers threatened by a study of their teaching methods is another. In both instances, the social dynamics of the data collection situation, if ignored, may destroy a study's validity. Project TALENT, a large longitudinal study, found this out the hard way when parents at one data collection location gleefully burned all their material because they believed the information sought was too personal. As with experimental design, the contingencies are too numerous to cover adequately. The following examples may, however, sensitize the reader to some of the pitfalls and suggest how to avoid them.

A most serious problem occurs when those familiar with the study are concerned that the untreated group is being discriminated against. This can be especially serious in therapy or other differential treatment situations where administrators, other professionals, or parents become upset when certain cases who badly need treatment are in the control group. This is often handled by setting up a waiting list to include the control subjects and then treating them later. Indications in the proposal that the cooperating agencies understand this situation and are prepared to cope with it are reassuring.

The more the experimenter will disturb the natural situation in which the data are to be collected, the more likely it is that only certain institutions or organizations will be willing to cooperate. This results in a selective factor, since the research sites are atypical; generalizability is reduced. Prior explorations to show that typical research sites will cooperate provide reassurance to the sponsor. Include assurance of your awareness of the problem and, in an appendix, evidence of the willingness of typical sites to cooperate.

For most studies, the more normal the situation, the more generalizable the results. Investigators show good training in field methods by noting their intent to avoid periods following holidays, a big athletic or social event, and so on.

Often overtaxed research sites may restrict or refuse new requests. Turning to new sites beyond the immediate locale may increase resource requirements as well as inconvenience but may have the advantage of greater generality. If institutional permissions are obtained before the proposal is submitted (a strongly recommended practice), then adjustment can be made in the design as well as in the budget for such sites and the rationale for their use well presented.

The likelihood of obtaining permission to do a study may be remote if one is studying a controversial topic; for example, provisions for collecting data may be far from routine if one is studying sexual attitudes or other highly personal matters. Even such apparently innocuous topics as school achievement in countries with tightly controlled, authoritarian governments may present problems. Inclusion of plans that anticipate these problems may prevent an unnecessary rejection.

Whenever data are gathered from more than one group, or in several situations, describe the provisions made to ensure that the circumstances for data collection are comparable.

The Hawthorne effect--that is, the effect that the very doing of a study has on the group involved--has already been mentioned as a design factor to be controlled. It has its implications for data collection as well. In some instances, these effects may be negative when one finds an "I'm a guinea pig!" or "What, again?" attitude. Such attitudes may be particularly strong in laboratory schools. State the means that will be used to control these variables, e.g., having the regular teacher unobtrusively administer tests as if they were part of the routine.

Using an observer, tape recorder, or television camera may markedly influence the experimental variables or create artificial situations. Describe the steps to be taken with respect to this problem, such as concealment of the camera, special rooms with provisions for concealed observation, or an adaptation period. Kounin (1970) left a box in the classroom throughout the year. Subjects never knew whether it contained an active videocamera and came to ignore it.

As noted earlier, observations of control and experimental groups should be made unobtrusively without the observer knowing which group is being observed. Research assistants may unconsciously bias results favorably if they know how the experimenter hopes the experimental group should act. Mention control of this factor if it is relevant.

Analysis

The method of analysis must be consistent with the objectives and design. For instance, when the study calls for finding the extent of a relationship, thus requiring a correlation, a common error in statistical analysis is the use of a difference statistic between high and low groups, such as a "t" test. A significant "t" test would indicate a correlation significantly different from zero but would not indicate whether the relationship is high enough to permit any kind of reasonable prediction.

The assumptions of the statistics should fit the data. If they do not seem likely to, tell what corrections can be made. For instance, analysis of variance assumes normally distributed populations, but corrections in the level of significance can be made for nonnormal data. The statistics selected should usually also match the quality of data (e.g., nonparametric statistics for categorical data).

In multifactor designs involving analysis of variance, the researcher should show awareness of the appropriate error term. A description of how missing data and/or unequal cell frequencies of a complex design are to be handled also displays a sophistication that is comforting to the reviewer.

When new statistical techniques, computer programs, or other unfamiliar analytic tools are to be used, they should be adequately described and their advantages over current methods clearly indicated so the reviewer may be assured of their appropriateness as well as their reliability. New software may present a special problem here if debugging is still taking place. Describing alternatives that provide backup if snags throw off the time schedule suggests that you are both prudent and realistic.

It is not always possible to completely anticipate the nature of the analysis that will be used; it may depend on the nature of the data collected. This is especially true of content analysis procedures, but it may also be true of statistical methods. As is probably obvious by now, the best strategy is to *reveal the depths to which these problems have been anticipated by describing the projected solution in sufficient detail to clearly convey its nature. At the same time, show awareness of where departures from plan may occur.*

Check to make sure the procedures will handle all the relevant data that will be gathered and will yield evidence bearing on *all the objectives.*

Work Plan

The work plan, or time schedule, is another sign of how carefully and realistically the project has been developed. Some readers turn to it first to get an overall perspective on the project. In other instances, a reviewer who is having difficulty understanding the flow of the procedure turns to the time schedule for the first real understanding of what the researcher intends to do. This indicates the importance of the work schedule as a clear, sequential statement of the operations to be performed.

It follows, of course, that the work schedule should give a *consistent and comprehensive presentation of the preceding material.* Omission of segments of the study makes projections of its length unreliable at best and indicates either carelessness, sloppiness, or disorganization; none of these is conducive to project approval.

Depending on the complexity of the project, various means may be used to describe the work plan. A simple time schedule with a list of dates for completion of various activities is one way. A more complete one lists the dates on which activities will begin and end. More often, however, the work plan is laid out graphically in flow charts or diagrams. Especially for complex projects, these are a better way of indicating the sequence of work than a list of events and dates. They make it possible to show the interrelationships among the different parts of the study and to demonstrate more clearly the relative length of various phases. They are increasingly being requested in federal and state proposal guidelines. Their advantages are these:

1. They require one to estimate the time required to meet all criteria appropriate for each activity (e.g., how long will it take to get a 65% questionnaire return?).
2. They force an exploration of the interrelationships between activities.
3. They require that each step be analyzed in sufficient detail (very helpful for the procedure section!) so that difficulties are uncovered that might have remained hidden in a less clearly specified proposal (only to arise later and bedevil the researcher when the proposal is approved).
4. They serve as a basis for resource allocation of personnel time to various parts of the proposal--and personnel is the major cost.
5. They serve as a justification for the allocation of resources (particularly useful in negotiations!).
6. They provide a basis for administrative control of the project.
7. By maintaining a total perspective, they provide a better foundation for making informed change decisions when those are required, since they more clearly show the implications of each change for the total operation.

If the work schedule is laid out well, the reviewer will have little question about what is to be done, and the major concerns will be problem significance and strength of design.

There are a number of ways of diagramming the schedule of work, each of which has developed a jargon of its own. They apply some sophisticated common sense and, in the more complex methods, some statistics and computerization to the tasks of planning and controlling progress and resource allocation.

Computer programs are now available that not only facilitate preparation of the work plan but also so tie together the work plan and the budget that the budget totals are created simultaneously. As one inserts activities into the work plan, their costs are estimated as well and the data placed into the appropriate places in the work plan spreadsheets. As is noted in the section on budget in the next chapter, the test of a good work plan is whether the budget is derived easily from it. With a carefully developed and detailed work plan, it is just a matter of assemblage and perhaps some addition to obtain the figures for the budget. Conversely, detailed budget preparation, such as that shown in figure 7, p. 100 is readily translated into a work plan.

Using computer software that ties together the budget figures and the work plan charts makes it possible to generate several kinds of displays of the project tasks and financial data to help the researcher focus on different aspects. The effects of various trade-offs between project duration and cost can then be explored. Since the programs use calendars for specific years, the effect of holidays, vacations, and other problems can be anticipated. Two such programs for IBM-compatible personal computers are *SuperProject* by SORCIM/IUS and Micro Software's *Microsoft Project.* Apple Corporation's *MacProject* is such a program for its MacIntosh computer. The illustrative charts in this book were made with the latter.

The choice of available charts varies with the program. Most such programs provide some form of PERT charts (called a schedule chart in *MacProject*, see figure 4), a project or activity table that lists the various activities and their time and resource requirements (figure 7, referred to above), and a precedence diagram (figure 5, called a task timeline in *MacProject*). Though not shown here, *MacProject*, for example, also provides tables for noting each task and its costs as allocated across each person or budget category, a table showing the costs for each resource used for each task, a resource timeline showing resources used each week (see workload analysis below), a week-by-week cash flow table, and a project table with tasks, dates, costs, income, and their accumulation. These are interconnected so that entries and changes in one are reflected immediately in the others.

MacProject and *Microsoft Project* differ in their entry point. To use *MacProject* you create boxes, enter the activities, interconnect them, and enter in a table task time, the project's beginning and end times, and resources used, and it creates all the interim dates as well as the other tables and charts. *Microsoft Project* is table-oriented and asks for the task, task time, resources used, and previous activity and then creates the schedule chart and other tables. These programs can provide substantial savings in computation and artist's time. Now that they are available, I can't imagine doing a complex project without them.

PERT—Program Evaluation Review Technique. Usually referred to by its initials, PERT or its modifications results in a flow diagram showing the sequence of the various activities and their interdependence in terms of completion dates. In a sense it is a road map to a destination to show the intermediate points and distances between them. Activities are sequenced from left to right.

In PERT, as it was originally developed, completed tasks are shown as circles and the activities required for their completion are shown by arrows leading to them. The circles are typically numbered, at random in complex charts, since with numerous changes it is almost impossible to sequence them logically. The numbers tie the circles to a list of activities. Starting date and required time are shown on each arrow.

For most of us, such charts are easier to interpret if the role of circles and arrows is reversed and labels inserted directly in the circles of the chart. Often boxes instead of circles are used to provide more room for activity description and arrows connect boxes to show their sequence and interdependence. Figure 4, a *MacProject* schedule chart, is an example. It displays the steps in a typical sample survey project. The numbers above each box show the estimated days required to accomplish the task. The date below the box on the left is the latest starting date and to its right the latest ending date. Important events that mark the end of a phase of the study are called "milestones" and are given special symbols, the rounded corners of certain boxes in figure 4. In *MacProject*, inserting the beginning and end calendar dates together with the time required for each activity provides enough information for the program to generate all the interim dates automatically, a tremendous time saving.

Some experts believe a better and more realistic work plan diagram is created if one begins with the project's outcomes and works backward. Working forward is said to be more likely to create an "ideal," or "model" set of steps. Having different individuals prepare charts from opposite ends and comparing them gives the advantages of both methods. For more information on PERT (and CPM which is described next), see Cook, 1979). Such charts usually are first laid out in terms of gross activities and then successively refined to ensure that a complete anticipation of what the project will require is at hand.

The thicker line connecting the boxes over the first part of the diagram is what is known as the critical path. In *MacProject* it is automatically generated between those boxes where there is no slack in the schedule. In figure 4, slack time appears with the duplication and sending of the questionnaire. One can see this better in figure 5, where

Figure 4. A schedule chart similar to a PERT chart for a sample survey.
Created by *MacProject*, reduced and cut into three sequences joined by hand to fit page.

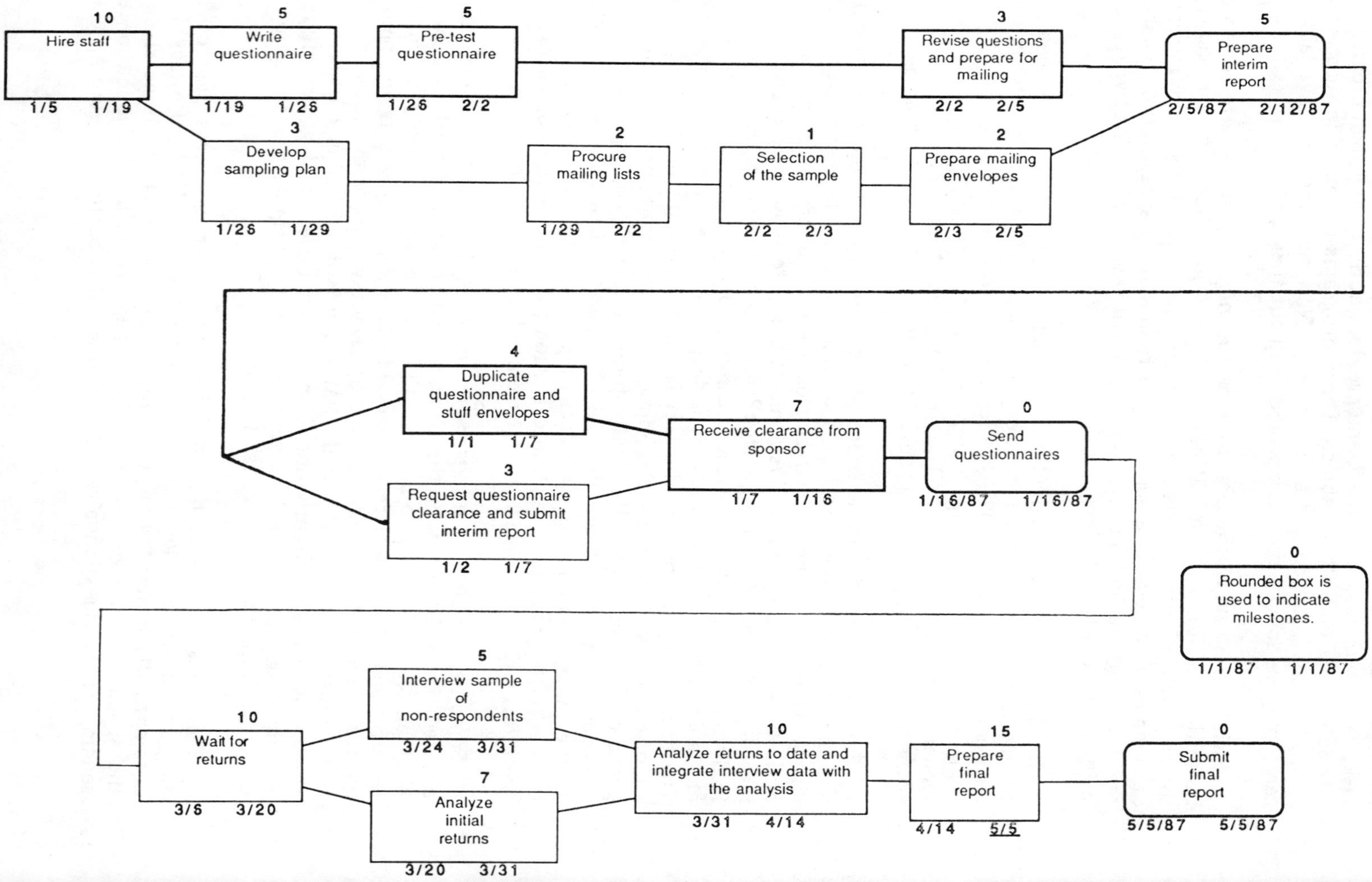

Figure 5. A task timeline showing the same project as figure 4.
Reduced in size from a chart created by *MacProject*.

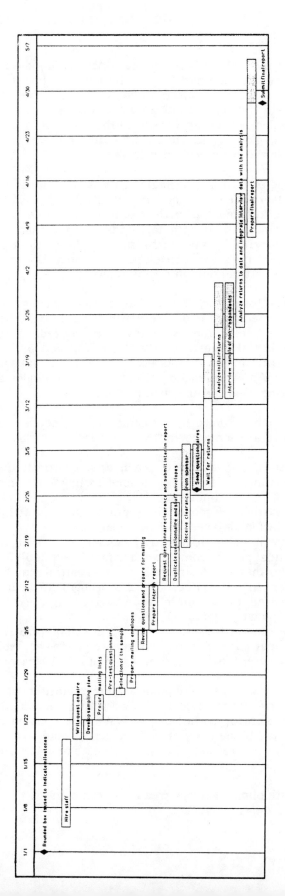

the area to the right of the vertical line dividing a bar shows slack time.[2] The critical path is that line continuously connecting two points which takes the longest required time to finish the interim events and, therefore, is the least time in which the project can be completed. In what is called the critical path method (CPM), such a line is generated from the beginning to the end of the project so the minimum time required for the total project is known.

This line or path is "critical" in the sense that if there is no slack time and the planned end of the project coincides with the deadline for its completion, keeping the critical path on schedule can be very important. If the interim critical path tasks take longer than estimated, the whole project is inevitably later in finishing. The critical path may or may not include what might be considered the most important, or "milestone," events; it is critical only in a time sense.

In actual practice, the initial critical path is often supplanted as various tasks encounter unforeseen difficulties and as dates on the chart are changed. New "longest paths" are created. Planners should expect that their initial adjustments will be followed by others, and the chart must be kept current if it is used for project management (as it almost always is!). An experienced project director includes slack in the schedule which may be used for just such occasions.

If the time required by a critical path exceeds the time allowed for a project, here are some corrective measures that may be taken:

1. Activities that were planned sequentially may, by appropriate adjustment either of personnel assignments or of the nature of the task, be run simultaneously.
2. Activities on noncritical paths can be stretched out, or their initiation delayed and personnel switched to more critical tasks. Sometimes critical activities can be divided into phases with less critical phases completed as staff is available.
3. Steps that are desirable but not essential may be omitted.
4. Additional resources may be brought to bear to reduce the time required to complete an activity (e.g., extra personnel, special equipment, overtime).
5. The scope of the activities of the whole project or of those on the critical path may be reduced (e.g., fewer subjects, shorter questionnaires, fewer hypotheses, simplified treatments).

Obviously such detailed plans are most sensible when the nature of the problem permits the steps in the work to be anticipated. When a project is highly exploratory, what one does next depends on what was just found, so PERT may be nearly impossible. One would have to anticipate all the possible alternatives associated with each possible outcome. Much cruder

---

[2]The stippling in these areas was removed in the reproduction so the type would show.

work plans are appropriate for exploratory projects.

Other work plan diagrams. Simpler diagrams such as task timelines, also called precedence or cascade diagrams, are also useful in showing the flow of work. Figure 5 translates the previous figure into a task timeline. It does not make as clear the interdependent relationships between tasks, but slack times are more visible and the time overlap between activities is quite clear. Both figures 4 and 5 provide different, but useful, perspectives of the same project. Usually only one, typically the task timeline, is shown in the proposal, although if there were no page limit problem, both could be included.

Gantt charts are named after Henry L. Gantt, the man who invented them. These simply list the operations and show the time required against a time scale, as in figure 6. Again, the activities of figure 4 are translated here into a Gantt chart. Additional notation such as triangles to designate a product or milestone event is usually added to give a more refined picture.

Figure 6. A simple Gantt chart, again for the same project.

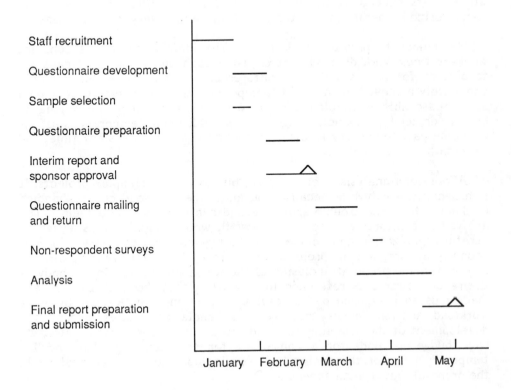

Workload analysis.   Some of the actions suggested for reducing the length of the critical path assume that personnel changes can be made to accommodate the work flow.   But sometimes staff availability is a problem.   A work plan tells the amount of staff time required for each task, but it does not compare personnel demands with available staff; that requires a workload analysis. *Therefore, these corrective measures should be undertaken only in connection with such an analysis, which, especially for large and complex projects, should be made in any case.*

The workload analysis determines the week-by-week (or other appropriate time unit) peaks and valleys in demand for personnel over the duration of the project. It often turns up instances where too much is expected of certain personnel in too short a time and other instances where there is unfilled time that either is an unnecessary expense to the project or could be utilized in other ways.   The workload analysis is computed by totaling the days of work for each week of the work plan for each person or, in the case of a large project, for each skill category, such as clerical, secretarial, and general professional.   These totals can then be compared with available staff to determine when and where problems exist and adjustments made to concentrate work, spread it out, move it to other parts of the network, and so on.   Workload analysis can be considered an interim step in achieving a satisfactory work plan. *MacProject* has a resource timelime table that provides the data for a workload analysis, since one can spot, starting from costs, those places where costs exceed available resources for the work.   Here again the computerized program facilitates what used to be a very laborious task.

Remember to provide slack time.   The ideal is to have a constant week-by-week work demand that is just enough under the staff capacity to provide for illness and other unforeseen events.   Since this is rarely completely achieved, plan ahead to cope with those problems that remain after reasonable work plan adjustments have been made: arranging to borrow or lend personnel, budgeting for additional temporary staff or overtime pay, temporary layoffs, scheduling vacations for slack time, and so forth.

A workload analysis is extra work; but for large, complex projects, it is especially worthwhile because you know the workload can be handled (or know where the trouble spots are and can plan to handle them).   The analysis is comforting to sponsors as well, who recognize it as a sign of careful organization and competence that gives them confidence in your capacity to carry out the project. Considering the load of reading already involved in the proposal, inclusion of the workload analysis in the body of the report is rare.   A reference to it showing that the analysis has been made plus an indication of its results is often enough: "A week-by-week workload analysis shows that we can handle all phases except the development of the sampling plan and the coding of the questionnaire. We have budgeted funds for a consultant for the sampling plan and for temporary help for the coding." If you include the workload analysis in the proposal, put it in an appendix.

When the project staff is small--or just one person, as for most dissertations--the work plan is the workload analysis except where consultant help, special skills, or secretarial assistance is needed.

Some general cautions. Regardless of which method of work plan analysis is used, keep such factors as the actual (not intended) submission date, the length of the review process, the availability of staff once project approval has been received, and other details in mind as you set the starting date. *Make sure the personnel section and the work plan schedule are consistent with regard to staff availability.* Consider that federal project review may be very lengthy, several months or more, and that contract negotiations come after that. These may be extended if such items as overhead, fringe benefits, and consultant pay become issues. Only after all this is resolved can the project be initiated. Without explicit authority *in writing*, it is difficult, if not impossible, to obtain federal reimbursement for expenditures made before the date of final project approval. If work must be begun before the expected date of final approval, the writer should indicate how it will be financed.

Allow extra time for phases not under your direct control. Data collection is often the most seriously underestimated phase, especially where contact with the field is involved. Control of subjects often rests with the parents and/or the institution rather than the investigator, and these agents often give research a lower priority than other time demands. Further, following up dropouts and incompletes, to prevent their having a selective effect on the data, may take as long as or longer than the original data collection. These phases must be planned realistically. Waiting for clearances of all kinds (e.g., approval of instruments in a federal project) and the return of questionnaires are other important examples of variables beyond one's control.

Similarly, analysis and interpretation of the data; writing the final report; and especially the secretarial, editorial, and duplicating time needed to produce the report tend to be underestimated. Authors frequently tend to end the time schedule at the point where they complete their writing, ignoring the editorial and production phases, which often extend three months beyond the date of completed draft. It is well to bear in mind that, in general, required time increases with greater complexity, magnitude, and difficulty and as control decreases.

Occasionally, when the project is too large to be granted all in one lump, or when the agency wishes to start the project and evaluate progress, it may use the time schedule to find a satisfactory breaking point in the project. Indicating phases in the work plan facilitates this process, especially when interim products are developed.

Expected End-Product and Dissemination Plans

This section is not required in all proposals but is a good section to include if there are products in addition to the usual report of results or if the report of results is other than routine. Sponsors want to know that their project will be remembered and, if possible, that it will have impact. Products help! Tests, evaluation instruments, curriculum materials, films, pamphlets, and the like, even though they may be only by-products of the project, are sometimes more important and more enduring than the project results. Describe them and their possible use outside the project.

Be sure to check the copyright policy of the funding agency. Some agencies require that all products whose development was supported by public funds be placed in the public domain. Others, under the same circumstances, require only that the government be given the right to use the product royalty-free. Still others are halfway between and permit protected publishing or production rights for a limited period. If there are restrictions, indicate awareness of them in this section by describing their expected effect, if any, on dissemination.

You may feel uncomfortable describing endproducts in a proposal, the results of which are to be found. In that case, perhaps you can describe the minimum that might result from the project if worst came to worst and the maximum if everything turned out beautifully. That provides the needed information, and the reader can make his own estimate of which of these is more likely.

The increasing concern with ensuring that study results reach the consumer means that dissemination plans are often given more weight in evaluating proposals than in the past. Plans for translating the results into highly readable form, drawing practical implications, and getting this information into dissemination networks (mental health clinics, school study councils, state departments, consortia, and so on) should be clearly described where dissemination is a stated or a possible criterion.

Give some consideration to the form of the report. It may be that videotapes, films, filmstrips, invitational seminars, workshops, and conferences would be appropriate additions to the printed report. A supplementary budget for such items may be included that could be funded should the sponsor so desire. More often, however, sponsors will make a separate award for dissemination after they are sure the results are worth it.

Requests for proposals (RFPs) may require reports in specified form; thus an article ready for publication may not suffice as a final report. In fact, if the RFP was so complete in its specification of design that the sponsor's monitor had as much responsibility for major decisions as the researcher, that officer may expect to be joint author on resulting publications. Money for RFPs is given as a contract, and since a contract implies the purchase of services, the contract may require that permission be obtained before the contractor publishes results in any public forum. Indicate awareness of these conditions in the RFP response.

5.

Proposal Development:
3. Resources

The chapter covers the description of the resources, those available and those needed to carryout the activities required by the problems set forth in Chapter 3 and the activities of Chapter 2. It also includes the sections on assurances and clearances, abstract, title, a final check, and duplication of copy.

The final sections of the proposal are supportive of the procedure section. They describe the resources in expert personnel and facilities already available to carry out the project, thus providing an inviting opportunity that can be realized if only the sponsor will provide the necessary money. This part of the proposal begins with a personnel section attractively describing the qualifications of the persons who will carry out the activities described in the procedure section.

The facilities section describes the advantages of the institution in which the personnel will work. It details available support--both the physical facilities and equipment and the bureaus, centers, and other units with personnel possessing relevant expertise.

The budget shows in considerable detail what contributions the institution is prepared to make and the resources that will be required of the sponsor for the project to become a reality.

The appendixes are an integral part of a complex proposal and often contain very important material not appropriate elsewhere in the text. They should not be an afterthought.

The next section describes the clearances for federally supported projects that the host institution is required to supply assuring compliance with civil rights regulations and certain ethical limitations. It assures the sponsor that cooperating institutions supplying subjects, personnel, equipment, and so on, have been contacted and are willing to fulfill their project responsibilities.

The final sections are concerned with the wrap-up of the proposal prior to submission: the development of the abstract, desirable characteristics of the title, a final check and review, and duplication.

PERSONNEL

Prepare the personnel section to meet this project's requirements; don't just reuse a write-up from an old proposal unless it is a good fit.

Tell who will direct the project. Give a picture of the person's competence, showing experience relevant to the abilities called for in this project. If experience is lacking, highlight training that might substitute (e.g., research training seminars, postgraduate fellowships, apprenticeships in other projects). Having the project director position filled is important to the sponsor. It is the key position; knowing the competence of that person is the main security a sponsor can have. Indeed, some sponsors prefer to fund more on the capabilities of the project director than the project write-up. A good investigator may pull "silk purse" results out of "sow's ear" projects. Ensuring that project leadership will be immediately available is critical if the project must get underway quickly. When time is not a problem, it indicates the existence of prior capability within the organization and a readiness that bodes well for the project's success. (Some projects are awarded contingent on the availability of certain staff and/or require sponsor approval of replacement of key staff members.)

Profile other key staff members. In a large project describe their qualifications and how the mix of expertise fits the project's requirements. State the responsibilities for key personnel in the narrative of the proposal and indicate the items in their vitae that support their appropriateness for the assignment. Put vitae in an appendix and keep them brief; a page per person is often enough. Emphasize relevant experience, skills, and training. Summarize in the vitae final paragraph other capabilities that indicate the breadth and scope of less relevant experiences. Reviewers are much more likely to be impressed with a résumé in which relevant background and experience are highlighted for their attention. For persons with minor roles, paragraph summaries of assignment, responsibilities, and relevant background will suffice. This will shorten and simplify this section, which can otherwise be overwhelming, especially if complete vitae are pulled from files for inclusion.

Make each person's assignment clear. Don't make the reviewer hunt for a person's relation to the project. An organizational chart is helpful for large projects.

Do not list persons without their permission. Discovery that the writer has used names without consent reflects very unfavorably; it is a kind of dishonesty. If the proposal is written as if such persons had agreed to serve, it suggests the writer can't be trusted and puts the whole project under a cloud of suspicion. If there isn't time to contact them, say that "persons such as _____ will be contacted to secure their cooperation if the project is approved." Depending on the agency, sometimes you can secure letters of willingness to work with the project and send them late, asking that they be appended. In many competitions, however, only what is submitted by the deadline can be considered in judging the proposal. Check with staff to find out.

Organization and management. In a large proposal, and sometimes in a small one where the staff are part of a unit with background and skills conducive to the conduct of this project, a section on organization and management is included in addition to the personnel section. Some RFPs require it. This section gives the opportunity to describe how the organization and management will support the project and are particularly facilitative of its conduct. It may indicate their record of successes and the background of experience that can be drawn on.

Multiple-staff projects are team efforts; if there is evidence to show that the members can work together effectively, that is particularly important. Perhaps a research team has worked together on previous projects; indicate how the sponsor can take advantage of the group's momentum and cohesiveness to save the cost and time of team building that is so often a part of new projects. This can be especially appealing to a sponsor if the team's past record is good.

This is also a good section in which to include the relation, if any, of this project to the ongoing program of the unit. Note here the relationships and areas of responsibility of subcontractors and consultants and show how they facilitate attainment of the project goals.

In general, competence has been judged by the vitae and what the reviewer knew about the reputation of the researcher. Recently one federal agency, the National Science Foundation, has required that researchers with a prior grant from it include a section in the proposal detailing the results of that study (or the one closest to the proposed work, in the case of multiple prior awards) in four single-spaced pages or less and listing resulting publications. Reviewers are being asked to comment on the quality of the work described. Clearly a new and important reporting requirement has been added to the proposal, one that, even more than the vitae, will determine the competence of personnel. It is too early to tell yet whether this requirement will be adopted by other agencies.

New researchers. In addition to applying to small-grant programs that are specifically established to encourage new researchers or choosing programs that have a history of supporting new as well as established ones, novice researchers can bolster their chances by asking an established researcher to work with them in some role. One such role is as an active consultant.

The borrowing of names per se can of course be abused, but evidence of experienced and active consulting participation does give the reviewer assurance that the probability of a successful project is increased. Where such a relationship has been established, the nature of the cooperation should be made clear in the personnel section. Refer to it elsewhere if that seems appropriate.

Another role is as co-researcher or as principal investigator, the writer taking a less senior position. In either instance, the appropriate roles should be made clear in the budget in terms of relative time assigned to the project and in the personnel section where their relative responsibilities are detailed. Indicate that the senior person is willingly assuming certain administrative and legal responsibilities with respect to the project and will oversee the work, which will be principally done by the junior investigator. This is an established practice, well respected by both institutions and sponsors. Make clear that the senior person wants to do this and thinks well of the junior person. A letter from the senior person regarding role, opinion of the junior staff, and willingness to actively oversee the project is very helpful. There have been instances recently where senior persons have not adequately carried out their oversight responsibilities and junior investigators have cut corners or been outright dishonest in order to meet self-perceived expectations. Although these instances are rare and so far confined to the biological and medical fields, everyone suffers when such an instance occurs.

Advisory committees and consultants. The expertise and approval of advisory committees and consultants can strengthen an otherwise weak proposal. But both must be used in their proper role. Use advisory committees only when it is clear that they are needed to legitimize the project in the eyes of the subjects or when their expertise will help legitimize the project's results among one's intended audience. Sometimes committees can be useful in helping to analyze a complex situation or a set of data, the interchange among members helping to enrich the ideas of any one researcher. But sponsors are often put off by the use of prominent leaders in a field if it appears they serve mainly to provide project appeal; the investigator gives the impression of hiding behind the committee. This is particularly true when the researcher saddles a committee with prerogatives for research direction that he should be exercising. We are all aware of the mediocrity that often results from the compromises that must be made in a group; reviewers would typically prefer that advice be sifted by a competent project director who wants to bear responsibility for the decisions.

Proper use of consultants may satisfy reviewers' concerns about specific shortcomings in background and experience of the project staff, especially technical competence (e.g., sampling plans, medical advice, software know-how). It is much less likely that managerial competence can be acceptably supplied by consultants. Further, be careful of the number of consultants employed. A few consultants used in the right places may score very positively. Too many consultants may indicate a weak staff and make the project's acceptance less likely. If possible, include letters from significant consultants (in an appendix) showing their willingness to participate.

Don't use consultants known to be your personal friends unless it is made clear that their expertise is required. Sponsors are suspicious of relationships where professionals hire each other as consultants, fearing these may be pay for past or future favors rather than a purchase of competence.

Congress has been critical of extensive use of consultants by federal agencies, since Congress believes it has authorized enough staff that the needed expertise ought to be in-house. This attitude carries over into restrictions on research funding as well. For example, the National Science Foundation has had a maximum daily rate for individuals for consultant services, linked to the maximum rate paid a federal employee with a personnel position rating of GS-18. Other agencies may follow this rule or have their own. Some programs require that special justification for consultants be included in the proposal. Be alert to this problem when reading the proposal preparation directions. If in doubt, and planning to hire consultants with public funds, check with the program staff about special restrictions or complications.

FACILITIES AND OTHER EVIDENCE OF COMPETENCE

The facilities section tends to be filled with a standard institutional description pulled from the file and included in every project. Unless the organization is unknown to experienced reviewers, they are likely to skip or very lightly skim it. Therefore, any particular advantages one would normally expect to describe here should probably also be noted in a section that will be read more closely, with reference made to the facilities section of the proposal. Alternatively, place them in the beginning of the section so it is immediately apparent this is not a routine description.

Institutional descriptions expressly tailored to the project are much less likely to be skipped or treated lightly. Special facilities that might have a bearing on the research should be listed: data processing and computer facilities, consultant aid such as a bureau of statistical consulting services, a survey research center, special equipment, especially relevant library holdings, test or research collections, advantageous building arrangements--all may be pertinent. If the project must get underway shortly after it is approved, ready availability of needed space and equipment should be noted. Established networks of relationships with schools or clinics, available panels of respondents, working arrangements with interviewers, and similar items--all may be relevant to particular projects and thus should be noted.

When field arrangements require the approval of schools, clinics, or other cooperating agencies, evidence of prior approval lends strength to the proposal. Experienced proposal writers duplicate copies of letters from responsible personnel in these agencies and include them in an appendix with good effect.

Institutional commitment to the research can often be shown in this section by noting the organization's willingness to allocate particularly good and useful space and/or equipment to the project if it is funded. This is reassuring to a potential sponsoring agency and suggests that it would be getting its money's worth.

If its cost is to be charged to the project, renovation of facilities for a research project raises red flags for reviewers. Sponsors are painfully aware that faculty use this means to improve space when they can't get their own institution to do it. As a result, whether correctly or not, sponsors believe the researcher's home institution should handle renovations. Often sponsors will negotiate ways to charge improvements back to the institution. One frequently used strategy is to require that renovation expenses come out of the indirect cost budget item. The researcher is usually caught in the middle, often not particularly caring who pays so long as the renovations are made. One possible way to prevent such a question from arising in the first place is to compare the institution's charge for renovation and overhead with the cost of renting comparable, locally available commercial space. Even if the costs are equal, the convenience of the institutional space is usually a factor in your favor.

Equipment availability may also be a problem. Find out the policy of the agency on renting equipment, especially whether it allows lease-purchase plans, and state in the proposal how your rentals conform to its policy. This avoids any misunderstanding and shows that you have done your homework.

BUDGET

The budget simply translates the work plan into costs. Discovering a good research idea and translating it into suitable operational terms is the hard work. Once that has been done and a careful work plan developed, creating the budget is primarily a matter of determining the costs of the planned activities, allocating them to the proper budget category, and seeing whether their total lies within the realm of possible sponsorship. If not, it is back to the drawing board to find where cuts can be made that will not affect the integrity of the project but will lower the cost.

Novice researchers fear their first budget preparation, but they quickly lose that fear as it fits together; experienced researchers may not like preparing the budget, but they take it in stride. If you are new at the game, take heart; this is one aspect where others can give you concrete help. If you have a research office at your institution, checking budgets is usually one of its main responsibilities, so turn to it. Otherwise, your accounting section can probably supply much of the needed information and expertise. The personnel there know the prices of things, the "ins and outs" of direct and indirect costs, and what is included in fringe benefits as well as how to calculate them; such things are mysteries to the newcomer. To give you an understanding of what they are doing and the ability to do it yourself if need be, this section will explain some of what is involved in budget making.

As an operational statement in monetary terms, each budgetary provision should have a counterpart in the project description and vice versa. Developing the budget is an excellent test of how clearly and completely the project has been described. A clearly described project and precise work plan will be easily translated into budgetary terms. A vague one will be translated only with slow guesswork. If much of the latter occurs, the proposal write-up should be reexamined; it probably needs sharpening.

Budgets are usually the last section to be developed. Researchers who are fascinated by the substantive rather than the fiscal tend to leave little time before deadline for budget development. Tired from their previous effort, they get that "what the heck" feeling and threaten to "rear back and pass a miracle," setting down figures that are, at best, crude estimates and, at worst, have no basis in fact. Don't you do it! Set a self-imposed deadline early enough that even if there is a hitch in this process, you allow time for carefully preparing the budget, writing the abstract, giving the proposal an overall once-over, getting internal clearances, and having the proposal duplicated and mailed. As you can see, budget isn't quite the last thing.

Preparing for Budget Development

Although you can start developing the direct-cost budget without the following information, to properly finalize it, you must have five pieces of information:

1. *What upper limit is reasonable?* If you know that you are well within the typical funding range for your target agency or program, skip this question. Set the budget for your project at whatever is reasonable in order to accomplish the task rather than in terms of the typical-size grant or all you can get. If you are well under the typical grant size, use what additional resources are necessary to build a solid study. If you skimped first time through, go back and build in what is needed. But don't build up the project size just to get the funds. Not only is this unethical in that it deprives another investigator of the funds for his research, but it also is likely to come back to haunt you when the project monitor discovers it, as is likely when the final report or product is evaluated.

You are interested in building a continuing relationship with sponsors; some sponsors trade information with one another. In some federal agencies, each project is to be judged strictly on its merits exclusive of the past reputation of the investigator; in many others and increasingly, as just noted in "Personnel," the past record is very important. Further, even when the past record is not supposed to affect the decision, it is very hard to say that is entirely the case (see quotation from Howarth, 1980, in Chapter 10). Obtaining funding over a period of years will be much more important to you than trying to get all you can any one time.

Assuming, however, yours is a project in which the upper limit is of concern, two factors are involved in that determination:

a. *What is the sponsor's likely limit?* Some digging may be required to find out what kind of funds is available and how these have been doled out to comparable projects. Program staff can certainly tell you the former and may help with the latter. The list of past years' grants can usually give an idea of what has been granted to comparable projects. (See Section IV)

If the proposal is for a contract rather than a grant (see p. 198 for the difference), there is usually a statement in the request for proposal (RFP) something like "This project is estimated to take 1½ person-years." A "person-year" is jargon for the typical cost of a professional person's work for a full year, including such expenses as routine travel, supplies, office equipment, secretarial help, and research assistant help. The estimated cost for a "person-year" varies from agency to agency, as well as over time with the effects of inflation. Beverly Kooi, in a study for *Federal Grants and Contract Weekly* (Oct. 25, 1977), found it varied in 1977 from about $41,000 for the Environmental Protection Agency to $177,000 for the Department of Defense. That is quite a range, but behavioral science figures were mostly in the $50-60,000 range. Again, some detective work on past contracts will give a current estimate for the agency of interest.

b. *How much will be available to run the project after your institution has reserved its share of the funds for indirect costs?* Indirect costs are explained in a later section, but for the moment it is enough for you to know that anywhere from a quarter to half or more of your funding may be absorbed by indirect costs or what is called "overhead." On the average, across institutions, investigators probably receive only about twothirds of their funding for day-to-day operational expenses. This comes as a rude shock to new researchers! It sometimes becomes a point of contention between administrative officers, who must try to recover all the actual costs of research to keep institutions solvent, and researchers, who perceive administrators as grabbing research funds for administrative purposes.

But indirect costs are as real as direct ones and are here to stay, so learn what they are and determine what proportion of your total asking price remains for your actual use on the project after indirect costs have been charged to it. That gives you a maximum direct-cost budget figure.

If your project is likely to approach the upper cost limit as described herein, some estimate should be in your mind from the beginning of project development so you can roughly gauge what is reasonable as you plan it. Finding you are substantially above the limit and having to extensively redesign is painful and wastes precious time.

2. *What rules and regulations must be observed regarding which costs can be charged to the project and which cannot?* Sponsors differ in what they will pay for. Some will not pay for alterations to buildings, some exclude equipment, *many foundations will not pay indirect costs,* some have limits on how much can be paid a faculty member in the summer, some have limits on consultant pay, and so on. In short, find out what sponsor restrictions apply to your proposal.

Your institution has regulations that may affect your budget as well. There is probably some set formula for computing the amount of vacation that can or must be taken, the summer pay from the academic year salary, and so on. Unfortunately, the more restrictive of the two tends to prevail. Institutions are typically unwilling to waive their regulations because a sponsor does, and sponsors set the restrictions under which their money can be spent.

3. *What kind of contract is envisaged?* If you are applying for a grant, you are, in essence, asking for a bank balance against which you

may charge reasonable costs, with anything left over returned to the sponsor. This sounds as though there might be little pressure to cut costs, since the sponsor gets the money back anyway. But Parkinson's law, that jobs expand to fill the time allowed, applies to costs as well. In addition, returned funds go back to the treasury and are rarely available for reassignment. The sponsor's staff get no credit if you come in under budget--they just have that much less to allocate to others for having given you too much and can be criticized by fellow workers for using up available funds. So a "sharp budget pencil" is important even for grants.

A contract is used by the federal government to purchase services or a product for which it provides specifications. The government wants to get the best price possible, so you will be bidding against others; all things being equal, the lower your bid, the better your chance of getting the contract.

Most contracts are of a fixed-price nature; you agree to do the project for a set price *even if it costs more.* So don't cut yourself short! With a fixed-price contract, you can keep the difference if it costs less. But not all contracts are fixed-price ones. Depending on circumstances, there are also cost-reimbursement, cost-plus-fee, and cooperative or cost sharing contracts. Each has its own features with budget implications; but since they are rarely used for research, they are beyond the scope of this book. (See also the section on kinds of contracts and grants, p. 198.)

With the three items above, one can construct the budget and determine what one's costs will be. There are, however, two additional items of information that are important to bear in mind. Question 4, on flexibility in moving funds among budget categories, tells how precise your budgeting must be; and question 5, on "cost sharing," tells whether you must find an institutional source for part of your budget.

4. *What flexibility is there to shift funds among budget categories once funds are given?* If money can be shifted from category to category after the funds are given, you don't have to be quite as precise initially. Usually there is some rule allowing 5 or 10% of the total to be shifted without the sponsor's approval. This isn't very much money in some categories with a small total, so these will have to be precise. But such rules vary with the agency. Find out how much flexibility you will have. This also determines how much contingency money can be moved across category lines if the unforeseen occurs.

5. *How much, if any, "cost sharing" or matching funds are required? Must they be "hard," that is, cash; or can they be "soft," that is, contributed services or use of equipment or facilities?* A small amount is required in most federal projects, but check the program announcement; some agencies require more. Matching funds in cash typically come from your own unit's budget, so if that is required, be sure you get authorization. "Soft" matching can be in contributions of your time that are not charged to the project, use of equipment without rental charges, and other forms. Since these represent forgone income, they may require

someone's authorization as well.

When answers to all five questions are in hand, one has the information needed to prepare a final budget.

Constructing the Budget

For a grant, one typically traces through the work plan, determining the out-of-pocket costs of each activity, as well as the staff time involved. The latter is then translated into its cost by using the rate of pay and adding entries rounded to the nearest dollar. Add all the costs, compare the total with whatever limit you have set, and then rework estimates or design to come in under it. Sometimes one decides to exceed the limit on the assumption that even though the sponsor hasn't supported projects at this level before, perhaps it will this one. Maybe, but be sure to provide a good reason for it to do so.

For a contract, one often starts with a figure that one expects would win the contract and works backward, crudely allocating what seem to be appropriate portions to phases and then figuring how to do them for that amount or less. Either way, be sure to allow sufficient resources for data collection and final report preparation, including data analysis. These tend to be the most underestimated activities.

Expenses are listed in the budget by category, but if the budget extends beyond one year, they are listed by category within fiscal year. Typical categories are the following:

> Personnel--salaries, wages, and fringe benefits
> Subcontracts and services--services such as test scoring,
>   computer use, and statistical analysis; subcontracts
>   with other organizations (for example, interviewing, a
>   sample survey, a sampling plan); consultants, and so forth.
> Expendable materials and supplies
> Communications--long distance calls, postage, and the like
> Reports and publications
> Travel
> Equipment rental
> Equipment purchase
> Indirect costs

Personnel cost. Personnel costs are probably the largest expense category, often 70% of direct costs. Each key staff person is shown with the percentage of time over the life of the project that he will be working on it. For example:

> Prof. Keith Cleghorn, $15,833
> 20% one academic year,
> full-time 2 summer months,
> @ $37,500 per academic year

The amount requested would have been determined by the following figuring:

20% of $37,500   = $ 7,500   (academic year cost)
2/9ths of $37,500   = $ 8,333   (summer 2 months' cost)
        Total $15,833

A secretary who is half-time on the project would be shown as:

Secretary, $ 7,500
50% 12 months
@ $15,000 per year

Include annual or semiannual wage increases that may occur before the project is approved for funding as well as such increases over the life of the project. Unless there is a salary schedule, these must, of course, be estimated. Allow enough, however, or you may have to cut into another category to provide for them.

Examination of the workload analysis will show whether student or other temporary help will be available at the times needed. Exams, vacations, and holidays make students unavailable at various times, and their replacement, if the project must be carried forward at that time, is often more expensive than rescheduling the project.

The secretarial requirements for the ordinary flow of work and for peak loads should be analyzed carefully in relation to the existing secretarial load pattern--e.g., class registration, end-of-semester problem, annual report times. Cooperative arrangements that share a secretary's time with other routine or special needs should be considered both pro and con in terms of their economy and efficiency and in relation to the investigator's own work habits.

After all entries are made, the personnel costs are summed, and a separate entry is made for fringe benefits. Fringe benefits are included in indirect costs in some institutions and broken out as a separate item in others. Follow the pattern required by your sponsors. Fringe benefits are usually figured as a percentage of personnel costs. Such benefits include, for example, retirement and medical insurance contributions, vacation time, sick leave allowance, national holidays, and personal leave days. In some institutions, fringe benefits also include the remitted tuition of staff and graduate assistants; in others those amounts are shown as direct costs. Some sponsors will not pay remitted tuition costs that are direct charges but will allow them as part of overhead or indirect costs. If tuition is part of your budget, be sure it is included in that part of the budget where the sponsor will pay it. There usually are separate fringe benefit rates for salaried and nonsalaried personnel. New peculiarities emerge from time to time with certain agencies. Your budget officer should know these; but if she doesn't, check with the sponsor's staff.

Subcontracts and services. Large subcontracts (currently greater than

$10,000) usually need approval by the sponsor. Therefore, enough detail of the need and arrangements for such a contract should have been included that it seems clearly justified. Further, it is helpful to show that the price is reasonable. There is always the sticky question of the subcontractor's indirect-costs. Should the sponsor pay your institution's indirect cost on that part of the project funding not carried out there? Most agencies either refuse to do so or reduce the indirect cost charges to an amount appropriate for accounting and auditing. Find out your proposed sponsor's policy.

Joint projects such as those between a social service agency, clinic, or school and a university are often handled as a subcontract with one agency (usually the one more likely to get the funds) serving as prime and the other as subcontractor. Negotiations between the parties for which shall be prime and who controls what can be tricky. Having as much as possible carefully considered beforehand and reduced to writing is very important. With such prior agreement, these arrangements can be hard on friendships; without them. . . .

As noted previously in the discussion of personnel, extensive use of consultants is frowned on in some agencies, and some link the maximum pay per day to federal salaries (currently the GS-18 level). Check to determine the current situation. Note that consultants are usually a separate category from other personnel costs; no fringe benefits are usually paid for consultant honoraria.

Costs of services such as test scoring, computer use, and statistical analysis should be obtained, if possible, as a written estimate. This ensures that there is no misunderstanding about what you need and also provides a basis for discussion if providers of services decide to charge more later.

Materials and supplies. Keep track of how you estimate supply costs of items that are considered expendable. These include various stationery and duplication supplies, audio- and videotapes, tests, and similar items. Items that might make the total unusually large should be either broken out as a separate entry or their justification noted in parentheses (e.g., 75 copies of *Quikset Intelligence Test* @ $2.75 = $206).

Communications. Long-distance calls, postage, and the like are budgeted here. Local calls and phone rental are typically included in indirect costs; if not, include them here. As in supplies, large entries, such as might be incurred in a survey project, should be explained (e.g., 225 follow-up calls averaging $1.50 per call = $338).

Reports and publications. Include the cost of producing the final report as well as any other publications produced during the project. Some journals require authors to share the costs of publication; they ask for "page charges." Include estimated page charges if you plan to use such a journal to publish your study results. Entries calling for many copies of the final report tend to be questioned on federal proposals.

Congress has attempted to confine large print orders to the Government Printing Office. Some agencies have limits on how many copies of the report or other items may be produced on project funds.

Travel. Travel intown as well as out of town should be considered. Considerable mileage can be incurred in visiting research sites. Anticipate contingent possibilities: Do you need a female driver to transport female subjects? Project reports at professional conventions are an important part of dissemination and are usually allowable costs; include the cost of attendance. Give some detail on out-of-town trips, especially if there are many of them: APA convention, New York City, air fare $150 plus 5 days per diem @ $100 = $650; 3 one-day trips to New York City Library, $185 air fare plus $45 per trip ground transportation = $690. Take special care to justify foreign travel, as sponsors want to be sure they are not paying for your vacation.

Equipment rental and purchase. Equipment for federal purposes is distinguished from supplies by cost (e.g., greater than $500) and expected service life (e.g., two years or more). Rental of equipment is often allowable when purchase would not be, especially for a short project. Check prior commitments to be sure that rental equipment will be available when you need it.

Many agencies have restrictions on equipment purchase. Some allow lease-purchase arrangements whereby the rental paid may be applied in whole or in part to purchase of the equipment when the project ends. This can result in acquiring expensive equipment at considerable savings. Some sponsors disallow lease-purchase arrangements, perceiving them as an institutional subsidy.

Your case for specialized equipment purchase or rental will be bolstered if you can assure the sponsor that you have checked the equipment inventory of both your own and neighboring institutions, and the equipment needed is not available.

Indirect costs. Institutions rarely charge a project directly for the costs of space, heat, institutional administration, accounting, library, basic phone service, and similar items. It would be difficult to calculate these for each project and impossible for the government to audit them. Guided by Bureau of the Budget Circular A-21, institutions choose which allowable costs will be charged indirectly and calculate these as a portion of the institution's total budget (or as a percentage of the institution's personnel costs). This figure is audited annually by the government and a figure established that represents the proportion of indirect to direct costs for that institution. It may then charge up to that percentage to each federal research project in indirect costs. These costs are commonly known as "overhead." Nonfederal public agencies and some foundations permit the federal auditor's indirect-cost figure to be used in calculating budgets for them as well.

Because of the competitive nature of many programs, some institutions do not charge the full percentage of indirect costs to which federal auditing has entitled them. This is an institutional prerogative. Sometimes, especially for a small grant or one from a foundation, fiscal officers will agree to waive all or part of the indirect costs to help the researcher get funded.

Because of the leeway allowed each institution to determine what is in the indirect-cost base and whether the full indirect-cost will be charged, it is difficult to compare institutional figures. Indirect cost rates of private universities are said to be higher than those of state institutions, but the American Council on Education's 1969 Report of the Ad Hoc Committee on Indirect Costs concluded that the facts do not bear this out; the average rates were almost identical.

Learn whether your indirect-cost figure is based on personnel or total direct costs and what items are included. (Equipment purchases are often excluded, as are subcontracts and tuition or training stipends, for instance.)

When facilities are to be modified or renovated for a project, sponsors may wish the funds to come out of indirect costs. Since project funds are usually paid in regular installments, and the work must be done at the start of the project, either the institution or the agency must advance the money. Where the institution is reluctant to do so, sometimes the costs can be charged directly and overhead costs reduced by an equal amount.

If space is to be rented, check to see whether there is a maximum rate: some federal contracts are limited to the rate that the General Services Administration (GSA) pays for space in your community. Full indirect costs would not be applicable if the project's space is directly charged.

Some foundations and an occasional public agency refuse to pay the indirect-cost figure or pay only a small percentage. Many items, such as phone and the equivalent cost of rental space and office equipment, can be charged directly in order to recover these costs.

Recovering indirect costs. If your project is approved, you will probably start receiving account sheets from your fiscal unit showing your available balances *minus indirect costs.* What happened to those funds? Did they disappear into the coffers of the institution? Policy varies; some institutions routinely return a portion of them either directly to the research unit that generated them or to one of the administrative levels to which it reports. Others simply put them in the general revenue stream. In many, the matter is negotiable.

When indirect costs are retained in some central administration office of the institution, it pays to try to negotiate some of them for your project. Since overhead charges usually include the cost of using space as well as that of the customary office furniture and equipment, charges for such items as remodeling, phone connections, furniture, and common office equipment are typically legitimate charges to an indirect-cost budget. You can ask that costs for these be charged against that line item rather than your operational budget. You may be able to get a new desk, for example.

In some instances, when there are requirements for cost sharing or when the budget is too high and you think you might have a better chance if the budget were smaller, indirect costs can be forgone and that amount used for cost sharing. Alternatively, the indirect-cost rate can be reduced for that project.

Remember, *you are always in a stronger negotiating position for the return of a portion of indirect costs before the project is submitted.* After internal budget approval and submission start the process for getting the money, if it is approved, your administrators realize the overhead will come to the institution without their having had to bargain away any of it to you.

Cost sharing. Cost sharing is expected in all federal grants and some foundation ones. Some time ago, Congress set cost sharing for federal research grants at 1% of the total cost of all grants to an institution in a year. Thus, not every project must cost-share so long as the institution meets that goal over all its grants. Further, it could be met by in-kind services, but such services must actually be charged and show in the accounting records. Your accounting office generally takes care of this aspect, but check to see what, if anything, will be charged to your project.

Some federal agencies require larger cost-sharing percentages. When their funds are tight, they like to stretch them by requiring you to share the load. New agencies are also more likely to require cost sharing than mature ones. Find out about the current requirements.

When in-kind contributions are accepted, what is known as "differential overhead," the difference between a higher federally approved rate and a lower rate that is actually charged the project, can be used as a contribution. If the institution has set its routine rate below the approved one, as many have for competitive reasons, it is a particularly advantageous way of handling cost sharing.

Researchers tend to believe that the larger the institutional contribution, the more likely the project is to be funded. This may be true in some programs, but usually the problem, design, and procedure are the determining factors. Colleagues or institutional research officers can be helpful on this score, having observed the effect of such contributions on the success rate for a sponsor.

Contingency allowances. Contingency allowances are not an explicit part of any sponsor's budget guidelines. Yet, it goes without saying that any project will meet some unexpected developments. Further, one can learn from others which agencies habitually try to negotiate budgets downward. There should be slack in the budget which permits the investigator to meet such situations with equanimity. Adding an extra graduate assistant, extra secretarial time, or other personnel costs will often do it. It is always more difficult for a sponsor to judge how much personnel is enough in contrast to other categories of expenditures. While that makes personnel a good place to put extra funds, sponsors' fiscal negotiators know it as an equally good place to cut for the same reason.

Remember, however, that there are limits on your ability to shift funds across categories, so be sure you put contingency funds where they are available at your institution. Many institutions will not allow personnel funds to be shifted to nonpersonnel categories, but the reverse is often permitted. In that case contingency funds must be included in your nonpersonnel items. Find out what institutional rules apply to your sponsored accounts.

In a large project, be careful to avoid the excess slack in both budget and work plan that may accumulate as various administrative levels contribute to budget and schedule estimation. Estimates sought from other persons, especially in complex projects, nearly always contain some leeway to protect against contingencies. That slack is added to and compounded if the person putting the whole budget and work plan together adds another few percent to provide for contingencies. If estimates come up through several administrative levels, the potential for compounding is increased. Adjust *both work plan and budget* if such overestimating is found; it is likely slack was buried in both.

Costs of proposal development. The personnel and material costs of proposal development may be substantial, but they can rarely be charged to the project. Some institutions, by keeping careful records of their proposal preparation costs, have negotiated them into their overhead rate. Alternatively, when cost sharing is required of the institution, it may be possible to use the costs of preliminary studies and proposal preparation as part of the institutional contribution. Whether this is allowed will be determined by the agency's regulations on cost sharing, in particular, and, in general, by whether its regulations prohibit charges of any kind incurred prior to the date of the funding agreement.

Keeping Track of Budget Rationales

It is critically important to document the way each budget figure was determined. Record the rationales in the working papers if not in the proposal itself. How did one arrive at 20% of the investigator's time, at the figure of $2.00 per person per week for supplies, and so on? These are the kinds of questions one will face if required to enter into budget negotiations.

It is tempting to assume that one can reconstruct one's thinking, and it is such a bother to get it all down in the heat of budget development. One has to get caught only once in budget negotiations to learn this lesson; learn it vicariously! Don't learn by *not* doing!

If the budget is multiyear, often only the first year is funded, with annual budgets required each year. You will be expected to be consistent from year to year. If you wish to change the basis for an item, you need to know how it was calculated so you can justify the change. This is particularly critical when the person preparing the first budget will not prepare later budgets. *For all these reasons, keep good budget notes!*

One way of tying the work plan and budget notes together besides that discussed in the work plan section (p. 73) is to lay out your budget on a big sheet of accounting paper as the Public Management Institute suggests in *The Grants Blueprint* (in Bauer, 1984). Basically the form consists of successive rows for the sets of activities involved in the objectives, each activity occupying a row (see figure 7). Cutting across each row are columns in which are recorded by whom the activity will be done and how many hours or weeks it will require. Moving across the sheet, successive columns record the costs of the staff involved, any consultants and contracts involved and their costs, nonpersonnel costs such as supplies and equipment, and finally a column for the results. As noted in the section on the work plan, Chapter 4, such a chart is provided for and tied to the plan figures by computer programs such as *MacProject*.

Figure 7 translates the preparation of the questionnaire (a goal of the project) into activities and costs. Thus the involvement of the director, graduate assistants (GA), and secretary for each of the five activities into which the goal is divided can be given with costs. Each activity corresponds to a box on the *MacProject* task chart (figure 4). The costs of each activity and the total for the goal can be determined and displayed. This information can be entered into *MacProject's* tables, as indicated earlier. Alternatively, any of the microcomputer spreadsheet programs would be ideal for developing such a cost chart.

A Sample Budget

Figure 8 shows the four-month questionnaire project, which was used as an example in the section discussing the work plan (Chapter 4), translated into a budget. To do so required setting some sample sizes; these would, of course, have appeared in the proposal. The budget assumes a 100-person pretest, and a 1000-person questionnaire sample with no mail follow-up but a phoned follow-up of 100 non-respondents. The budget shows how the individual totals were computed. Note that in most instances the estimated cost is rounded up slightly when entered into the budget. Ten percent was added to the computer center estimate. This budget contains considerable detail; it shows the basis for each figure. Many researchers submit this detail to forestall questions by negotiators. If you wish to do this, you can attach justifications in an appendix even if budget forms do not provide for it. But some researchers and fiscal officers believe this gives the game away by providing the other side too much information if they want to cut your budget. Negotiation is a game; decide with your fiscal officer how you want to play it!

Figure 7.
Sample budget worksheet showing translation of
first steps in work plan, figure 4, into costs.

Goal	Personnel				Consultants Subcontracts Service	Expendable Supplies		Communications	Travel	Equipment	Total Activity Cost	Total Cost	Product or Outcome
Prepare questionnaires													
Activity	Person	Day	Rate	Cost									
Write questionnaire	Dir GA	1 4	259.50 57.30	259.50 229.20		supplies	10				498.70		Draft quest.
Pretest questionnaire	Secy GA	1 10	60.40 57.30	60.40 573.00		400 pages @ 6¢	24		650mi @.22/mi=143		300.40		Prelim. results
Revise questionnaire and prepare for mailing	Dir Secy GA	.5 .5 2	259.50 60.40 57.30	129.75 30.20 114.60							274.55		Final quest.
Prepare mailing envelopes	Secy	2	60.40	120.80		envelopes labels	40 35				195.80		Envel. address.
Duplicate quest. and stuff env.	Secy GA	1 2	60.40 57.30	60.40 114.60		400 pages @ 6¢	24	postage 220			419.00		Quest. ready for mailing
Total cost of prep. of quest.	Dir Secy GA	1.5 4.5 18	259.50 60.40 57.30	389.25 271.80 1031.40 1692.45			133	220	143		2188.45	2188.45	

Figure 8. Sample budget translating work plan of figures 4-7 into costs.

Budget

Principal investigator: Dr. Elizabeth Grace 1/3 time for 4 of 9 months, academic year of 185 working days at salary of $48,000-- about 27.4 working days	$ 7,111
2 research assistants Each ½ time for 4 of 9 months, academic year salary $10,600--about 82.2 total working days	4,711
Secretarial 3/4 time for 4 months at $16,000 per calendar year of 265 working days--about 65 working days	4,000
Total salary and wages	15,822
Fringe benefits (incl. tuition--29.4%)	4,652
Total	20,474
Consultant for sampling plan at $400 per day, 1 day	400
Computer services	450
Supplies (includes 1100 machine-scored answer sheets)	400
Duplicating Questionnaire and letter = 4 pp. x 1000 subjects = 4000 Reports, 50 copies of 50-page report = 2500 Tryout forms and misc. = 750 = 7250 at 6¢/cy = $435	435
Postage 22¢ per questionnaire x 1000 plus misc. postage	250
Phone Long-distance follow-up of 100 cases at $1.25 per case = $125	125
Local travel for tryouts--distance to institutions and return averages 50 miles; 6 trips = 300 miles x 22¢ per mile	66
Convention travel Air fare to Chicago and return, $700 Hotel and meals, $110 x 3 days, $330	1,030
Total	$23,630
Negotiated overhead rate = 57.25%	13,528
Total to nearest $50	$37,150

Budgets for foundation proposals. Although there is some variation among foundations, budgets for foundation proposals rarely need to be as detailed as those for public agencies. In the initial approach, often the estimated total cost alone will suffice. If the foundation is interested and asks for a follow-up proposal, your foundation contact person will indicate how much detail is wanted.

APPENDICES

Appendices have already been referred to as the place to put material which provides detail but which is too bulky and/or gets in the way of the flow of the copy. If the maximum number of pages in the proposal is restricted, be sure to find out whether appendices are included in the page count. As shown below, an appendix is an important section, not just an afterthought. Use it for:

- Copies of letters from administrators of sites promising cooperation.
- Copies or sample items of new or unfamiliar tests or questionnaires as well as technical information on validity and so on.
- Descriptions of unfamiliar statistical or other research procedures.
- Samples of intended products.
- An index, helpful to reviewers, especially during panel consideration of complex proposals, may help a supportive reviewer turn the tide if she can quickly locate the proper spot during discussion; very easy to create if the project is typed with certain word-processing software.
- A variety of very important charts:
  - Proposal sections indexed to evaluation criteria. *This is particularly useful for RFPs* since it helps reviewers to see quickly where and how you have met specific criteria. Refer to it on the title page or somewhere prominent early in the proposal; alert the reviewer to its presence.
  - Personnel by required experience. Like the above, especially useful for RFPs; refer to it in the personnel section.
  - A detailed work plan analysis. Where a simplified one is included in the proposal's text, a PERT chart or more detailed one may be put here.
  - Personnel by task chart; the result of the workload analysis.
  - Organization chart.
  - Technical or conceptual charts that will be referred to repeatedly. Tab them for easy access.

ASSURANCES AND CLEARANCES

Local Requirements. Universities, governments, and foundations want to be assured that their sponsorship of a project will not get them into trouble. Thus, even though no university funds are involved, projects that involve human or animal subjects and are carried out by faculty, staff, students, or persons in any type of employee relationship require clearance (more on this in the next section). Further, some universities, in order to maintain good relations with local agencies that could be overburdened with university requests, may require a university clearance before they are approached. This keeps those agencies from being overused and attempts to ensure priority access for especially deserving projects.

Because the university's protection is often insufficient and because they have no role in that decisionmaking, schools, counseling centers, mental health clinics, social agencies, and other institutions often erect their own "fences," establishing approval committees as well. Failure to observe the procedures required by those committees may result in snarls that take many, many times the initial clearance effort to unravel--if, indeed, they can be unraveled after the fact. Often a project site is lost not only for this project but for any research for a period of time. Such resource polluters make research more difficult for everyone; don't be one.

Even though you'll feel in a more certain position to know what you are about after you are ready to start the project, if possible, obtain site use approvals in advance of submitting proposals. It makes those involved feel more a part of the effort, and they are more likely to be cooperative. To approach them afterward makes their concerns an afterthought; if they want to change things or make a suggestion for improvement, the needed flexibility may be lost. Further, such approvals tell the sponsor that you have the places in which to work if the project is approved and, that those agencies see enough merit in the project to cooperate with you. Put evidence of their approval of your proposal in an appendix.

Sponsor and federal requirements. Beyond those clearances required by the local scene are those required by sponsors. In the case of foundations, required assurances are usually limited to giving assurance that the receiving organization is certified as nonprofit by the Internal Revenue Service.

The federal government, however, seems to require an unending stream of clearances (Affirmative Action, Title IX, sex discrimination, and so on). Usually, when they get too burdensome, efforts are made to cut back; so their number and nature go in cycles. Most competition announcements or requests for proposals list the assurances required. Be sure to include these, since lack of one may prevent your proposal from being considered.

The one commonly required assurance of all federal programs is that of the protection of human or animal subjects. In fact, institutions receiving federal funds of any kind must require approval of *all human or animal subject research* by protection committees regardless of whether federal funds are involved. Failure to do so threatens their access to federal funding. They must establish a committee of five or more members (the composition of the committee is also specified) to ascertain whether proposals adequately protect human subjects from mental as well as physical harm. A similar committee is specified for animals.

Among other concerns, the human subjects committee must ensure that informed consent of the subject is obtained if she is "at risk." Such consent is obtained in writing in a form approved by the committee. Many committees have established standard forms. A sample appears in figure 9. Certification of approval of the project by the committee must be received by a federal sponsor usually within a specified period after project submission. A sample Department of Health and Human Services form is shown in figure 10. Details are currently available in the *Protection of Human Subjects*, (45 CFR46). It is available from the Office for Protection of Research Risks, National Institutes of Health, Bethesda, Md. 20205.

Proposals involving the use of animals should include full explanation of 1) arrangements for their acquisition and breeding, 2) personnel caring for the animals (including veterinarian), 3) facilities for care, feeding, disease control, and so on. Like use of human subjects, use of animals must conform to accepted principles. Information is currently provided in *Principles for Use of Animals* and, for warm-blooded vertebrates, *Guide for the Care and Use of Laboratory Animals.* Both are available from the National Institutes of Health, address given above.

Other assurances must usually also be given, but the institution usually needs to file them only once. Figure 11 shows the list of required assurances that were included in a recent Department of Education research announcement. Following institutional filing, one indicates on the checklist form that the required assurances have been filed. A sample checklist appears as figure 15 in Chapter 6.

State or local agencies often follow federal guidelines for human or animal subject clearances and may require others as well, but their requirements are usually less complex than federal ones. Again, the program announcement should give the required information.

Figure 9. A sample of a consent form.
Items 3 and 4 are completed by the researcher.

STATEMENT OF CONSENT

1. Subject's name_____

2. Address_____Tel.No._____

3. Purpose of study. (Be sure it is clearly stated in layman's terms so that the subject will understand what you are attempting to accomplish.)

4. Experimental methods--risks involved, if any.

5. I have been informed of the nature of the research and the risks, and I voluntarily agree to be a subject. I am at least eighteen years of age, having been born on _____. I understand also that I may withdraw from the study at any time or refuse to answer a particular question without penalty.

6. _____
   Signature of subject

7. _____
   Signature of person obtaining consent

8. Date_____

The above statement is to be signed in duplicate with one copy being kept by the researcher and the other by the subject.

NOTE: If you have questions about the research, do not hesitate to ask the researcher, whose phone number is _____. If you have questions about your rights as a subject, please contact the chairman of the Human Subjects Committee, Syracuse University, Professor William Johnson, 423-4288, or his secretary, Linda Smith, 423-4289.

Figure 10. A DHHS human subjects protection assurance form.

OMB No. 0925-0637

DEPARTMENT OF HEALTH AND HUMAN SERVICES	☐ GRANT ☐ CONTRACT ☐ FELLOW ☐ OTHER
PROTECTION OF HUMAN SUBJECTS ASSURANCE/CERTIFICATION/DECLARATION	☐ New ☐ Competing continuation ☐ Noncompeting continuation ☐ Supplemental
☐ ORIGINAL ☐ FOLLOWUP ☐ EXEMPTION (previously undesignated)	APPLICATION IDENTIFICATION NO. (if known)

POLICY: *A research activity involving human subjects that is not exempt from HHS regulations may not be funded unless an Institutional Review Board (IRB) has reviewed and approved the activity in accordance with Section 474 of the Public Health Service Act as implemented by Title 45, Part 46 of the Code of Federal Regulations (45 CFR 46—as revised). The applicant institution must submit certification of IRB approval to HHS unless the applicant institution has designated a specific exemption under Section 46.101(b) which applies to the proposed research activity. Institutions with an assurance of compliance on file with HHS which covers the proposed activity should submit certification of IRB review and approval with each application. (In exceptional cases, certification may be accepted up to 60 days after the receipt date for which the application is submitted.) In the case of institutions which do not have an assurance of compliance on file with HHS covering the proposed activity, certification of IRB review and approval must be submitted within 30 days of the receipt of a written request from HHS for certification.*

1. TITLE OF APPLICATION OR ACTIVITY

2. PRINCIPAL INVESTIGATOR, PROGRAM DIRECTOR, OR FELLOW

3. FOOD AND DRUG ADMINISTRATION REQUIRED INFORMATION *(see reverse side)*

4. HHS ASSURANCE STATUS

☐ This institution has an approved assurance of compliance on file with HHS which covers this activity.

_____ Assurance identification number   _____ IRB identification number

☐ No assurance of compliance which applies to this activity has been established with HHS, but the applicant institution will provide written assurance of compliance and certification of IRB review and approval in accordance with 45 CFR 46 upon request.

5. CERTIFICATION OF IRB REVIEW OR DECLARATION OF EXEMPTION

☐ This activity has been reviewed and approved by an IRB in accordance with the requirements of 45 CFR 46, including its relevant Subparts. This certification fulfills, when applicable, requirements for certifying FDA status for each investigational new drug or device. *(See reverse side of this form.)*

_____ Date of IRB review and approval. *(If approval is pending, write "pending." Followup certification is required.)*
      (month/day/year)

☐ Full Board Review   ☐ Expedited Review

☐ This activity contains multiple projects, some of which have not been reviewed. The IRB has granted approval on condition that all projects covered by 45 CFR 46 will be reviewed and approved before they are initiated and that appropriate further certification *(Form HHS 596)* will be submitted.

☐ Human subjects are involved, but this activity qualifies for exemption under 46.101(b) in accordance with paragraph_____ *(insert paragraph number of exemption in 46.101(b), 1 through 5),* but the institution did not designate that exemption on the application.

6. Each official signing below certifies that the information provided on this form is correct and that each institution assumes responsibility for assuring required future reviews, approvals, and submissions of certification.

APPLICANT INSTITUTION	COOPERATING INSTITUTION
NAME, ADDRESS, AND TELEPHONE NO.	NAME, ADDRESS, AND TELEPHONE NO.
NAME AND TITLE OF OFFICIAL *(print or type)*	NAME AND TITLE OF OFFICIAL *(print or type)*
SIGNATURE OF OFFICIAL LISTED ABOVE *(and date)*	SIGNATURE OF OFFICIAL LISTED ABOVE *(and date)*

HHS 596 (Rev. 1/82)

(If additional space is needed, please use reverse side under "Notes.")

Figure 11. A sample list of assurances.

PART V
ASSURANCES

The Applicant hereby assures and certifies that it will comply with the regulations, policies, guidelines and requirements, as they relate to the application, acceptance and use of Federal funds for this federally-assisted project. Also the Applicant assures and certifies:

1. It possesses legal authority to apply for the grant; that a resolution, motion or similar action has been duly adopted or passed as an official act of the applicant's governing body, authorizing the filing of the application, including all understandings and assurances contained therein, and directing and authorizing the person identified as the official representative of the applicant to act in connection with the application and to provide such additional information as may be required.

2. It will comply with Title VI of the Civil Rights Act of 1964 (P.L. 88-352) and in accordance with Title VI of that Act, no person in the United States shall, on the ground of race, color or national origin, be excluded from participation in, be denied the benefits of, or be otherwise subjected to discrimination under any program or activity for which the applicant receives Federal financial assistance and will immediately take any measures necessary to effectuate this agreement.

3. It will comply with Title VI of the Civil Rights Act of 1964 (42 U.S.C. 2000d) prohibiting employment discrimination where (1) the primary purpose of a grant is to provide employment or (2) discriminatory employment practices will result in unequal treatment of persons who are or should be benefiting from the grant-aided activity.

4. It will comply with Section 504 of the Rehabilitation Act of 1973, as amended, 29 U.S.C. 794, which prohibits discrimination on the basis of handicap in programs and activities receiving Federal financial assistance.

5. It will comply with Title IX of the Education Amendments of 1972, as amended, 20 U.S.C. 1681 et seq., which prohibits discrimination on the basis of sex in education programs and activities receiving Federal financial assistance.

6. It will comply with the Age Discrimination Act of 1975, as amended, 42 U.S.C. 6101 et seq., which prohibits discrimination on the basis of age in programs or activities receiving Federal financial assistance.

7. It will comply with requirements of the provisions of the Uniform Relocation Assistance and Real Property Acquisitions Act of 1970 (P.L. 91-646) which provides for fair and equitable treatment of persons displaced as a result of Federal and federally-assisted programs.

8. It will comply with the provisions of the Hatch Act which limit the political activity of employees.

9. It will comply with the minimum wage and maximum hours provisions of the Federal Fair Labor Standards Act, as they apply to hospital and educational institution employees of State and local governments.

10. It will establish safeguards to prohibit employees from using their positions for a purpose that is or gives the appearance of being motivated by a desire for private gain for themselves or others, particularly those with whom they have family, business, or other ties.

11. It will give the sponsoring agency or the Comptroller General through any authorized representative the access to and the right to examine all records, books, papers, or documents related to the grant.

12. It will comply with all requirements imposed by the Federal sponsoring agency concerning special requirements of law, program requirements, and other administrative requirements.

13. It will insure that the facilities under its ownership, lease or supervision which shall be utilized in the accomplishment of the project are not listed on the Environmental Protection Agency's (EPA) list of Violating Facilities and that it will notify the Federal grantor agency of the receipt of any communication from the Director of the EPA Office of Federal Activities indicating that a facility to be used in the project is under consideration for listing by the EPA.

14. It will comply with the flood insurance purchase requirements of Section 102(a) of the Flood Disaster Protection Act of 1973, P.L. 93-234, 87 Stat. 975, approved December 31, 1976. Section 102(a) requires, on or after March 2, 1975, the purchase of flood insurance in communities where such insurance is available as a condition for the receipt of any Federal financial assistance for construction or acquisition purposes for use in any area that has been identified by the Secretary of the Department of Housing and Urban Development as an area having special flood hazards. The phrase "Federal financial assistance" includes any form of loan, grant, guaranty, insurance payment, rebate, subsidy, disaster assistance loan or grant, or any other form of direct or indirect Federal assistance.

15. It will assist the Federal grantor agency in its compliance with Section 106 of the National Historic Preservation Act of 1966 as amended (16 U.S.C. 470), Executive Order 11593, and the Archeological and Historic Preservation Act of 1966 (16 U.S.C. 469a-1 et seq.) by (a) consulting with the State Historic Preservation Officer on the conduct of investigations, as necessary, to identify properties listed in or eligible for inclusion in the National Register of Historic Places that are subject to adverse effects (see 36 CFR Part 800.8) by the activity, and notifying the Federal grantor agency of the existence of any such properties, and by (b) complying with all requirements established by the Federal grantor agency to avoid or mitigate adverse effects upon such properties.

Figure 12. An example of an institutional checklist.

REVISED DECEMBER 1981

SYRACUSE UNIVERSITY
OFFICE OF SPONSORED PROGRAMS
PROPOSAL INFORMATION CHECKLIST

Note: A completed and signed copy of this form must accompany all
proposals when brought to the Office of Sponsored Programs and
before the proposal can be submitted.

Submitted by: _____ Dept. credited: _____
Proposal title: _____
_____ Sponsor _____
If applicable, submitted in response to RFP No. _____

PLEASE CIRCLE YOUR ANSWERS

1. (a) Have you ever submitted this as a preliminary
        proposal?   YES   NO
    (b) If the answer to (a) is "yes", please fill in
        the following.
        Sponsor(s) _____
        When _____
2. (a) If this proposal is supported, is there space
        available (without renovation) to house your
        propsal adequately?   YES   NO
    (b) If not, have you discussed the problem with
        the Associate Vice Chancellor for Academic
        Affairs?   YES   NO
    (c) How was it resolved? _____
3. (a) Do you have access to the office furniture,
        machines and other office equipment needed
        by your program?   YES   NO
    (b) If not, have you made arrangements with
        your chairperson or dean to satisfy these
        needs?   YES   NO
4. Will your program require scientific equipment
    not readily available on campus?   YES   NO
    (a) If the answer is "yes", have you included
        the equipment in your budget request?   YES   NO
    (b) If the answer to (a) is "no", explain where
        the equipment is to come from. _____
    (c) Will space or renovations be necessary to
        house the equipment? If the answer is "yes,"
        explain. _____

5. (a) Will your program require the services of the
        S.U. Academic Computer Center or the
        purchase of computer equipment?   YES   NO
    (b) If the answer is "yes", has your proposal
        been reviewed with the Computer Center
        to make certain sufficient funds and
        correct equipment are being requested?   YES   NO
    (c) If the answer to (b) is "no", please explain
        why it has not. _____
6. Will your program require any additional   YES   NO
    or unusual library facilities which have not
    been included in your budget? If the answer
    is "yes", explain in detail. _____

(continues)

figure 12 continued

7. (a) Will your program require any additional
        or unusual audiovisual equipment or services?   YES   NO
    (b) If the answer to (a) is "yes", have your
        needs been discussed with the Director of
        Audio and Visual Support Services?   YES   NO
8. (a) Will your proposed program involve the
        use of human subjects (clinical testing,
        questionnaires, interviews, etc.)?   YES   NO
    (b) If the answer to (a) is "yes", has it been
        reviewed by the Human Subjects Committee?   YES   NO
        If not, check with O.S.P. for further
        information. Full instructions may be
        found in Section 14, of the O.S.P. Manual.
9. Does the proposed program involve any long-
    range financial commitment by the University
    after sponsor support ceases?   YES   NO
    If the answer is "yes", explain the nature of
    the commitment and how it is to be met. _____

    _____

10. Does the program involve any "overload" for
    faculty during the academic year? Note:
    Overload requires S.U. and (usually) sponsor
    approval. Also the proposal budget should
    clearly indicate those salaries which are on
    an overload basis. If the answer is "yes",   YES   NO
    please explain. _____

    _____

11. Does the proposal include full S.U. negotiated
    indirect costs (overhead)? If the answer is   YES   NO
    "no", what compensating benefits would the
    University receive in lieu thereof, or what
    other justification exists? Explain. _____

    _____

12. Is it certain (or probable) that the program
    will require cost-sharing, (i.e., certain costs
    to be paid from S.U. funds)?   YES   NO
    If the anwwer is "yes", please fill in the
    following information.
    A. Faculty Academic Year Salaries   Non-Federal Account
        ____% Prof. _____   _____ $_____
        ____% "   _____ $_____
    B. Staff Salaries
        ____% Name _____   _____ $_____
        ____% Name _____   _____ $_____
                                           Subtotal $_____
    C. Fringe Benefits @ ____% $_____
    D. Other. Specify _____ $_____
                                           Subtotal $_____
    E. Indirect costs on the above @ ____% $_____
    F. Difference between proposed rate and full
        negotiated rate, to be completed if answer
        to 11 is "no", ____% $_____
    G. Tuition   No. of hours ____ @ ____% $_____
        In addition to sponsor allocation
                                           Total $_____

Approved by:
    Department Chairman or Director _____ Date _____
    Dean*   _____ Date _____
    O.S.P.   _____ Date _____
    *Exception: College of Arts and Sciences

In addition, large institutions, wanting to be sure the project's requirements of space, equipment, computer processing, cost sharing, and so on have been considered, often have their own checklist. The applicant submits this checklist at the same time institutional approval is sought. On approval, the project is forwarded to the agency for consideration. A sample of such a form used at Syracuse University appears in figure 12.

If you have questions about these clearances, agency personnel can usually help you. You may wish to consult a reference such as the section on "How to Comply with 'Strings Attached' to Federal Grants" in *Federal Grants Management Handbook*. (See Appendix B for reference)

ABSTRACT

There are two points of view on when the abstract should be written: 1) at the outset of proposal preparation or 2) as a last step. If one could state the project succinctly and accurately at the outset, that would be great; it would make the remainder of the process a straightforward deductive exercise. This may be possible in some instances, especially where one has the project well in mind from the beginning. Most projects, however, seem to change considerably during the proposal development process. Therefore, even if you write the abstract at the outset, carefully review it at the end to be sure it is faithful to the proposal as fully developed.

Most often the abstract is formulated at the end of writing, after the proposal is completed. In a page, or at most two, it describes the objectives of the study and gives a condensed view of the procedure. Length of the abstract is usually specified in the guidelines (see figure 13) and is designed to fit the particular computer-based information system used to keep track of projects once they are funded.

Keep in mind that the abstract serves at least five purposes: 1) Project reviewers read it before the rest of the proposal to gain a perspective on the study. 2) Panel members and administrative staff use it to remind themselves of the nature of the study when the project comes up for panel discussion. 3) The project title and abstract are the basis for inserting the project in a computerized system of project record keeping (e.g., the Smithsonian Institution's Science Information Exchange). It will be catalogued with terms that are routinely used for indexing projects. Don't forget that such terms are usually the commoner rather than the abstruse technical terms in a field, and the information system is frequently used by persons who are unacquainted with even the most common of such terms. 4) It is usually the only part of the proposal read by administrators reviewing funding recommendations by Congressional staff or by others who are studying the agency's program. 5) It is usually the basis for press releases and information sent to the media and to the recipient's Congressional representatives whenever funding of a federally sponsored project is formally announced.

Given these many uses, it is clear that one should:

Figure 13. Sample abstract and instructions.

SUGGESTED PROJECT ABSTRACT FORMAT AND INSTRUCTIONS

The abstract must be prepared on *one page* according to the following instructions and in the format suggested on the next page. The narrative should be typed single-space. This abstract will be reproduced and used to disseminate information to a variety of people including educators, researchers, Education Department and other government agencies and congressional staff officers.

1. Title: the title of the study.

2. Eligible research area and subtopic

3. Business Address and Telephone: include the name of the department with which the investigator(s) is (are) affiliated.

4. Project Duration: enter the beginning and ending dates being requested.

5. Total Funds Requested: enter the total Federal funds requested. If project is for more than one year, show the amount requested for each year, followed by the total.

Abstract: The narrative should be a succinct, *non-technical description* of the research. It must not exceed 250 words in length, should be typed single-spaced, and should be so clearly written that the following questions could be answered by a member of the general public who reads it:

Paragraph (a) What is the specific purpose of this study? What information is being sought?

Paragraph (b) How is the study to be conducted? (A non-technical description of the general methodology and statistics to be used. Should include complete information on subjects – numbers, sex, age, ethnicity, etc. Location if research is to be done at a location other than the business address of the investigator)

Paragraph (c) What difference might the results make? – to whom? (What might we know or be able to do as a result of this work that we do not know or cannot do now? To whom will this be important?) It is important that the abstract shows justification for the project in terms of its implications for increasing educational equity and/or the improvement of educational practice.

This abstract is distributed to a wide public if an award is made. The title of the project and the abstract often form the primary basis on which belief about educational research develops. Clear titles and well-written abstracts are important in communicating the value of work being supported.

TITLE: A Qualitative Sociological Study of Mainstreaming

IIC Practice
Eligible Research Areas

INVESTIGATOR(s): Robert Bogdan and Ellen Barnes

BUSINESS ADDRESS AND TELEPHONE: The Center on Human Policy, Syracuse Univ., Syracuse, N.Y. 13210. Tel: (315) 423-1870

PROJECT DURATION: 9/30/79 - 9/29/82

TOTAL FUNDS REQUESTED: 1st Yr: $46,146 2nd Yr: 62,505 3rd Yr: 67,052

Total : $175,703

NARRATIVE

What is mainstreaming? What does it look like in practice? Public Law 94-142 has mandated services for handicapped children in the least restricted environments possible. This has been translated by some into the concept of mainstreaming.

Although professionals have written about the concept, and definitions from a legal and professional perspective exist, little is known about how mainstreaming actually is carried out in the day-to-day school operation. How do teachers define mainstreaming? What do they do when they go about it? By finding out answers to these and related questions, the researchers in this study are attempting to get information that can help in designing staff development activities for teachers and administrators.

Many parents and professional, teachers and administrators, will be asked to nominate programs in the Central New York area that have good mainstreaming practices. From the list, 25 programs will be chosen for detailed investigation. The classrooms will be visited regularly for a 6-week period, and interviews will be conducted with teachers, administrators, and staff development experts.

Using an open-ended approach, the study aims to produce 25 case studies of mainstreaming as it is practiced and experienced in schools. From this material, generalizations can be made concerning the nature of mainstreaming and what activities might be developed to help teachers in their efforts. Materials developed can be used in designing staff development activities.

- *Prepare the abstract with great care.*
- *Paraphrase the objectives and procedure* using broad but accurate strokes and keep parts in proper perspective with appropriate emphasis.
- *Employ the key terms* used in the body of the material so as to prepare the reader for them.
- Include key terms that are likely to be commonly used for indexing projects in the field.
- Write so as to communicate to such persons as Congressional staff members, foundation officers, reporters, and press secretaries--in short, the casual lay reader.
- Indicate in positive terms what will be done, not what one will "try to do."

An example of the instructions for a program abstract as well as a sample abstract is shown in figure 13.

TITLE AND TITLE PAGE

The title is as important as the abstract, for it serves many of the same purposes in an even briefer way. In some information systems, *only* the title is entered, scanned, and indexed; and length is confined to a certain number of characters (e.g., 200). Therefore, follow any directions for title strictly. The suggestions for abstracts are also applicable when writing titles. In addition, keep the title short but descriptive even for the casual reader (who just may be a member of Congress). Fit the title to the mission of the sponsoring agency. Use some imagination when appropriate; make your title memorable so it stands out from your competition. An acronymn is helpful in drawing attention to a project: "Development of a New Grantsmanship Curriculum: PROF--Proposal Requirements Optimally Fulfilled." In general, avoid jargon, inappropriate double entendres, flippancy, and controversial terms. Politicians have used titles to select projects to ridicule a program (e.g., the Golden Fleece Award). Sponsors don't want their projects to be susceptible, so consider whether your title might be vulnerable and, if so, change it.

Title page. Even when the format of the rest of the proposal is unspecified, most federal agencies require that the first page be prepared on their special form. A generic form in wide use is shown in figure 14. Applicants complete the first two sections of the form (see sectioning on left side). With a couple of exceptions, the form is self-explanatory. Item 5, the employer identification number, can be supplied by your institution. Item 6 refers to the reference number and title of the program to which you are applying. It can be found in the *Catalog of Federal Domestic Assistance* (CFDA). (See p. 189.)

Note that items 9 through 13 are designed to assist staff in giving useful information to members of Congress, letting them know where something to their benefit is going on in their districts. While this request may seem more appropriate to community projects, research projects have local benefits; and this information is required of them as well.

Figure 14. Sample application pages.

Form Approved Through 9/30/89
OMB No. 0925-0001

DEPARTMENT OF HEALTH AND HUMAN SERVICES
PUBLIC HEALTH SERVICE

GRANT APPLICATION

FOLLOW INSTRUCTIONS CAREFULLY

LEAVE BLANK		
TYPE	ACTIVITY	NUMBER
REVIEW GROUP		FORMERLY
COUNCIL/BOARD (Month, year)		DATE RECEIVED

1. TITLE OF PROJECT *(Up to 56 spaces)*

2. RESPONSE TO SPECIFIC PROGRAM ANNOUNCEMENT ☐ NO ☐ YES *(If "YES," state RFA number and/or announcement title)*

3. PRINCIPAL INVESTIGATOR/PROGRAM DIRECTOR — NEW INVESTIGATOR ☐

3a. NAME *(Last, first, middle)* | 3b. DEGREE(S) | 3c. SOCIAL SECURITY NUMBER

3d. POSITION TITLE | 3e. MAILING ADDRESS *(Street, city, state, zip code)*

3f. DEPARTMENT, SERVICE, LABORATORY OR EQUIVALENT

3g. MAJOR SUBDIVISION | 3h. TELEPHONE *(Area code, number and extension)*

4. HUMAN SUBJECTS
4a. ☐ No ☐ Yes { ☐ Exemption # ______ OR ☐ IRB Approval Date ______ }
4b. Assurance of Compliance # ______

5. VERTEBRATE ANIMALS
5a. ☐ No ☐ Yes IACUC Approval Date ______
5b. Animal Welfare Assurance # ______

6. DATES OF ENTIRE PROPOSED PROJECT PERIOD
From:
Through:

7. COSTS REQUESTED FOR FIRST 12-MONTH BUDGET PERIOD
7a. Direct Costs $ | 7b. Total Costs $

8. COSTS REQUESTED FOR ENTIRE PROPOSED PROJECT PERIOD
8a. Direct Costs $ | 8b. Total Costs $

9. PERFORMANCE SITES *(Organizations and addresses)*

10. INVENTIONS *(Competing continuation application only)*
☐ NO ☐ YES { ☐ Previously reported ☐ Not previously reported }

11. APPLICANT ORGANIZATION *(Name, address, and congressional district)*

12. TYPE OF ORGANIZATION
☐ Public, Specify ☐ Federal ☐ State ☐ Local
☐ Private Nonprofit
☐ For Profit *(General)*
☐ For Profit *(Small Business)*

13. ENTITY IDENTIFICATION NUMBER

14. ORGANIZATIONAL COMPONENT TO RECEIVE CREDIT TOWARDS A BIOMEDICAL RESEARCH SUPPORT GRANT
Code ☐☐ Identification ______

15. OFFICIAL IN BUSINESS OFFICE TO BE NOTIFIED IF AN AWARD IS MADE *(Name, title, address and telephone number)*

16. OFFICIAL SIGNING FOR APPLICANT ORGANIZATION *(Name, title, address and telephone number)*

17. PRINCIPAL INVESTIGATOR/PROGRAM DIRECTOR ASSURANCE: I agree to accept responsibility for the scientific conduct of the project and to provide the required progress reports if a grant is awarded as a result of this application. Willful provision of false information is a criminal offense *(U.S. Code, Title 18, Section 1001)*.
SIGNATURE OF PERSON NAMED IN 3a *(In ink. "Per" signature not acceptable.)* | DATE

18. CERTIFICATION AND ACCEPTANCE: I certify that the statements herein are true and complete to the best of my knowledge, and accept the obligation to comply with Public Health Service terms and conditions if a grant is awarded as the result of this application. A willfully false certification is a criminal offense *(U.S. Code, Title 18, Section 1001)*.
SIGNATURE OF PERSON NAMED IN 16 *(In ink. "Per" signature not acceptable.)* | DATE

REMOVE AND USE FOR DRAFT COPY

OMB Approval No. 0348-0006

FEDERAL ASSISTANCE

1. TYPE OF SUBMISSION *(Mark appropriate box)*
☐ NOTICE OF INTENT (OPTIONAL)
☐ PREAPPLICATION
☐ APPLICATION

2. APPLICANT'S APPLICATION IDENTIFIER — a. NUMBER; b. DATE Year month day 19
Leave Blank

3. STATE APPLICATION IDENTIFIER — a. NUMBER; b. DATE ASSIGNED Year month day 19
NOTE TO BE ASSIGNED BY STATE

SECTION I—APPLICANT/RECIPIENT DATA

4. LEGAL APPLICANT/RECIPIENT
a. Applicant Name
b. Organization Unit
c. Street/P.O. Box
d. City
e. County
f. State
g. ZIP Code
h. Contact Person *(Name & Telephone No.)*

5. EMPLOYER IDENTIFICATION NUMBER (EIN)

6. PROGRAM *(From CFDA)*
a. NUMBER ☐☐.☐☐☐
MULTIPLE ☐
b. TITLE

7. TITLE OF APPLICANT'S PROJECT (Use section IV of this form to provide a summary description of the project.)

8. TYPE OF APPLICANT/RECIPIENT
A—State
B—Interstate
C—Substate Organization
D—County
E—City
F—School District
G—Special Purpose District
H—Community Action Agency
I—Higher Educational Institution
J—Indian Tribe
K—Other (Specify)
Enter appropriate letter ☐

9. AREA OF PROJECT IMPACT *(Names of cities, counties, states, etc.)*

10. ESTIMATED NUMBER OF PERSONS BENEFITING

11. TYPE OF ASSISTANCE
A—Basic Grant
B—Supplemental Grant
C—Loan
D—Insurance
E—Other
Enter appropriate letter(s) ☐☐

12. PROPOSED FUNDING		
a. FEDERAL	$	.00
b. APPLICANT		.00
c. STATE		.00
d. LOCAL		.00
e. OTHER		.00
f. Total	$	.00

13. CONGRESSIONAL DISTRICTS OF: a. APPLICANT | b. PROJECT

14. TYPE OF APPLICATION
A—New
B—Renewal
C—Revision
D—Continuation
E—Augmentation
Enter appropriate letter ☐

15. PROJECT START DATE Year month day 19

16. PROJECT DURATION Months

17. TYPE OF CHANGE *(For 14c or 14e)*
A—Increase Dollars
B—Decrease Dollars
C—Increase Duration
D—Decrease Duration
E—Cancellation
F—Other (Specify)
Enter appropriate letter(s) ☐☐☐

18. DATE DUE TO FEDERAL AGENCY ► Year month day 19

19. FEDERAL AGENCY TO RECEIVE REQUEST
a. ORGANIZATIONAL UNIT (IF APPROPRIATE)
b. ADMINISTRATIVE CONTACT (IF KNOWN)
c. ADDRESS

20. EXISTING FEDERAL GRANT IDENTIFICATION NUMBER

21. REMARKS ADDED ☐ Yes ☐ No

SECTION II—CERTIFICATION

22. THE APPLICANT CERTIFIES THAT ► To the best of my knowledge and belief, data in this preapplication/application are true and correct, the document has been duly authorized by the governing body of the applicant and the applicant will comply with the attached assurances if the assistance is approved.

a. YES. THIS NOTICE OF INTENT/PREAPPLICATION/APPLICATION WAS MADE AVAILABLE TO THE STATE EXECUTIVE ORDER 12372 PROCESS FOR REVIEW ON:
DATE ______

b. NO. PROGRAM IS NOT COVERED BY E.O. 12372 ☐
OR PROGRAM HAS NOT BEEN SELECTED BY STATE FOR REVIEW ☐

23. CERTIFYING REPRESENTATIVE — a. TYPED NAME AND TITLE | b. SIGNATURE

SECTION III—FEDERAL AGENCY ACTION

24. APPLICATION RECEIVED Year month day 19

25. FEDERAL APPLICATION IDENTIFICATION NUMBER

26. FEDERAL GRANT IDENTIFICATION

27. ACTION TAKEN
☐ a. AWARDED
☐ b. REJECTED
☐ c. RETURNED FOR AMENDMENT
☐ d. RETURNED FOR E.O. 12372 SUBMISSION BY APPLICANT TO STATE
☐ e. DEFERRED
☐ f. WITHDRAWN

28. FUNDING		
a. FEDERAL	$	.00
b. APPLICANT		.00
c. STATE		.00
d. LOCAL		.00
e. OTHER		.00
f. TOTAL	$	.00

29. ACTION DATE ► Year month day 19

30. STARTING DATE Year month date 19

31. CONTACT FOR ADDITIONAL INFORMATION *(Name and telephone number)*

32. ENDING DATE Year month date 19

33. REMARKS ADDED ☐ Yes ☐ No

NSN 7540-01-008-8162
PREVIOUS EDITION IS NOT USABLE

424-103

STANDARD FORM 424 PAGE 1 (Rev. 4-84)
Prescribed by OMB Circular A-102

In addition to the federal form, if it is required, prepare a conventional title page. It should include your project title; proposers' name(s), address, and phone; if different from the preparer, the person to contact with business questions, with his address and phone; and a reference to the location of the table listing criteria and where the proposal addresses each and/or the location of the proposal index. It should be followed by a table of contents.

Disclosure of your ideas to competitors. It is rare that material in rejected proposals is either made public or used in an unprofessional manner. But it does occasionally occur. If you are concerned about this possibility, some protection may be gained by including on the cover page or placing prominently, near the beginning, a statement to the effect that "This proposal contains material considered to be the proprietary property of Dr. David R. Krathwohl, Syracuse University. It has been prepared for the exclusive review and consideration of the National Science Foundation in response to the announcement of the Social and Developmental Psychology Program, NSF Brochure 84-9. No further distribution or subsequent disclosure of the materials is authorized." Some RFPs include the exact statement of this kind they wish you to use; it is usually longer and provides for government use in certain circumstances. Check RFPs for it.

A FINAL CHECK AND REVIEW

Fine, the draft is finished. Now the researcher can check to make sure that the proposal is a consistent chain of reasoning. Each section should reflect the previous material and carry it a step further in a consistent and coherent way. Make sure that ends are not dropped--objectives slighted, data to be collected but no analysis plan, and so on.

Even the best proposal writers benefit from having someone not familiar with the write-up criticize it. Don't be embarrassed to ask one or more friends to read it; choose ones who will be frank, but only if that's what is *honestly* wanted. Give them a copy of the criteria that will be used in judging the proposal. Let them interpret those criteria on their own with no help from you. They may interpret them in a way you missed!

If you can allow the time, put the draft aside and then come back to it afresh after a long enough period to look at it in perspective. You'll be amazed at what you'll find.

DUPLICATION

How important is the appearance of the proposal? Some organizations do a very careful and complete job of preparing the proposal in attractive form. Their proposals arrive in spiral bindings with printed covers and offset-printed text. We cannot say that the reader will be unimpressed by this. Yet, simple dittoed proposals have been and will continue to be approved (although other duplication processes providing more contrast are preferable). The major effort should be on legibility, lucidity, and clarity of presentation.

Here is the statement often included in RFPs but more generally applicable:

> Unnecessarily elaborate brochures or other presentations beyond those sufficient to present a complete and effective response to this solicitation are not desired and may be construed as an indication of the offeror's or quoter's lack of cost consciousness. Elaborate art work, expensive paper and bindings, and expensive visual and other presentation aids are neither necessary nor wanted.

Use tabs or colored paper to convey the structure of a large proposal and make sections accessible. Colored paper has an advantage over tabs (which can get torn off or bent in transit), but tabs convey the organization more readily. When using color coding, place the coding key in a prominent and accessible place (front cover, table of contents, or first pages). Don't put text on dark colored paper; that makes reading difficult.

Other than the time required for assurances, clearances, and letters of support, the place where the writer is most likely to underbudget time is that required for accurate, careful, and clearly legible duplication. Be sure to use a word processor if at all possible; it makes rewriting text and editing so very much easier. Even with word processing and rapid duplication services, a carefully proofread document requires time. Remember that word processing's best dictionaries will not pick up typographical errors that form a correctly spelled word. These are the worst kind of errors, since they may make enough sense that they are not immediately spotted as typos, and the reader must stop to decipher your meaning. They are eliminated only by time-consuming, careful proof-reading. Most of us who read a lot are so used to skipping past errors that we are terrible proofreaders. If possible, find someone who is good at it and treasure that person. Usually the less familiar the proofreader is with the proposal, the better.

If time and resources are available, an attractive cover design that will make the proposal stand out may be worthwhile. It helps to impress that particular proposal on the staff's and readers' memories. An attractive cover treatment distinguishes your proposal from all the others on the desk; it calls attention to itself as the one to pick up and examine.

Before duplicating, review the advice in Chapter 2, question 8--"Is the hasty reader signaled to the critically important parts of the proposal?" (p. 32). There is no point in reprinting that section here, but some selected quotations may make you want to read them if you have not already done so: "Make the proposal look as though it wanted to be read!" "Good writing, like good acting, uses nonverbal gestures." "Avoid . . . jazzing the copy with jargon or more gesture than sense."

As a final warning about duplication, consider this version of Murphy's law, which appears over our duplicating machine:

WARNING

This machine is subject to breakdowns during periods of critical need. A special circuit in the machine called a "critical detector" senses the operator's emotional state in terms of how desperate he or she is to use the machine. The critical detector then creates a malfunction proportional to the desperation of the operator. Threatening the machine with violence only aggravates the situation. Likewise, attempts to use another machine may cause it to also malfunction. They belong to the same union. Keep cool and say nice things to the machine. Nothing else seems to work. Never let anything mechanical know you are in a hurry.

* * * * * *

It is always helpful to examine sample proposals. Already funded proposals can be obtained from federal programs under the Freedom of Information Act. In addition, there are a number of other sources; see the "Sample Proposals" section in Appendix A.

6.

Submission, Review, and Negotiation in Federal Programs

SUBMISSION

Assemble *all* the materials needed for proper review of your proposal. Some programs prepare a checklist to help you; indeed, some require that it be enclosed with the proposal. Such a list is shown in figure 15.

Acknowledgment cards. Federal programs that ask you to submit proposal acknowledgment cards with your application include them in the application packet. Addressed to yourself, the card is sent back with the file number of your application along with the date the application was received. It is your assurance that the application was received in time. The file number facilitates follow-up correspondence, since projects are usually arranged in file number order rather than by researcher's name. There may be separate notification cards for you and for your business office. A sample of a returned card is shown below:

We have received your proposal. It has been recorded for the Teaching and Learning grants competition and assigned the following identification number:

A4230

All proposals are filed by identification number in order to facilitate rapid retrieval. Please refer to the number recorded in the space above should you have need to communicate regarding this proposal.

Proposal Clearinghouse
National Institute of Education
Washington, D.C. 20208
Telephone: (202) 254-5600

Letter of transmittal. Strictly speaking, a letter of transmittal is unnecessary; the proposal presents itself. But if one is used, the letter of transmittal should identify the competition in which the proposal is entered and be signed by a responsible institutional administrator such as a dean, vice-president for academic affairs, or director of the office of grants administration. Where the number of pages in the proposal is restricted by the competition's rules, the letter, as not properly part of the proposal, can be used to convey additional information. There is, of course, no assurance that the staff will send the letter to the reviewers with the proposal; that is a chance one takes. Sometimes it can be used by a superior to indicate the institution's pride in and support of both the investigator and the proposal. Such a letter has to be done well to have any impact, since judges and staff tend to view such a letter as routine

Figure 15. Sample proposal checklist.

CHECKLIST

Complete this sheet and forward one copy with the application.

Principal Investigator: _____

A.   Type of application

_____ Large grant   _____ Small grant

B.   Auxiliary information exists concerning:

Civil rights

_____ Assurance of compliance with Title VI of the Civil Rights
Act of 1964 *already filed* (HEW Form 441). Date of
Assurance: _____
_____ Assurance of compliance with Title IX of the Education
Admendments of 1972 *already filed* (HEW Form 639A).
Date of Assurance: _____
_____ Assurance of compliance with Section 504 of the
Rehabilitation Act of 1973 *already filed* (HEW Form 641).
Date of Assurance: _____

Cost sharing

_____ Institutional agreement dated _____
_____ No institutional agreement; tentative proposed percentage
of project cost to be shared by applicant if an award is
made: _____%.

C.   Contents of package

_____ 15 copies of the application, each containing:

Cover sheet, with all items filled in, and one copy with
original ink signatures of the Principal Investigator and
Institutional Official
Narrative description of the project
Resumes of all professional staff
Project Budget Summary and supplementary information
_____ One self-addressed Acknowledgment Card (on back cover of
announcement)
_____ One copy of this checklist (attached to signature copy of
proposal with paperclip)

D.   Mailing

Address the package to Proposal Clearinghouse, NIE, 1200 19th
Street, N.W., Washington, DC 20208. Hand-delivered packages will
be accepted only in Room 804, 1200 19th Street. Mark the outside
of the package: Teaching and Learning and show the selected area
letter designation.

administrative blarney. After all, the administration can be expected to support the applicant.

Where the proposal is submitted in separate parts, list them in the letter of transmittal to alert staff to assemble them for the review. If you have one, give your institution's contracts person's name and phone number, so budgetary inquiries may be made.

Delivery. Double-check the address against that required; don't miss the deadline for a simple error at this stage of the effort. Sending the proposal by certified mail with a return receipt provides evidence of the dates of mailing and of receipt. Proof of mailing by a deadline date is enough in some competitions—a legibly dated postal receipt, for instance. Such a deadline is usually five days prior to the deadline for receipt at the proposal clearinghouse. Others require actual receipt by the deadline. If the receipt deadline is close, it may be well to use one of the air courier services; although remember, they are occasionally grounded by weather. The typical federal deadline is usually 4:00 p.m. EST; projects arriving at 4:01 on the deadline day *cannot* be legally considered in most competitions. It is foolish to spend hundreds of dollars in personnel time to prepare a proposal and then risk missing the deadline to save a few dollars. Bear this in mind in choosing a time and means of transmittal.

In a few years, this step may be simplified. Bill Wilson, Director of Sponsored Programs at Syracuse University, plans within two years to enable faculty to transmit proposals to his office by electronic mail for internal clearance, review, duplication, and submission. NSF's EXPRES Project (EXPerimental Research in Electronic Submission) is similarly geared toward receipt, internal review, external review, approval and negotiation by electronic mail, initially using NSFNET.

THE REVIEW PROCESS

What happens after the proposal is submitted for federal funding? It is helpful to understand the review process while preparing the proposal, since accommodation to the judging process is an important goal of proposal preparation. Further, one feels more comfortable engaging in an activity if one understands all the parts of it.

Your proposal will probably be received by an office such as the National Science Foundation's Office of Applicant Management and Organization, which accepts proposals, certifies when they were received, and keeps track of their processing. Such offices came into being to ensure that deadlines were fairly and uniformly observed.

Screening. The initial screening ascertains that the necessary information has been included. If the agency supplies a checklist and it has been followed, the proposal will pass this screening. The next screen ensures that the proposal falls within the scope of what the agency is authorized to fund and is appropriate for the program or competition in which it is entered. A surprisingly large number of proposals fail these two screens owing either to carelessness in assembling the proposal or to not having adequate information about the program. Proposers rejected at this level often receive no word that they have been screened out early, being notified along with all the other proposers when judging is completed.

Types of reviews.   The technical review of the proposal can be conducted entirely by the staff of the agency, by external reviewers, or by some combination of these two. Agencies with a strong sense of mission--they know exactly what it is they wish to support--are more likely to opt for internal review, possibly using staff from other programs to assist them. These are more likely to be programs funding demonstrations of particular ideas or seeking other tightly specified goals.

"Peer review" systems prevail where the goals are more open-ended, as they are in most research programs. Usually this means using nongovernment personnel who have special expertise and are close to the research process. Government staff may have expertise but typically have not actually done research recently. External reviews may be done by individual reviewers, by panels especially established for the competition, by standing panels or committees, or by some combination of these.

An external reviewer will usually be sent only one proposal at a time, although she may review several over the course of a year. When all reviews have been returned, the government staff must synthesize the recommendations and prioritize the proposals for funding. Standing committees usually meet to discuss their evaluations and then give a final rating to the project. Staff may, for good reasons, recommend action contrary to the reviewers. Since their recommendation is subject to scrutiny by their superiors, they document defense of their decision clearly. As Cavin (1984) notes, "What may appear an innovative and novel idea to a reviewer who reads a handful of proposals in a year may not be new at all in the experience of a program director who reads hundreds of proposals annually" (p. 8).

The staff recommendations may go to a standing advisory group for approval or to more senior agency officials. As noted earlier, such officials rarely have time to read the full proposal, so the abstract, perhaps together with the work plan and budget, must convey the project's essence. Before it is forwarded upstairs, the project officer may have been in touch with the researcher to clarify certain questions. Such calls ring joyfully in the researcher's ear, but this is no assurance the project will be funded. Read on.

Two typical review process examples.   The exact review process depends on the program. The descriptions that follow are of recent review practices at a competition in the National Institute of Education (NIE) and the general process at the National Institutes of Health (NIH). Both give you an idea of what the review process can be like. Cavin (1984) provides an excellent summary of the processes of several other programs: the Department of Education's Fund for the Improvement of Postsecondary Education (FIPSE), Office of Special Education and Rehabilitation Services (OSERS), and Office of Postsecondary Education (OPSE); the National Science Foundation (NSF); and the National Endowment for the Humanities (NEH). Quarles (1986) in a chapter giving inside reviews of funding agencies provides descriptions of the review process at NSF by Felice S. Levine, at NIH by Janet M. Cuca, and at ADAMHA (Alcohol, Drug Abuse, and Mental Health Administration) by Susan Quarles and Salvatore N. Cianci.

The review process for an unsolicited proposal competition of the National Institute of Education began with screening by the professional staff for relevance to education. Proposals that qualified were sent to at least two outside reviewers. Proposals relevant to an established program were also reviewed by NIE professional staff members. The outside reviewers included educational practitioners and were drawn from a wide range of disciplines. (Note the breadth of audience to be considered in proposal writing!) Reviewers gave each proposal a numerical score as well as comments. The highest-ranked proposals were then submitted to a panel of outside judges for review. A typical unsolicited proposal competition judged this way reduced over 400 proposals to the best 100 for the panel. The panel members' recommendations and supporting documents were then studied by an administrator of the program who put together a set of funding recommendations for the director of NIE, who made the final funding decision. In this instance, 26 of the 100 proposals were funded. Clearly there is considerable room for the professional staff to exercise their judgment in this process: in their initial reading, in their choice of field and NIE staff reviewers, in their reactions to the reviews, and in their reactions to the panel's judgments.

In the National Institutes of Health, a proposal is assigned to the most relevant institute by the Division of Research Grants. An investigator may indicate which institute is preferred, but the request is not binding. An Initial Review Group or Division of Research Grant Study section, composed of outside reviewers evaluating proposals on their scientific and technical merit, either approves, disapproves, or defers for additional information. Study sections typically consist of 15-20 members nominated by the executive secretary of the group, who is an NIH scientist. She also designates the chair. Approved projects are ranked using a 5-point scale in half unit intervals from the best, 1.0, to the least acceptable, 5.0. The scores given by individual reviewers are averaged and multiplied by 100 to obtain a priority score ranging from 100 to 500. The executive secretary makes a summary report, which, together with the proposals and priority scores, is reviewed by the institute's National Advisory Council. The council (which includes lay members) judges the project's relevance to the institute's goals. Note again the inclusion of lay members, which considerably broadens the audience for which one must write. A proposal not approved by the council is rarely funded. The membership, authority, and function of all these groups are given in an annual publication, *NIH Public Advisory Groups*.

Figure 16 shows peer review score sheets designed by the National Institute for Handicapped Research for use with a range of project types (research, development, training, and so on), which are typical of the task confronting a reviewer and of the criteria used. (See also pages 108-109 re review criteria.)

Determining who will review the proposal. Even though all members of a panel will have copies of the proposal, a proposal is usually assigned to two or more principal reviewers who lead the discussion of it. The reviewers' names are often not available, but the pool from which reviewers and field readers is drawn usually is, as is the composition of past panels. Ask for information about panels; it gives you clues to the nature of your reviewing audience.

Researchers may find out to which panel their proposal has been sent for review. It is unethical to contact the reviewers on the panel, but if one believes that the proposal has been assigned to the wrong panel, and there is another that would be more appropriate, one may appeal the assignment and ask that it be changed.

Project withdrawal. It is possible in some agencies, such as the National Institute of Mental Health, to withdraw a proposal that has received low panel ratings so that it is not recorded as being turned down. It is not clear how much of a difference this makes, unless the reviewer remembers the previous version and is prejudiced by it. A panel should be primarily concerned with the quality of the proposal before it and some of our best researchers were not funded on the first submission of a project.

If the writer's research record on past grants is bad, that is another matter. As noted in the section on personnel, one's record on past grants seems to be increasing as an important factor, but Howarth's research (1980) indicates it has always been important. Ethical transgressions may result in a researcher's being barred from applying to a program for a certain period, but these decisions are usually a staff rather than reviewer responsibility.

NOTIFICATION AND NEGOTIATIONS

If you are lucky enough to be funded, you will probably first learn of it when they phone with questions about your budget. Don't open the champagne yet. Usually that means you are going to succeed, but sometimes they run short of money before they fund all those queried. If you should find out through the informal grapevine that you are to be funded, keep it to yourself. Under no circumstances leak it to the media. Congressional offices are automatically notified of funds to their districts *before that information is publicly released.* They may wish to take the credit for it, notify you, or congratulate you; they consider this their prerogative whether or not they exercise it. They are very, very sensitive about reading it in the papers or hearing it on TV first, and they hold the funding agency responsible! On occasion an award has been held up, and

Figure 16. Sample Peer Review Score Sheet

NIHR Peer Review Score Sheet
Field Initiated Research Projects
FY 1986

Applicant's Name_____ Application No._____

Reviewer's Name (please print)_____

Reviewer's Signature_____ Date_____

_____

GENERAL INSTRUCTIONS: The selection criteria to be used in the evaluation of
NIHR Field Initiated Research Projects program for FY 1986 were published in the
Federal Register on March 12, 1984.   These same criteria are reflected on the
attached score sheet.   The rating scale is as follows: Outstanding (5); Superior (4);
Satisfactory (3); Marginal (2); and Poor (1).   Each rating is then multiplied by the
weight assigned to the criterion.   Applicants who receive an average score of
superior or outstanding (4-5) will be considered for funding.   Please include
comments on the strengths and weaknesses of the applicant's proposal which
substantiate your ratings.   USE BLACK INK ONLY.

If the reviewer elects to make changes in a score or comment, make the necessary
change in the item.   Indicate which item has been changed below and initial the
change in the space provided.   Cross out those spaces below which are not used.
Initial the cover sheet only.

        Criterion #   Changes Made
                                                        Initials
    1. _____   _____   _____
    2.

NIHR Peer Review Comment/Score Sheet   page 1 of 9

I. Potential Impact of Outcome—Criterion 1: Importance of Problem (Weight 15%)

Apply criteria as appropriate/relevant to all proposed activities viz. Research (R), Development/Demonstration (D), Training (T), and Utilization (U).	Comment both on strengths and weaknesses relating comments to score. Avoid pejor-ative comments. Write legibly in BLACK INK only.	Assign a single score for this summary criterion using a scale of 1-5.
To what degree does/do/is/are:	Comments:_____	Outstanding 5___
1. proposed activity related to announced priority? (All) proposals on priority announced; does not apply to Field Initiated Research.	_____ _____	Superior 4___ Satisfactory 3___
2. research likely to produce new and useful information? (R)	_____	Marginal 2___ Poor 1___
3. need and target group(s) adequately defined? (All)	_____	Absent from ___ proposal
4. outcomes likely to benefit defined target groups? (All)	_____	
5. training needs clearly defined? (T)		
6. training methods and developed subject matter likely to meet defined need? (T)		
7. need for information exist? (U)		

NIHR Peer Review Comment/Score Sheet   page 2 of 9

I. Potential Impact of Outcome—Criterion 2: Dissemination/Utilization (Weight 15%)

Apply criteria as appropriate/relevant to all proposed activities viz. Research (R), Development/Demonstration (D), Training (T), and Utilization (U).	Comment both on strengths and weaknesses relating comments to score. Avoid pejor-ative comments. Write legibly in BLACK INK only.	Assign a single score for this summary criterion using a scale of 1-5.
To what degree does/do/is/are:	Comments:_____	Outstanding 5___
1. research results likely to become avail-able to others working in the field? (R)	_____ _____	Superior 4___ Satisfactory 3___
2. means to disseminate and promote utili-zation by others defined? (All)	_____	Marginal 2___
3. training methods and content to be pack-aged for dissemination and use by others? (T)	_____	Poor 1___ Absent from ___ Proposal
4. utilization approach likely to address defined need? (U)		

NIHR Peer Review Comment/Score Sheet   page 3 of 9

II. Probability of Achieving Proposed Outcomes-Criterion 3: Program/Project Design (Weight 25%)

Apply criteria as appropriate/relevant to all proposed activities viz. Research (R), Development/Demonstration (D), Training (T), and Utilization (U).	Comment both on strengths and weaknesses relating comments to score. Avoid pejorative comments. Write legibly in BLACK INK only.	Assign a single score for this summary criterion using a scale of 1-5.

To what degree does/do/is/are:

1. are objectives of project(s) clearly stated? (All)

2. hypothesis sound and based on evidence? (R)

3. project design/methodology likely to achieve objectives? (All)

4. measurement methodology and analysis sound? (R) (D)

5. conceptual model (if used) sound? (D)

6. sample populations correct and significant? (R) (D)

7. human subjects sufficiently protected? (R) (D)

8. device(s) or model system to be developed in an appropriate environment?

9. training content comprehensive and at an appropriate level? (T)

10. training methods likely to be effective? (T)

11. new materials (if developed) likely to be of high quality and unique? (T)

12. target populations linked to project? (U)

Outstanding   5___
Superior   4___
Satisfactory   3___
Marginal   2___
Poor   1___
Absent from   ___
proposal

NIHR Peer Review Comment/Score Sheet   page 4 of 9

II. Probability of Achieving Proposed Outcomes-Criterion 4: Key Personnel (Weight 20%)

Apply criteria as appropriate/relevant to all proposed activities viz. Research (R), Development/Demonstration (D), Training (T), and Utilization (U).	Comment both on strengths and weaknesses relating comments to score. Avoid pejorative comments. Write legibly in BLACK INK only.	Assign a single score for this summary criterion using a scale of 1-5.

To what degree does/do/is/are:

Comments:

1. principal investigator and other key staff have adequate training and/or experience and demonstrate appropriate potential to conduct the proposed research, demonstration, training, development, or dissemination activity?

2. principal investigator and other key staff familiar with recent pertinent literature or methods or both? (All)

3. all required disciplines effectively covered? (All)

4. staff time commitments adequate for project? (All)

5. the applicant likely, as part of its nondiscriminatory employment practices, to encourage applications for employment from persons who are members of groups that have been traditionally underrepresented, such as-
   (i)   Members of racial or ethnic minority groups;
   (ii) Women;
   (iii) Handicapped persons; and
   (iv) The elderly   (All)

Outstanding   5___
Superior   4___
Satisfactory   3___
Marginal   2___
Poor   1___
Absent from   ___
proposal

NIHR Peer Review Comment/Score Sheet   page 5 of 9

II. Probability of Achieving Proposed Outcomes-Criterion 5: Evaluation Plan (Weight 5%)

Apply criteria as appropriate/relevant to all proposed activities viz. Research (R), Development/Demonstration (D), Training (T), and Utilization (U).

Comment both on strengths and weaknesses relating comments to score. Avoid pejorative comments. Write legibly in BLACK INK only.

Assign a single score for this summary criterion using a scale of 1-5.

To what degree does/do/is/are:

Comments:_____

Outstanding   5___

1. there a mechanism to evaluate plans, progress and results? (All)

Superior   4___

Satisfactory   3___

2. evaluation methods objective and likely to produce data that are quantifiable? (All)

Marginal   2___

3. evaluation results, where relevant, likely to be assessed in a service setting? (All)

Poor   1___

Absent from proposal   ___

NIHR Peer Review Comment/Score Sheet   page 6 of 9

III. Program/Project Management-Criterion 6: Plan of Operation (Weight 10%)

Apply criteria as appropriate/relevant to all proposed activities viz Research (R), Development/Demonstration (D), Training (T), and Utilization (U).

Comment both on strengths and weaknesses relating comments to score. Avoid pejorative comments. Write legibly in BLACK INK only.

Assign a single score for this summary criterion using a scale of 1-5.

To what degree does/do/is/are:

Comments:_____

Outstanding   5___

1. there an effective plan of management that insures proper and efficient administration of the project(s)? (All)

Superior   4___

Satisfactory   3___

2. the way the applicant plans to use its resources and personnel likely to achieve each objective? (All)

Marginal   2___

Poor   1___

3. interinstitutional collaboration, if proposed, likely to be effective? (All)

Absent from proposal   ___

4. there a clear description of how the applicant will provide equal access and treatment for eligible project participants who are members of groups that have been traditionally underrepresented, such as-
   (i)   Members of racial or ethnic minority groups;
   (ii) Women;
   (iii) Handicapped persons; and
   (iv) The elderly

NIHR Peer Review Comment/Score Sheet   page 7 of 9

III. Program/Project Management-Criterion 7: Adequacy of Resources (Weight 5%)

Apply criteria as appropriate/relevant to all proposed activities viz. Research (R), Development/Demonstration (D), Training (T), and Utilization (U).

Comment both on strengths and weaknesses relating comments to score. Avoid pejorative comments. Write legibly in BLACK INK only.

Assign a single score for this summary criterion using a scale of 1-5.

To what degree does/do/is/are:

Comments:_____

Outstanding   5___

1. the facilities that the applicant plans to use adequate? (All)

Superior   4___

Satisfactory   3___

2. the equipment and supplies that the applicant plans to use adequate? (All)

Marginal   2___

Poor   1___

3. the commitment of the institution evident? (All)

Absent from proposal   ___

NIHR Peer Review Comment/Score Sheet   page 8 of 9

III. Program/Project Management-Criterion 8: Budget and Cost Effectiveness   (Weight 5%)

Apply criteria as appropriate/relevant to all proposed activities viz. Research (R), Development/Demonstration (D), Training (T), and Utilization (U).	Comment both on strengths and weaknesses relating comments to score. Avoid pejorative comments. Write legibly in BLACK INK only.	Assign a single score for this summary criterion using a scale of 1-5.

To what degree does/do/is/are:

Comments:_____

Outstanding   5___

1. the budget for the project(s) adequate to support activities? (All)

_____

Superior   4___

_____

Satisfactory   3___

2. costs reasonable in relation to the objectives of the project(s)? (All)

_____

Marginal   2___

_____

Poor   1___

3. budget for subcontract (if required) detailed and appropriate? (All)

_____

Absent from   ___
proposal

NIHR Peer Review Score Computation Sheet   page 9 of 9

Application No._____   Date_____

Instructions: 1. Enter summary criteria scores (0-5) in first column.
              2. Mutiply by weighting factor, enter results in third column.
              3. Add weighted scores, enter total score.
                 PLEASE CHECK ARITHMETIC!

Summary of Criteria	Score 0-5	Multiply by Weight Factor	Weighted Score
I. Potential Impact of Outcomes			
1. Importance of Problem	_____	x 3 =	_____
2. Dissemination/Utilization	_____	x 3 =	_____
II. Probability of Achieving Proposed Outcomes			
3. Program/Project Design	_____	x 5 =	_____
4. Key Personnel	_____	x 4 =	_____
5. Evaluation Plan	_____	x 1 =	_____
III. Program/Project Management			
6. Plan of Operation	_____	x 2 =	_____
7. Adequacy of Resources	_____	x 1 =	_____
8. Budget and Cost Effectivness	_____	x 1 =	_____
		Total Score	_____

in severe instances not made, because of premature release of the information. Remember, it is not official until you or your business office receives *written* notice. Only then are you sure you are authorized to spend the money.

Budget negotiations. Typically, if the project is approved, there will be a negotiation of the budget. Many budget discussions are initiated by the program officer, who wishes to assure herself (and you) that the budgetary basis for the project is sound before turning the project over to the fiscal officer to negotiate. Remember it was suggested you save your budget notes? This is where you will need them; your budget notes are essential for a sensible discussion. If you have "loaded" the budget and/or cannot defend a certain item in these sessions, *you undermine your credibility for other items which may then be questioned.* In addition, you show yourself a careless and possibly poor manager as well.

When negotiating a grant, it is sometimes possible to increase the budget if one remembers an important forgotten item. Don't count on it, but it is always worth a try if the omission is serious. If you are low bidder in a competition, it is even more difficult. Remember, however, the sponsor wants you to be able to do the project. While saving money is important, even more important are results! The problem is to find that balance point where you have just enough.

Once the program officer is satisfied, the budget is usually passed to the sponsor's fiscal officer, who may repeat the process with the fiscal officer in your institution who handles the research projects. The fiscal officers on both sides are the ones who do the legal paperwork to set up the grant or contract. Keep yours informed so explanations are consistent. With larger projects, and some sponsors, nearly all negotiations may be with fiscal officers from the outset. Remember, it is the fiscal officer who makes the commitment; oral requests by program officers to do more need to be backed up by fiscal officer action before the required resources are assured.

Sometimes the negotiation is nothing more than a short telephone call. When these turn into more extensive negotiations, bring in your institution's fiscal officer, particularly if you are dealing with theirs. This is especially important if there is a site visit that includes a fiscal review, a common part of the approval process for very large projects. Fiscal types know each other's lingo and communicate with each other more easily than with you. Your institution's fiscal officer isn't going to give the game away, but he doesn't know your project as well as you do. He will need your help; stick with him. Frequently he knows better than you the strings to pull to get your own institution to make additional contributions; let him do it if added funds are needed.

If large sums are at stake, you may want to role-play a bargaining session with your fiscal officer before you enter the real negotiations. This gives you the opportunity to anticipate questions, to prepare your strategy, and to have in mind the trade-offs you are willing to make, especially if the scope of work must be pared to fit a reduced budget. Don't let the negotiations wear you down to the point where the resources are inadequate to properly carry out the project. *You won't get any credit for saving money; the whole point is to complete the project successfully!* Taking on a project with inadequate resources is irresponsible and could color your career.

During the negotiations, remember this is not the only business you and/or your institution expect to do with this sponsor. *You are not just negotiating this project, you are building a relationship!*

Along these same lines, develop a good working relationship with your institution's fiscal officer. You'll work as a team in negotiating. It will help you to understand his position if you realize that the grant or contract is with the institution, not with you as a person. In the case of a contract, the institution can be held liable for its fulfillment if you fail. Even though this accountability is not always exercised with research projects, one such expensive occasion can be enough to make a fiscal officer nervous for life. Be sympathetic if you can; he is trying to protect you and the institution. Such accountability is more often exercised in new research projects.

Here is a summary to emphasize the important points above:

- Have your budget notes handy to explain any questions.
- Have in mind the trade-offs in reduction of the scope of work commensurate with budget cuts.
- Ask about adding omitted budget items that are critical.
- Don't let them reduce your budget below what is reasonable to do the project properly. It may be necessary to negotiate a cut in the scope of work if the budget is tight; it is better to do that than to spread resources too thinly. It is better not to attempt the study at all with a seriously inadequate budget. You get no points for trying to save money if your project fails.
- Use your fiscal officer to talk to their fiscal officer; they are more likely to be "simpatico."
- Remember you are building a continuing relationship; you'll probably be going back to this agency for other projects.

Unless you have *prior written approval,* your project expenditures become an institutional contribution until there is a formal award.

Suppose your project was approved but no negotiations have been scheduled; you are in the "approved but not funded" category, so be patient. Sometimes, program staff hope that after a first round of negotiations, there may be some funds left as a result of "sharp penciling" the budgets. A second round of negotiations with the projects next in priority order is then initiated until the funds are expended. With luck, the funds will hold out until yours is reached.

Notification of rejection. You will typically receive your rejection by letter. Alternatively, you may learn you are in the "also ran" category of "approved but not funded." That means you need to raise your priority score or your sponsor's equivalent. The letter writer will typically offer feedback if you wish it. Take her up on it; if the proposal is in the turned-down category, the important thing is to benefit from the reviewers' comments. Even if not offered in the letter, these comments, exclusive of information that could identify the reviewer, can be obtained verbatim under the Freedom of Information Act from federal agencies.

Your letter inviting a collect return phone call to discuss the reviewer's evaluations will often bring important insights and perspectives. (Federal staff typically won't call collect, but inviting collect calls reinforces your seriousness of intent.) Alternatively, arrange with the staff member's secretary to call at an appointed time when she will be free. It is most helpful if you can discuss the reviewers' comments with a professional staff member who was present during the panel meetings. There is no substitute for this kind of feedback, especially if one is to resubmit the proposal to the same group.

One word of caution with respect to these contacts. As noted in Chapter 2, question 3 (p. 20), researchers should understand the role of the staff in the funding decision. In some instances the entire decision is the responsibility of the reviewers, and the staff has very little role in the decision. In this situation it is important that the staff member distinguish those comments that are her interpretations from those of the reviewers. The staff member's opinion is useful as that of another professional who, like yourself, is trying to predict the reactions of reviewers to appropriate changes. The staff member usually has had the additional advantage of having watched the reviewers in action or having corresponded with them over a period of time. Staff advice should be considered from this perspective.

In most agencies, however, the reviewer or panel judgments are not determinants of action but are recommendations to the staff. The weight of these recommendations varies with the agency and the relative professional expertise of reviewers and staff. When the reviewer is expert and the staff is not familiar with the area, the reviewer's recommendations are likely to be determining. In most philanthropic foundations, however, or in government programs where the staff assumes the role of trying to build or mold the program in certain directions, staff members are almost always keys to funding. Their advice should be taken very seriously.

When a staff member conveys a reviewer's comments, it is always helpful, if possible, to find out how much consensus existed among the reviewers for specific recommendations. A recommendation may be unique to a single reviewer, and a change in this direction may even negatively affect other reviewers.

Knowledge of consensus also avoids a situation in which the writer makes all the recommended changes only to find a new set of recommendations for change on resubmission. This is an infrequent but unfortunate situation. The reviewers may be ambivalent or basically negative toward the problem, and their "nitpicking" objections are an indirect way of rejecting the proposal. An experienced staff member, surmising this situation, may not encourage resubmission. (See also p. 212 re appeals)

Typically you can do the follow-up by phone, particularly if you and the staff member both have the comments of the panel members before you. However, if you happen to be in Washington or can find an opportunity to get there, so much the better. Face-to-face conversations often give clues that are not available over the phone.

Above all, if you think your idea is a good one, do not be discouraged by a rejection. The approval rate on resubmitted projects is as high as or higher than on those submitted for the first time. This is especially true if one understands what the reviewers are trying to convey and follows their advice. Some programs selectively encourage resubmissions by having a judgment category entitled "resubmit." In these programs the approval rate of proposals revised to take care of initial reviewers' objections may be three or four times the rate for initial submission.

On resubmitting a rejected proposal, it is well to remember that the reviewers are likely to bring their initial reaction to the new proposal. If the initial reaction was severely negative, resubmission may be more appropriate after the yearly turnover of part of the panel has occurred; it will then be considered afresh by at least a portion of the group. Typically, federal appointments are three- or four-year terms, so roughly a quarter to a third of the panel turns over yearly.

When changes were minor, specific, and concrete, a cover letter summarizing the changes is essential. When basic rewriting is required, the cover letter may still be helpful but is less important. If changes are pointed out, readers may review only those sections. When it is desirable to have the entire proposal reread, indicate this in the cover letter, or ask that the project be treated as a new one rather than a resubmission.

Section III
Aids to Proposal Preparation

This chapter is a collection of aids to help you achieve the goal that you should have set for yourself in the previous section--writing the best possible proposal! Here is what is provided to assist you:

Chapter 7 customizes the material in Chapters 3 through 5 for particular kinds of proposals such as evaluations, longitudinal studies, case and qualitative method studies, nonresearch proposals, and others.

Chapter 8 translates the material in Chapters 3 thourgh 5 into a checklist for use in critiquing a proposal. Use it to find problems in your drafts.

Chapter 9 is a checklist of the steps required in a large and complex proposal. Though some steps are unique to complex ones, the list will be found helpful for proposals of any size.

Chapter 10 summarizes the results of research on disapproved proposals so you can see where common errors have been made and avoid them.

Chapter 11 provides background on how research findings become knowledge and describes the criteria applied to findings as they are judged for acceptance as knowledge. It also describes how behavioral scientists differently view the importance of various criteria. Understanding this larger picture of science puts the advice of Chapters 3 through 5 and 7 in a helpful perspective, a perspective that facilitates your understanding of why the advice was given in the first place, and the relative importance of different points.

Chapter 12 summarizes tips on writing style to help you communicate your ideas more effectively.

7.

Comments on Proposals for Particular Kinds of Studies

As you must realize by now, the goals and methods of a study shape the proposal; different kinds of studies will emphasize different things. Some may fit the standard proposal format beautifully; others may require adaptation. Still others may be best described when the standard format is abandoned almost entirely. This section highlights the problems and opportunities of a variety of kinds of proposals and suggests how they might be better presented.

Consider proposals designed to attract sponsor support for:

1. Following one's hunches wherever they might lead in the search for new knowledge.
2. Systematically observing a predefined situation or exploring certain points of view with the intent of finding a new organization or set of relationships.
3. Systematically trying to create a technique, tool, or effect.
4. Creating a convincing experiment to show that something works as hypothesized.
5. Providing a demonstration of an established technique.

These projects span a continuum from discovery and exploration through validation to dissemination and installation. Given the usual pressures for success, if sponsors are free to choose, they will more likely fund projects at the latter than the former end of the continuum. By contrast, the chances of a new discovery with widespread impact lie at the discovery end. But such projects are inherently riskier and much more difficult to assess, leaving the sponsor with considerable uncertainty.

To help relieve their uncertainty and improve their decision making, sponsors' guidelines, particularly federal ones, are frequently structured for projects at the validation, demonstration, and installation end of the continuum. This means that the closer the proposal is to the exploratory end, the more difficulty one will have meeting the requested proposal format and the further one will have to deviate from it.

Although the usual range of social science projects encountered fits the continuum only crudely, arranging them in such an approximate order helps to get a sense of how the nature of the proposal varies along the continuum. Eleven common categories of proposals have been identified:

1. Exploratory studies
2. Qualitative methods studies, including participant observation and ethnographic studies
3. Philosophical and historical studies
4. Predictive studies
5. Equipment, instrument, and curriculum development

6. Methodological studies
7. Evaluation studies
8. Longitudinal studies
9. Survey studies
10. Experimental studies
11. Demonstration and action projects (nonresearch studies)

In a chapter that highlights some of the problems of the proposal process, it is only fair to note that sponsors are aware of and concerned about its weaknesses, including the difficulties of writing attractive exploratory proposals. Ideal conditions for research are hardly created by the necessity of writing proposal after proposal to keep one's research progressing. Further, the hiatus between proposals may result not only in a loss of momentum but also in the loss of one's carefully recruited and trained research staff to projects with certain funding.

Experimental programs involving long-term grants (so-called career research grants) have been tried to avoid the hiatus, but they reduce the program officer's flexibility. Occasionally, other efforts have been made to deal with these problems, so we make some slight progress. Still, we seem to be fundamentally committed to the proposal system until a better way of allocating funds can be found. Therefore we must learn to use the system to get the best decisions possible. That means adapting the proposal to the kind of project being described. The following material discusses the particular characteristics of each of the 11 categories of projects noted above. Consult the discussions on each side of a project type to get a sense of the problems and opportunities in that region of the continuum.

EXPLORATORY PROJECTS

The extensive planning and the mass of detail required by most federal programs have tended to discourage the submission of exploratory studies. As someone has pointed out, could Archimedes, anticipating an insight, have requisitioned his government for a bathtub three-quarters full of water? It is hard to be convincing when one cannot with certainty describe what is to be discovered. *It is possible, however, for many programs to sponsor exploratory research, even though their application format discourages them.* Approval may be harder to win; it may be harder for reviewers to commit themselves to an exploration than a concrete outcome. Nevertheless, do not hesitate to submit such proposals; you never know unless you try!

For most of us, exploratory projects are much more exciting than validating ones. And although the risks are greater, when projects are successful, the rewards are proportionately greater as well. In addition, by your application, you indicate the importance of such directions to program staff; they always want to stay ahead of the field. Even if you are not successful, you may hasten the day when the approach you wish to use is more routinely accepted and maybe even the time when programs routinely encourage exploration as one of a variety of approaches.

Such projects will win approval more easily if the writer includes adequate pilot studies that make clear there is potential in a larger, more expensive exploration. If feasible, it also helps to develop the study in phases so that the project can be supported a phase at a time as the results justify continued support.

In some instances, though not all, a truly bold exploratory study may win readier approval than one that tries to straddle the fence between being definitive and being exploratory. But when this is tried, reviewers have been known to move the whole project back to safer ground by asking for resubmission as a definitive study with the hypotheses neatly laid out and the appropriate techniques for testing them delineated. When this occurs, reviewers have sometimes assumed that the author, under time or other pressures, unintentionally left the exploratory part un-planned. To avoid this, explain why sheer exploration is the preferable approach.

Such an approach can sometimes be justified when the work in a field has become so muddled by confusing terminology that it is wiser to start almost anew. The field of empathy in counseling is an example of such a tangle of conflicting definitions and concepts. Definitions range from reports of feelings to predictions of the actions of a stranger and to descriptions of common themes of a culture. An exploratory study that would tease out the major dimensions of the concept, so that the previous work could be untangled in terms of these dimensions, is probably overdue. (Or maybe it's been done, and I'm not aware of it!)

QUALITATIVE METHODS STUDIES

Qualitative methods studies, including participant observation and ethnographic studies, are often at a disadvantage in competitions that seem to require clear-cut, prior specification of project objectives. This requirement particularly rankles the researcher who believes in entering a situation with as few biases as possible. Participant observers may bring a mental model of what is going on to help guide their observations, but they also want to be open to new orientations. To insist that the whole project be laid out at the start, as many program outlines seem to require, violates a basic premise of the method.

How does one convince a potential reviewer that an investigation so open-ended is worth supporting? Admittedly, it is difficult, but here are some suggestions.

Show the reader you have an innovative notion or approach. Probably this "sells" a qualitative proposal more than any other factor. Bogdan (1985), for instance, in studying mainstreaming of handicapped children, proposed doing a series of case studies of programs nominated as exemplary by parents, administrators, and teachers. With a positive approach, his sampling had a high likelihood of tapping and evaluating successful programs. This interested the sponsor in contrast to the usual evaluation of a random sample.

Much has been written about qualitative methods; show that you have mastered the principles that apply to your study. For example, techniques of interviewing have been studied extensively. How you structure your interview should be related to what you intend to find out.

Be sure that you are aware of previous literature on the phenomena you intend to study. Here, as in any review of literature, you demonstrate your competence in your conceptual mastery of that material.

Do some pilot studies and report the results. Too often, one's pre-conception of a situation differs from what one finds in the field. Bogdan (1971), for instance, began studying unemployment training programs as examples of adult socialization into the world of work. He found, however, that the program's difficulty in filling the classes was so great that the study became one of how people maintain programs that don't do the task they were created to do. Pilot studies might have uncovered this reconceptualization of topic before a proposal was submitted. Such prior knowledge helps show that your proposal is solidly grounded and that you are competent in both content and method.

Not everyone who believes she can enter a situation with an open mind can do so. Or even if she can, she may not be a sufficiently keen observer to catch what is significant. The evidence that is of most value here is prior experience--you who have already successfully done participant observation work can, obviously, do it again! Cite your previous work, especially if there are positive reviews of it. Novice researchers without previous published research can use references of established researchers with whom they have worked to tell how keenly sensitive they are, how openly observant, and how well trained and organized. Experience and/or references are probably critically important to getting such a grant.

How does one cite one's own work without seeming boastful? First of all, use the third person. Some will say this is false modesty, and they are correct. You are playing the odds, however, and there seem to be more persons who are rankled by too many "I's" than persons who are seriously bothered by use of third person. Second, put yourself in the reviewers' place and ask yourself the questions they should be asking. Point out the strengths and weaknesses of your past research in relation to what is anticipated in this new setting.

Indicate how you enter the problem with a "well-prepared mind." (Purists of the "approach the situation with a blank slate" school may not like this suggestion, but most reviewers are not purists.) It has been demonstrated that discovery favors the prepared mind, one that brings useful background to the situation. Indicate that background by sug-gesting the applicable theories, analogous situations, points of view, and hypotheses that might be useful in the proposal. This is an extremely helpful exercise in preparing for the project as well, so it is time well spent. As Wax and Wax (1980) note, prior preparation is a mark of respect to the hosts, as it demonstrates that one considers their affairs of sufficient importance to learn whatever one can about them before formal introduction..... Preparation is also a mark of respect to the scholars who have studied the community... in the past. True, when one enters the field, one may be hampered by inaccurate ideas gained from prior studies, but... the researcher will always be entering with some jumble of expectations so that it is better that these be grounded in past scholarship, rather than in what passes for conventional information. (p. 31, 32)

Follow to their conclusion the implications of some of the outcomes forecast above. Indicate the importance of these implications and whatever changes in viewpoint, operations, or organization might stem from them. This suggests the potential importance of the findings.

Let us pull these suggestions above together into recommendations that summarize and add some points. First, be sure to answer the questions relevant to your method that are implied by the usual proposal structure, even though you discard that structure as inappropriate to qualitative research. For example, address whatever theoretical issues underlie your project. This conveys both a deeper understanding of the problem and a command of the background knowledge that underlies it.

Second, describe the basis for selecting sites, cases, and data sources. If it is not obvious, describe the special appropriateness of those choices. When using records as sources, where their authenticity, accuracy, and appropriateness are suspect, provide the basis for allaying such concerns or outline the steps to be taken to do so.

Third, describe your method of observation, reasons for that choice, expertise with the method, and how you will ensure, insofar as possible, accuracy of information and description. Triangulation, comparing multiple points of view and data sources, may be very important in detecting and avoiding bias.

Fourth, pulling together your voluminous data is often a special problem for the novice; many fail this step. Indicate your plans; QUALOG (Shelly and Sibert, 1985) or similar computer-based analytic tools may be helpful in organizing data. Evidence of past success is important here, as noted above. Unless you have pilot data describing the creative process of data interpretation, you may have to await data collection. But steps to ensure that your interpretations are adequately tested can be described ahead of time. You want them to withstand similar critiques when they are published.

Finally, somewhere in the text describe the substantive problems you expect to encounter, what you plan to do to protect against them, and the seriousness of problems about which little or nothing can be done as the study is now conceived. How, if at all, will the latter affect the findings? Sharing such concerns shows professional competence, assures the reader of your integrity, and indicates foresight and planning. All that is good. The danger is that reviewers may believe you have underestimated the seriousness of such problems or their impacts. Avoid this insofar as possible by trying out your write-up with a very critical reviewer. Then rewrite this section until you are convinced that you have adequately answered her concerns. In developing your proposal, however, remember that it is easier to prevent such concerns from arising in the first place than to remove them once they are fully formed.

PHILOSOPHICAL AND HISTORICAL STUDIES

Typical proposal formats are probably as poorly suited to philosophical and historical studies as any. Hence, the proposer should feel free to depart as far as necessary from them to describe the project. Since such studies differ widely in their nature and direction, it is difficult to know what specifically to suggest. Bear in mind that unless this is a competition designed for projects of the kind you are preparing, you are writing for persons who are likely to be operationally oriented, who may have little tolerance for mystical or fuzzy descriptions, but who in all probability respect scholarship. Show clearly the origins of the study, the implications (to the extent to which they can be anticipated), and the operations involved, describing the entire project as precisely as possible so that those outside the field can understand and appreciate it.

If the proposer is likely to be unknown to the reviewer, evidence of scholarship may be critical. Include in the appendix a sample of writing, such as a draft of the first chapter of the study if that is possible. If not, send along a copy of a previous paper similar to what you propose, preferably one published in a journal that uses peer reviewing. Do not overdo it by sending whole books, unless these are requested.

Suggest, insofar as possible, the basis for confidence that the study is likely to be successful. For example, a study of the manuscripts of the Roman Curia to determine the mnemonic techniques used to help monks remember manuscripts before the dawn of printing may well have considerable present-day significance--if there is any reason to believe that those techniques were set down in useful form and are retrievable. Give the reader what facts there are that lead the writer to be hopeful about the project.

PREDICTIVE STUDIES

Predictive studies that attempt to improve our ability to forecast a person's future success or failure are not so frequent as they once were; and despite the historical abundance of such studies, some are still poorly designed. To be of maximum value to future decision makers, the sample used in the study must be similar to future groups whose success is to be predicted. Unfortunately, researchers too often use whatever subjects are available rather than carefully constructing their sample.

Acceptability of the measure of success or failure that is to be predicted is essential. If there are questions about it, the study is of little value. In too many instances, this measure lacks desirable psychometric characteristics (e.g., use of teachers' grades that combine attendance, deportment, and achievement with different emphasis from teacher to teacher and from subject to subject).

As indicated in the section on design, predictive studies must be cross-validated. Too many proposals omit this step, despite its importance.

Most predictive studies are based on some rationale about why the predictors ought to work. But an occasional study is proposed that suggests throwing all kinds of marginal possibilities into the prediction equation to see what will happen. Such studies probably run second in approval rate to those that select predictors on a reasoned basis. State the basis for inclusion of variables, even though the rationale may not be strong; it need not be if you are following the validation pattern of the Minnesota Multiphasic Personality Inventory, the Strong-Campbell Vocational Interest Inventory, or similar tests.

EQUIPMENT, INSTRUMENT, AND CURRICULUM DEVELOPMENT

Sponsors support the development of new equipment, instruments, and instructional materials as a means for achieving an end. You will want to stress the consequences of a successful project for achieving that goal. "A new measure of anxiety will lead to better estimates of psychotherapy success and to better diagnoses of mental health problems." How important is it to achieve these goals? Tell them!

If the relevance of the equipment or instrument isn't apparent to the program area being asked to consider it, make clear why the project should appeal. For instance, one may ask a program on research for the handicapped to support development of a body image self-report test. Show why this project should be undertaken by this agency; why won't it be developed without their support? Since a body image test has relevance for both handicapped and nonhandicapped, support of this project might well be undertaken by another agency. But body image may be a special problem for many of the handicapped, and support will hasten the day when a useful instrument is available to help such persons.

In many projects of this type, success is assured; the problem has been lack of resources rather than lack of knowledge to do the job. In others, the chances of success may be less certain. Indicate the likelihood of success and the basis for your estimate.

Check the copyright, patent, and publication policy of the agency from which funds are sought to determine its implications for your ownership of the products and your ability to get them disseminated and used. Be sure you can accept its policy. These policies have varied from time to time but so far have not been retroactive. They also vary from agency to agency, being much more lenient in some than in others.

Work plan sections are especially closely scrutinized in development studies, since they typically follow prototypical paths and can be charted in detail. Your inclusion of a well-laid-out work plan that gives every indication it will do the job fills the sponsor with confidence that you know what you are about. Along the same lines, the demands of a particular product may require divergence from the prototypical development process and hence introduce some uncertainty about how completely the plan can be charted. Again, your overt recognition of this fact in the proposal indicates your competence.

METHODOLOGICAL STUDIES

Clearly one of the major points to stress in a method development project is the newness of the approach to be studied and its potential advantages over present methods. If a different way of measuring, a new computer program, a different way of observing, has important consequences, point them out.

Support for new approaches is sometimes asked of agencies which are largely applied in their orientation or which have a particular applied research concern, such as schools, or mental health clinics. When possible, the value that will accrue to the area of their concern should be stressed. A new psychometric model or computer language might well benefit handicapped children, but reviewers in that program area would need to be convinced of that benefit to legitimize their support of such a project. They need not be the only beneficiaries, but they should benefit substantially. Telling why this project might not be developed if they don't support it also helps. If its value is marginal to a certain program that would appear to be a normal source of funds for it, sometimes a joint project can be suggested; a program unwilling to carry the full cost may nonetheless be willing to contribute some funds.

Writers of methodology proposals may find the outline of the procedures section almost totally irrelevant to method development but appropriate for evaluation. Development and evaluation may be two quite separate phases; describe them as such. Ignore the headings and write a description of the development procedure in a straightforward, logical manner; a set of sequential steps is usually easiest to follow and to explain. Return to the outline for the evaluation phase.

EVALUATION STUDIES

There have been many evaluations of government programs over the recent past, and evaluation as a part of government programs seems here to stay. A substantial body of evaluation literature has resulted, including new journals and many attempts to summarize methodological directions in the field, reflect on its problems, and prepare new solutions. A prospective evaluator should ensure that some mastery of this literature is appropriately displayed in the proposal.

An excellent set of standards for evaluations has been prepared by a committee of professional association representatives (Joint Committee on Standards for Educational Evaluation, 1981). Although these standards are addressed to the problems of educational evaluation, their applicability is much greater. They are worth studying, and when the standards address problems relevant to your situation, following their recommendations will help you build appropriate comment into your proposal.

Some special points to be noted:

1. Since many projects establish a program's goals as the basis for its evaluation, how you select those goals is critical. If the evaluation is to determine whether certain goals were achieved, where did these goals come from? Were they the original goals of the project? Has the project changed goals as it developed? Are they the goals of the agency that granted the funding? Were those goals accepted by those involved in the project? Do the goals reflect those of the personnel who came to control and administer the project? Were goals based on a needs assessment to determine the discrepancy between what is and what is needed or wanted? Whatever goals are used, it is important to provide a justification of why one has chosen particular goal sources.

2. Are there opponents of the project? Advocates? Are they informed or acting from stereotypes? How are they to be involved, if at all, in the development of the evaluation?

3. Advocates of "goal-free" evaluation suggest entering the scene without knowing the program's goals. The program is evaluated on the basis of whatever changes resulted. They argue that this permits greater sensitivity to important but sometimes unintended effects. For example, the family break-up that resulted from the guaranteed-income experiment was an unintended but important consequence (Rossi and Lyall, 1976). Whether goal-free evaluation is used or not, provisions for observing and recording unintended consequences and side effects may be important.

4. Indicate the orientation of the evaluation. Is it a formative evaluation? Will it be used to plan or to improve new programs, products, or ways of carrying on the project? If so, how will the information be made available to those who will use it? How will they be helped to understand it? What steps will be taken to ensure acceptance and utilization? Is it a summative evaluation? Will it be used to justify past activities? Are you following a particular evaluation model? In some or all respects? Why? Is it a meta-evaluation--an evaluation of someone else's evaluation?

5. What is the expected effect of the evaluation on the staff of the project? On the agency? On similar projects in the future? How are positive effects being enhanced?

6. How will the evaluation's conclusions be communicated and disseminated to the participants, the agency, future project participants and directors, and relevant policy makers?

LONGITUDINAL STUDIES

A longitudinal study is typically extremely expensive. Before reviewers will consider such a study, they need to be certain that 1) information already collected in data banks is inadequate and 2) a much less expensive cross-sectional study will not suffice. Directories of data bases are now available. If you believe adequate data have not already been collected, tell what directories and sources (Census Bureau, National Center for Education Statistics, and so on) were checked and why their data will not serve the purpose.

There are advocates of longitudinal research who argue that one never knows the real comparability of cross-sections of individuals at different ages; one is sure that they grew up under different social conditions, which may have affected what is being studied. So, depending on what is being investigated, longitudinal research may, indeed, be the method of choice. If you believe that, make the case and show why a cross-sectional study is no substitute.

To ensure continuity, longitudinal studies require a stable administrative base throughout the length of the study. Although the future can never be projected with certainty, tell why you think the administrative structure can be kept together across the period of time required to complete and interpret the study. If possible, include letters of support and commitment from administrative officials associated with the institutions involved. Their willingness to continue the study even in the face of funding and personnel changes can be an important factor in getting the study started. But such a commitment may be very difficult to obtain. It helps if staff costs can be reduced by keeping the cadre of professional staff small, with data gatherers trained and added during collection periods and then released.

The relation of data to objectives should be made quite clear. It makes sense to include some variables based on reasonable hunches rather than any really good evidence--the opportunity is too good to miss. But they should not load down the project or constitute too large a part of the costs. The best case can be made for the targeted variables, and the study is carried by their relevance. Stress their importance.

Three particularly troublesome problems in longitudinal studies should be noted and addressed in the proposal. First of these is the need to adapt the study's design as the project progresses. This occurs no matter how careful the initial planning. Not all reviewers will be sympathetic to procedural and budgeting elasticity that provides for this continual revision, but any who have actually *done* longitudinal studies will. It is wise to provide some flexibility in both plan and budget and to indicate, if possible, how new aspects will be integrated without disturbing the ongoing continuity.

Second is the problem of selecting measuring instruments that are easy enough for the poorest subjects at the beginning and yet difficult enough for the best subjects at the end. Use pilot tests to check for "ceiling" and "floor" effects with a cross-sectional sample. When different forms of an instrument are used, each with increasing difficulty, some indication of comparability of content and/or factor structure is appropriate. Such comparability cannot be taken for granted across different levels of commonly used standardized achievement tests. They usually change content from level to level to fit the curriculum.

Third is the problem of continued loss of cases through illness, moving, and so on. Start with enough cases at so that even with normal attrition, there will be a reasonable sample size at the end. Some estimate of likely attrition should be given and the basis for the estimate justified. Note also the expected effect of attrition on the characteristics of the sample. Since those who are stable members of a community often differ significantly in socioeconomic class and other characteristics from those who move in and out, attrition can have an important selective effect on the sample.

Where it is impossible, or undesirable, to include enough cases at the outset to offset attrition, it may be desirable to substitute cases as the project progresses. But, depending on what is being studied, it is sometimes hard to be convincing that there is sufficient similarity between the original cases and the substitutes. The grounds on which the assumption of similarity is advanced should be carefully explained.

SURVEY STUDIES

One of the first questions a reviewer is likely to ask about a proposal for a piece of survey research is "Why?" So many surveys have been completed with absolutely no impact and very little, if any, use of findings that the reviewer is likely to want to be convinced that this is indeed a worthwhile venture. This is not to say that gathering facts about society--social bookkeeping--is not worthwhile. Rather, it is to indicate that when funds are limited and the variety of entries on the "books" is unlimited, the selection of items must be made carefully. If the proposer can show that the survey is likely to have some important consequences, it is much more likely to be supported than if it is proposed simply because "we ought to know the facts--but so far there has been little demand for them." Indicate the need for the information and what group, if any exists, will be in a position to use the information and follow up on it. If one can tie into the increasing interest in social indicators, the importance of the study may be enhanced.

Is social action, then, always the expected result of a survey? No; it is just as important to gather information in support of a theory or point of view. But in those instances, it is the use of the information in the development of theory that is the important point to be emphasized.

Clearly the sample on which the data are to be gathered is critical to interpreting the generality of the findings. Perhaps more than in any other kind of study, the nature of the sample and sampling procedures should be described in detail. Be sure the sampling unit used is consistent with the hypotheses.

Often the instrument will have to be developed as a part of the study. Give examples of the kind of instrument that will be used--e.g., sample questions or examples of existing instruments similar to the one to be developed. Describe your plans to test the instrument's effectiveness.

Data collection procedures, particularly follow-up of nonrespondents, are an especially important part of a survey proposal. Give details.

In some instances it may be worthwhile to subcontract to a professional polling organization to collect the data. Some, such as the National Opinion Research Center at the University of Chicago and the Survey Research Center at the University of Michigan, occasionally merge questions from several studies in a single survey if the sampling plans are compatible. This markedly reduces the cost to each researcher. Since government agencies have different rules about the proportion of a grant that can be subcontracted and since most require advance permission for subcontracts, it is well to determine the ground rules before the proposal is developed. Work through all the important details with the subcontractor before the proposal is submitted.

Claiming that they are solely descriptive, many surveys state no hypotheses about what they expect to find. Although the point can be debated, it seems likely that the researcher who has thought through what to expect will be in a much better position to delineate fortuitous and chance tendencies in the data from generalizable ones. Such careful consideration is also more likely to impress the reviewers favorably than the study that omits it.

Budget and sample size are interrelated, but they are critical decision points in planning. Surveys can be large or small, and their size depends on many factors. Use of previous trials to estimate needed sample size is highly desirable. Some explanation of the basis for the sample size selected should be given.

Assuming your sample size is ten or greater and yours is a federal project, do not forget to allow time for the required clearance of instruments.

EXPERIMENTAL STUDIES

Since much of Chapters 3-5 applies without change to experimental studies, there is little to add here except to emphasize a few points. The rationale, hypotheses, and design are three of the major aspects that need extra attention in an experimental proposal. The rationale for the study is important, since the value of an experimental study lies in its contribution to knowledge (or its opposite, showing that what seems to have been a reasonable contribution to knowledge was wrong, thus warning others about it). The writer's rationale will explain how the study relates to previous findings and what is to be added to them. Place the rationale in the problem statement with related research or even in the objectives section; but be sure it is there. Studies have been submitted that had no rationales. To reviewers, they seemed to be careful plans to try something to see what would happen. These studies are not as likely to gain approval as studies that build on what is known. Put yourself in the place of a reviewer; unless you can tell why it is worth "seeing what would happen," why support it over a study that *does* tell why? Your study isn't a random collection of activities. You chose them; give your reasons.

If the study builds on what is known (or challenges it), the outcome can be anticipated--translate it into directional hypotheses, hypotheses that predict what will occur; they are important.

Since the interpretability of an experimental study depends on adequate controls over possible contaminating variables, the design is always subject to scrutiny. Be especially careful to explain what is and what is not controlled and the reasoning behind the choice of variables to control and the choice of methods to control them.

A common problem is lack of congruence between the unit of analysis and the sampling procedure. If conclusions are to be drawn about teaching methods, then the unit is the smallest group that is uniformly exposed to the method. In most instances, this is the classroom rather than individual students, although it is tempting to use students because this gives a much larger sample. The sample of classrooms is likely to be very limited, yet it is the proper sampling unit in this instance if the class as a whole will be exposed to the method. Make the unit of sampling match the unit of analysis.

NONRESEARCH STUDIES--DEMONSTRATION AND ACTION PROJECTS

Demonstration and action projects show that something works and works well enough to achieve some result. For instance, the new counseling center that you'd like the sponsor to support is expected to reduce teenage suicides by 50%. Such an effect will cause it to be copied by other institutions in your communication network. The application format will likely call for a description of what is to be done together with its rationale. This leads into how it is to be done, for whom, and when. Finally, one is likely to have to judge effectiveness. Thus it has many of the parts of a research proposal.

Demonstration projects show others what can be done so they will copy it. Therefore the generalizability of your demonstration and the dissemination aspects of your project plan should be stressed. Why is yours a good site for the demonstration? In what way is your site typical of those to which transfer is intended? Help reviewers see the parallel. Would installation problems be the same? Different? In what ways? If people are expected to visit your site, is it easily accessible to those who are the dissemination targets? If visits are not involved, how will the

Figure 14. Sample application pages.

REMOVE AND USE FOR DRAFT COPY

Form Approved Through 9-30-89
OMB No. 0925-0001

DEPARTMENT OF HEALTH AND HUMAN SERVICES	LEAVE BLANK			
PUBLIC HEALTH SERVICE	TYPE	ACTIVITY	NUMBER	
GRANT APPLICATION	REVIEW GROUP		FORMERLY	
FOLLOW INSTRUCTIONS CAREFULLY	COUNCIL/BOARD (Month, year)	DATE RECEIVED		

1. TITLE OF PROJECT (Up to 56 spaces)

2. RESPONSE TO SPECIFIC PROGRAM ANNOUNCEMENT ☐ NO ☐ YES (If "YES," state RFA number and/or announcement title)

3. PRINCIPAL INVESTIGATOR/PROGRAM DIRECTOR   NEW INVESTIGATOR
3a. NAME (Last, first, middle)
3b. DEGREE(S)   3c. SOCIAL SECURITY NUMBER
3d. POSITION TITLE
3e. MAILING ADDRESS (Street, city, state, zip code)
3f. DEPARTMENT, SERVICE, LABORATORY OR EQUIVALENT
3g. MAJOR SUBDIVISION
3h. TELEPHONE (Area code, number and extension)

4. HUMAN SUBJECTS
4a. ☐ No   ☐ Yes   ☐ Exemption #_____   OR   ☐ IRB Approval Date _____

5. VERTEBRATE ANIMALS
5a. ☐ No   ☐ Yes   IACUC Approval Date _____
5b. Animal Welfare Assurance #_____

6. DATES OF ENTIRE PROPOSED PROJECT PERIOD
From: _____ Through: _____

7. COSTS REQUESTED FOR FIRST 12-MONTH BUDGET PERIOD
7a. Direct Costs $_____   7b. Total Costs $_____

8. COSTS REQUESTED FOR ENTIRE PROPOSED PROJECT PERIOD
8a. Direct Costs $_____   8b. Total Costs $_____

9. PERFORMANCE SITES (Organizations and addresses)

10. INVENTIONS (Competing continuation application only)
☐ NO   ☐ YES   ☐ Previously reported   ☐ Not previously reported

11. APPLICANT ORGANIZATION (Name, address, and congressional district)

12. TYPE OF ORGANIZATION
☐ Public, Specify ☐ Federal ☐ State ☐ Local
☐ Private Nonprofit
☐ For Profit (General)
☐ For Profit (Small Business)

13. ENTITY IDENTIFICATION NUMBER

14. ORGANIZATIONAL COMPONENT TO RECEIVE CREDIT TOWARDS A BIOMEDICAL RESEARCH SUPPORT GRANT
Code _____   Identification _____

15. OFFICIAL IN BUSINESS OFFICE TO BE NOTIFIED IF AN AWARD IS MADE (Name, title, address and telephone number)

16. OFFICIAL SIGNING FOR APPLICANT ORGANIZATION (Name, title, address and telephone number)

17. PRINCIPAL INVESTIGATOR/PROGRAM DIRECTOR ASSURANCE: I agree to accept responsibility for the scientific conduct of the project and to provide the required progress reports if a grant is awarded as a result of this application. Willful provision of false information is a criminal offense (U.S. Code, Title 18, Section 1001).
SIGNATURE OF PERSON NAMED IN 3a (In ink. "Per" signature not acceptable.)   DATE

18. CERTIFICATION AND ACCEPTANCE: I certify that the statements herein are true and complete to the best of my knowledge, and accept the obligation to comply with Public Health Service terms and conditions if a grant is awarded as the result of this application. A willfully false certification is a criminal offense (U.S. Code, Title 18, Section 1001).
SIGNATURE OF PERSON NAMED IN 16 (In ink. "Per" signature not acceptable.)   DATE

OMB Approval No. 0348-0006

FEDERAL ASSISTANCE

| 2. APPLICANT'S APPLICATION IDENTIFIER | 3. STATE APPLICATION IDENTIFIER | 4. NUMBER a. NUMBER |

1. TYPE OF SUBMISSION (Mark appropriate box.)
☐ NOTICE OF INTENT (OPTIONAL)
☐ PREAPPLICATION
☐ APPLICATION

Leave Blank

a. DATE   Year month day   19____
b. DATE ASSIGNED   Year month day   19____

4. LEGAL APPLICANT/RECIPIENT
a. Applicant Name
b. Organization Unit
c. Street/P.O. Box
d. City   e. County
f. State   g. ZIP Code
h. Contact Person (Name & Telephone No.)

5. EMPLOYER IDENTIFICATION NUMBER (EIN)

6. PROGRAM (From CFDA)   a. NUMBER   ☐ MULTIPLE   b. TITLE

7. TITLE OF APPLICANT'S PROJECT (Use section IV of this form to provide a summary description of the project.)

8. TYPE OF APPLICANT/RECIPIENT   Enter appropriate letter

9. AREA OF PROJECT IMPACT (Names of cities, counties, states, etc.)

10. ESTIMATED NUMBER OF PERSONS BENEFITING

11. TYPE OF ASSISTANCE   Enter appropriate letter(s)

12. CONGRESSIONAL DISTRICTS OF
13. a. APPLICANT   b. PROJECT

14. TYPE OF APPLICATION   Enter appropriate letter

15. PROJECT START DATE   Year month day   19____
16. PROJECT DURATION   Months

17. TYPE OF CHANGE (For 9c or 9e)   Enter appropriate letter(s)

18. DATE DUE TO FEDERAL AGENCY ►   Year month day   19____

19. FEDERAL AGENCY TO RECEIVE REQUEST
a. ORGANIZATIONAL UNIT (If appropriate)
b. ADMINISTRATIVE CONTACT (If known)
c. ADDRESS

20. EXISTING FEDERAL GRANT IDENTIFICATION NUMBER

21. REMARKS ADDED   ☐ Yes   ☐ No

PROPOSED FUNDING
a. FEDERAL $_____ .00
b. APPLICANT $_____ .00
c. STATE $_____ .00
d. LOCAL $_____ .00
e. OTHER $_____ .00
f. TOTAL $_____ .00

22. a. YES THIS NOTICE OF INTENT/PREAPPLICATION/APPLICATION WAS MADE AVAILABLE TO THE STATE EXECUTIVE ORDER 12372 PROCESS FOR REVIEW ON:
DATE _____
b. NO ☐ PROGRAM IS NOT COVERED BY E.O. 12372
☐ OR PROGRAM HAS NOT BEEN SELECTED BY STATE FOR REVIEW

THE APPLICANT CERTIFIES THAT ► To the best of my knowledge and belief, data in this preapplication/application are true and correct, the document has been duly authorized by the governing body of the applicant and the applicant will comply with the attached assurances if the assistance is approved.

23. CERTIFYING REPRESENTATIVE
a. TYPED NAME AND TITLE
b. SIGNATURE
c. DATE SIGNED   Year month day   19____

24. APPLICATION RECEIVED   Year month day   19____

25. FEDERAL APPLICATION IDENTIFICATION NUMBER

26. FEDERAL GRANT IDENTIFICATION

27. ACTION TAKEN
☐ a. AWARDED
☐ b. REJECTED
☐ c. RETURNED FOR AMENDMENT
☐ d. RETURNED FOR E.O. 12372 SUBMISSION BY APPLICANT TO STATE
☐ e. DEFERRED
☐ f. WITHDRAWN

28. FUNDING
a. FEDERAL $_____ .00
b. APPLICANT $_____ .00
c. STATE $_____ .00
d. LOCAL $_____ .00
e. OTHER $_____ .00
f. TOTAL $_____ .00

29. ACTION DATE►   Year month day   19____

30. STARTING DATE   Year month day   19____

31. CONTACT FOR ADDITIONAL INFORMATION (Name and telephone number)

32. ENDING DATE   Year month day   19____

33. REMARKS ADDED   ☐ Yes   ☐ No

NSN 7540-01-008-8162
PREVIOUS EDITION IS NOT USABLE

424-103

STANDARD FORM 424 PAGE 1 (Rev. 4-84)
Prescribed by OMB Circular A-102

SECTION I—APPLICANT/RECIPIENT DATA
SECTION II—CERTIFICATION
SECTION III—FEDERAL AGENCY ACTION

Outstanding	5__
Superior	4__
Satisfactory	3__
Marginal	2__
Poor	1__
Absent from proposal	

Outstanding	5__
Superior	4__
Satisfactory	3__
Marginal	2__
Poor	1__
Absent from proposal	

Outstanding	5__
Superior	4__
Satisfactory	3__
Marginal	2__
Poor	1__
Absent from proposal	

3. budget for subcontract (if required)   _____   Absent from
   detailed and appropriate? (All)   proposal

another means that unless resource limits are sufficiently large (they rarely are), simultaneously maximizing problem formulation, the weighting of internal validity(LP) and external validity(GP), audience credibility, and information yield is impossible, regardless of the skill with which resources are allocated.   Hence the researcher must settle for something less than the optimum in designing and carrying out the research; she must make judgments about the desirability and appropriateness of various trade-offs.   One's choices in the various facets of design (subjects, situation, and so forth) and one's allocation of resources give operational expression to these trade-off judgments.

Although not all trade-offs come from resource constraints, once one's plans reach the resource limit, further adjustments to strengthen one aspect can be made only at the expense of another.   As game theorists put it, one enters a "zero sum game."   Hence resources used to strengthen internal validity(LP) not only cannot be used for building external validity(GP), they may have to be taken from allocations for further refining one's problem definition, building audience credibility, increasing information yield, or enacting various facets of design to build a strong chain of reasoning.   So one tries to optimize one's judgment of the appropriate balance of all these choices.   Let us next, then, examine in greater detail what optimization means in these five decisions.

Since we have just been examining internal validity(LP) and external validity(GP), we begin with the decision to optimally weight them, the second of the decisions to be optimized in figure 19.   In addition to the resource limit problem, there is a second reason that this weighting is optimized rather than both simultaneously maximized.   They work in opposite directions.   Methods of strengthening internal validity(LP) tend to weaken external validity(GP) and vice versa.

One increases internal validity(LP) by doing a very tightly controlled study that, among other things, eliminates all possible contaminating alternative explanations.   That would probably mean doing the study with specially selected individuals in a laboratory-like setting.   It is because psychologists have frequently done this that Bronfenbrenner (1977, p. 513) has characterized developmental psychology as "the science of strange behavior of children in strange situations with strange adults for the briefest possible time."   Clearly, in strengthening internal validity(LP), one can markedly limit external validity(GP).   Conversely, one could do the study in a natural setting, but there one's control over the situation is minimal and internal validity(LP) suffers.   So these two characteristics tend to be antithetical.

Typically we first tend to do studies with high internal validity(LP) to determine the nature and strength of the relationship and then investigate external validity(GP), the extent of generality, later.   But policy makers are often more interested in external validity(GP), the generality of a policy to all parts of the electorate.   Therefore many policy studies begin by demonstrating external validity(GP) and later studies are refined to emphasize internal validity(LP) in order to determine the variables that are causing the effect. Once these are known, then still better policy or treatments can be designed. So *determining the appropriate weighting of internal validity(LP) and external validity(GP)* for a study is one of the five decisions to be optimized.

We began with the second, but *problem formulation* is usually the first of these decisions; a problem well formulated is half solved. How long does one work and rework one's problem before proceeding to do the study? How long does one search for the ideal formulation, not knowing whether it will ever come and, worse, whether one will recognize it as the best or keep on looking for a still better one? So another optimization is that of deciding when to stop the reformulating and begin doing the study.

A third set of judgments is those involved in building credibility with one's intended audience. The prime one, of course, is integrity, showing that the researcher can be trusted to interpret the data without bias--he has looked at the question and the data fairly and intelligently. Telling the audience why one has left certain variables uncontrolled helps to convince them of the researcher's competence. The omission was not an oversight! Sometimes an accepted instrument or method may not be quite as precise as a new experimental one, but if there are insufficient resources to use both, then perhaps the choice of the one better accepted by the audience will result in more easily obtaining consensus about the interpretation of the result even though it may not show the result as precisely as would the newer or more sophisticated instrument. Alternatively, one may allocate resources to show the efficacy of a new instrument, assuming, of course, that one can make an adequately convincing case. This, however, uses up resources that adopting the old one would not. Is the increased efficacy worth it? That is the trade-off.

In the case of a research proposal, the sponsor is the audience, and the proposal writer is seeking credibility in the perception of the sponsor. Allocating resources to aspects of the proposal such as the review of previous literature to illustrate one's ability is a common example of appropriate allocation of proposal preparation resources to build audience credibility.

Information yield involves the problem of allocating resources so as to be sure to sense the main effect of interest, to be aware of aberrations in the data-gathering process that might affect the validity of the data, to observe side effects, which sometimes are more important than the main effect, and, in some instances, to gather data that will help one design the next study.

Resource allocation refers to the set of decisions that determine the strength of the links of the chain of reasoning. How one allocates one's resources determines the strength of each link. You will recall that the links are to be of equal strength. Thus it makes no sense to allocate the preponderance of one's resources to develop a sampling plan when the instrument that will be used for data collection is not adequately developed. Allocation of resources to bring these into balance is essential to a strong study.

Together these criteria provide an integrated perspective for conceptuali-
zing, analyzing, and implementing research studies.   Its complexity,
combined with the possibilities for different trade-offs, suggests why
researchers arrive at different "optimal" approaches to the same problem.

So now you have a picture of the whole set of decisions with which
the researcher is confronted--a set that is applicable regardless of the
method involved. The picture is more easily understood with respect to
experimentation, but wherever one is concerned with a generalizable
relation, this seems to be the model that applies.

Seems complicated? In some sense it is, but nothing has been added
that isn't involved in research. Even before they have had a research
course, classes asked to critique research studies come up with comments
that illustrate all the parts of this framework. We have all used these
concepts and made these judgments, but we have had no conceptualization
to hold them together. This model organizes these judgments into an
integrated framework.   That makes it easier to make sure all the
judgments have been made that ought to be, to see where there are built
in trade-offs in the research process such as that between internal and
external validity, and to understand why there are so many ways of
achieving an acceptable study design--different choices and trade-offs.
The truth of the matter is that designing or critiquing a research study or
proposal *is* a complex task and needs to be recognized as such.

The framework also makes it easier to see why designing a study is
as much an art as a science. That helps explain why reviewers may differ
in their judgments of the design of a study, why consultants may differ in
their advice about how to improve a study, why there are preferences for
certain designs and, most important of all, why research proposals need to
be constructed with so much care--there is so much to cover and so many
decisions to document as carefully made, not carelessly decided or
ignored. Further, one can appreciate the proposal writer's dilemma in
trying to anticipate the expectations of sponsors and reviewers with
regard to how much and what kind of explanation to include to gain
audience credibility.

Use of the criteria is further complicated by different researchers' views
of what a social or behavioral science should be and therefore what is
important to emphasize.   These differences may be conceptualized as
seven different orientations into which researchers are socialized, many
playing multiple roles for differing problems and circumstances.

In actuality, the picture is more complex than already painted. We
have more or less assumed to this point that all social scientists have
similar views of what their research should be like and what a social
science ought to be. Of course this is not true. Some, let us call them

analysts, typically seek to validate explanations. Their model for the social sciences is very close to that of the natural scientists, finding rules, laws, and principles that permit one to predict and control. This model is common among psychologists; many sociologists follow it as well. A second group, let us call them pragmatists, are much like the analyzers, but they have so often seen researchers advance explanations that are later proved wrong that they prefer to deal only in operational definitions--what works. Skinner (1957), in avoiding all constructs one can't directly sense, is assuming the role of the pragmatist.

Some sociologists believe that analyzers cut the problem to fit their experimental method. They prefer to work from the bottom up to a correct specification of the problem, developing wholistic explanations of phenomena from their observations--grounded theory. Let us call this third group synthesizers.

Then there are those like Piaget who are keen observers of the world. On the basis of their observations, often systematic but sometimes casual ones, they propose very useful explanations that are set forth with very convincing examples. A fitting title for the fourth group is theorists. Skinner (1954), in proposing programmed instruction based on his daughters' experiences in school, assumed the theorist's role. Theorists often drive analysts "up the wall" with their unproved claims, and analysts spend much time and energy trying to validate or invalidate those claims.

A fifth group, multiperspectivists, like Graham Allison (1971) in his explanations of the Cuban missile crisis, try to explain phenomena from different points of view, each covering a different aspect of the phenomenon. Allison looked at the crisis from the standpoints of the rational, political, and bureaucratic mind.

As we have described these different points of view, you may have noted a progressive disassociation of explanation from prediction. The sixth group, humanists, go still further, as many historians do, in explaining a particular concatenation of circumstances. In doing so they hope to find the stories that will be useful to their audience. Life is seen as so complex that the best they can do is to explain situations, tell useful stories, help us to build cognitive maps of how the world works (a long way from rules or principles).

Finally, the particularist believes the world is so complex and each person is so unique and precious that a social science is impossible. I can learn from you and you from me, but this information instructs the persons involved rather than building a science.

Obviously such differing points of view have implications for the model developed here in terms of what is considered good research and what research methods are preferred. Students choose areas for graduate study on the basis of the methods they use and their view of science and the world. Thus analyzers are more likely to like statistics and to use quantitative methods. Synthesizers are likely to be more verbally skilled

Figure 21. The Synthesizer
(from Krathwohl, 1985)

Figure 20. The Pragmatist
(from Krathwohl, 1985)

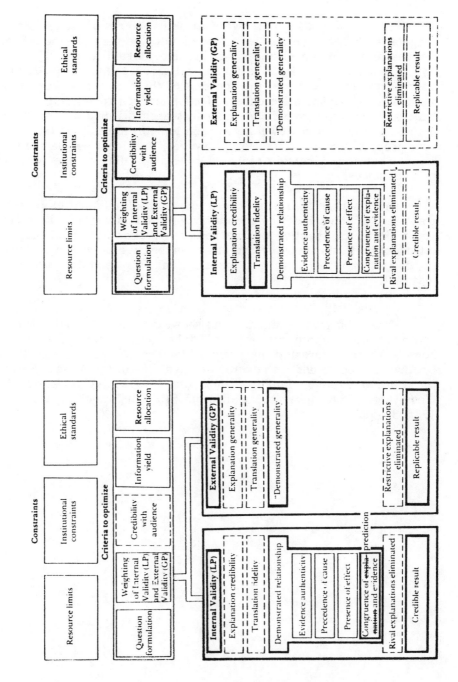

and to use qualitative methods.   Students' advanced training further socializes them into ways of doing research and of looking at what their discipline's knowledge base ought to be.   Many   researchers, especially those in the professions, are eclectic and take different roles depending on the problem.

Figures 20 and 21 show two contrasting points of view, those of the pragmatist and the synthesizer, mapped onto the parts of the model they emphasize (heavy lines) and de-emphasize (dotted lines).   There is not enough space here to describe further all seven points of view and relate them to the model.   From the contrast of these two, however, it is clear there are significant differences.   That is enough to suggest that if your beliefs about what constitutes good research differ from those of your proposed sponsor or reviewers, you need to be aware of that fact and build your proposal accordingly.   Note, however, that most people are not pure "types" but play a certain range of roles depending on the problem and circumstances.

This chapter is a very brief summary of a much more complete treatment of the subject by the author.[1] But this much of it should give you a better perspective on the research process.   As indicated in the introduction to this book, if one has a perspective on where one wants to go, it is much easier to get there.   That has been the intent of this material.

---

[1]The book gives examples and shows the model's application to the critiquing of research articles with fuller explanation than is possible here.   Those interested in reading further should consult David R. Krathwohl, *Social and Behavioral Science Research: A New Framework for Conceptualizing, Implementing, and Evaluating Research Studies* (Jossey-Bass Publishers, 433 California St., San Francisco, Calif. 94104, 1985, 324 pp).

12.

Some Writing Tips

Obvious errors in writing undermine other evidence of competence. If basic English is a weakness, that is beyond our scope. Ask a friend for help or hire an editor. There are, however, simple things each of us can do to improve his or her writing.

Assume the writer's task is to capture, hold, and lead the attention of busy but committed people to the important points in the proposal. Make their reading easier by organizing ideas clearly. Increase the impact of what they are reading by suitably direct and simple language.

Make the structure of the proposal clear. Use a variety of "road signs" to guide the reading and to highlight important points. Foreshadow what is coming and indicate what has been. Devices for doing this include headings, marginal notes, sectional introductions and prefaces, summaries and appendixes, outlines, charts, and diagrams. Overusing the latter, however, clutters the visual field. Don't!

Look for large, black sections of text. Break them up with paragraphing and headings. If titles and subtitles are difficult to assign and/or are not in proper sequence, refine the organization of the text. Similarly, skim such blocks for periods. *Simplify sentences*; find sentences that go on and on and break them up. But keep an interesting rhythm of long and short sentences; don't let the writing become too choppy, too staccato.

Diagrams and arrows can help show the flow of ideas and highlight important points. Take care when using boxes; if possible, leave the sides open so the reader has visual entry. Some people read around closed boxes, intending to come back but then forgetting.

Make the proposal easy to skim. Clear organization with distinct "road signs" eases skimming. In addition:

- Set a topic sentence into every paragraph. If an important topic sentence does not begin the paragraph, show where it is embedded with underlining, italics, or boldface type.
- Establish a set of headings with three or four levels and consistently follow that format. With word processors you can set heads in italics or boldface, as done here. Some printers have additional typefaces. Use only a few for good effect--too many gives a cluttered look.
- Use white space to set off and highlight significant items.
- Make correspondences self-evident. Set parallel structures and comparisons side by side in tables or figures or in multiple columns of text.
- Use white space to provide visual relief and to frame the text pleasingly. Double-space or use space and a half, if possible. Do not go overboard, however. Keep within the page allowance, if

- there is one.
- Use bullets like these to identify important points.
- Skim the proposal yourself, or better yet, ask someone for whom the proposal is new to skim it. Be sure that the "road signs" lead the reader to the correct meaning.

Make transitions smoothly. Do not let the reader get lost at junction points. To ensure easy shifts of perspective between sections, paragraphs, and even sentences, use:

- proper sequencing
- clear reference to earlier discussions
- selective repetition of key phrases and words

Use active verbs and simple constructions. Active verbs bring lucidity to sentences. Complex, passive constructions diminish the intensity of the communication; they lead the reader into grammatical bottlenecks, thus breaking his concentration. By striking out words and phrases and rearranging the remainder as needed, good technical editors markedly clarify meaning. Try it!

Change passives to actives. For example, compare "The necessity of replacing passive words with active ones is emphasized in every book on writing" with "Books on writing stress replacing passive words with active ones" (example modified from Becker, 1986, p. 59). Another example, "Reductions in excess verbiage were more noticeable than reductions in clarity," can become: "Verbiage declined more noticeably than clarity." Locate such constructions by checking for extra "to be" verbs.

There is a temptation to try to sound erudite, using complex sentence construction and lots of extra words. One uses phrases like "a majority of," "as a consequence of," and "at this point in time" in place of simply "most," "because," and "now." Simplify and your ideas will come through more clearly. Day's Appendix 4 (1983, pp. 166-169) lists "Words and Expressions to Avoid" together with their simpler substitutes; it is worth examining. The examples above are taken from that list.

Becker (1986) notes another example of complexity--the tendency to add a third phrase or modifier when we already have two, often having to "scratch" for the third: "This book excites our curiosity, gives us some answers, and convinces us the author is right" (p. 81). Contrast this with "This book excites our curiosity and gives us some convincing answers."

Use concrete "picture" language. Except when you want to show your familiarity with technical terms, substitute everyday words for the more abstruse (e.g., "end" instead of "terminate"; "begin," not "institute"). Use metaphors and analogies. Organize concepts into a model whenever possible.

Be positive. Emphasize the positive aspects; talk about opportunities rather than needs. Avoid being too tentative (e.g., "It is to be hoped" statements) and overqualifications.

Convey liveliness and enthusiasm.   This marks the proposer's commitment to the project.

Imitate the best writers.   Have you ever noticed in talking to a person with an accent that soon, to your embarrassment, you are unconsciously imitating her?   Writing is like that, too; one learns from and may copy some of the things one has recently read.   For this reason some writers deliberately read good writing, for example, the essays of E. B. White, before they start their own writing.

* * * * *

The tips above may not completely change a writer's style; by the time one is mature enough to be writing proposals, writing style is largely set. Make a list of personal weaknesses and post it where it will spark renewed effort--on the desk or wall where you cannot avoid it.   Consult books on writing and find suggestions.

Be sure to read the additional material on the writing process in Chapter 16 (pp. 244-248).   Though addressed to writers of dissertations, the advice will be found useful in a wide range of situations.   In addition, there is much good advice for writers.   Some of this is referenced in Appendix A.   Look at the annotations for Becker, Day, and Dugdale.

Section IV
Finding Funding

Which is better, public funding from the federal, state, or local government or money from a foundation? Each has advantages, but most of those who have used both routes prefer foundations. The application procedure is so much simpler, there are fewer strings attached to what one can do with the money, there are few if any reports to file except a final one, and there is little likelihood that the foundation's auditors will come in and disallow expenditures, demanding that money be returned. The opposites of these conditions are possibilities, some even certainties, with public funding. They result from the necessity to be publicly accountable, a characteristic that you may appreciate less as a researcher than as a taxpayer. The government's problem is to allow you the freedom you need as a researcher yet have sufficient information to be able to answer Congress's and others' questions intelligently, to sense when things are going awry, and to be able to maintain appropriate control in case something goes wrong. This means the government wants an extensive proposal to know what you are going to do, extensive reports to ensure you are doing it, and final reports to show you did it. Every time the government staff is caught by a complaint--abuse of subjects, nondelivery of products, and so on--it must provide safeguards for the future. This results in compliance assurances, reports, paperwork, auditing, and all the various other "overseeing" activities, which can become a serious burden.

Nevertheless, the fact remains that the government is the major source of funds for behavioral science research, for development, and social action projects. Morrill and Duby (1986) estimate it provided $225 million in 1985. Depending on one's definition, the government gives 7 to 10 times as much as foundations, or more. Further, 20% of the foundations have 97% of the assets, so the target base is narrowed. Finally, the average grant for small foundations has been under $2000. Foundation benefactors tend to be more interested in action projects that provide immediate relief for a social problem than in the basic research that might help us understand it.

When it comes to controversial projects, however, foundations are more likely to be able to take the heat than public agencies. That doesn't mean that many will or that those that do will like it. But given the realities, they can handle projects that governments, being sensitive to political pressure, cannot. The politics of funding are such that controversial projects can be used by a politician to gain popular attention as a defender of all that is "good and holy." In addition, such projects provide an excuse to politicians, competing administrators or anyone needing one, to switch those funds to a "better" use. The Science Education Program in the National Science Foundation took years, and a perceived crisis shortage of science teachers, to recover from criticism of its funding "Man, a Course of Study." This science curriculum was roundly criticized in Congressional hearings for showing the values of a primitive culture as though they might be understandable in their context. Politicians argued it taught acceptance of those values in our culture and for years eliminated curriculum development for all sciences. Such enduring effects of single incidents make federal staff very wary of funding potentially controversial topics.

Foundations, who in the past have also had their turn on the hot seat of Congressional hearings, are not eager to have to repeat that performance. So they may also not be eager to support a controversial project. If you can find a foundation that really believes in your project, however, it can and probably will do so.

Whether you decide to seek government or foundation funding, many in the field believe that researchers would be better off sending in fewer proposals and spending more time making contacts to find what is wanted, who is looking for it, and, in particular, who is interested in their project. The latter is particularly important at all times but especially when it turns up pockets of unused funds, especially end-of-year funds that will be lost if not spent; they can be real bonanzas. Such searches take good "people" skills, but they also require, as *Behavior Today* (Nov. 8, 1971) put it, "an investigator with some fire in his belly who wants to answer something and who can communicate his zeal to others."

Agency staff know that new ideas will always come through the front door if they keep it open. The best of the staff have an ear for such ideas. One's problem is to find these people when they have the time to listen. This may take some patience and may mean talking to other than the first person met in the agency. Listening first to what that staff member is seeking may give clues to how to shape the presentation. A good presenter is first of all a good listener!

"But if communicating zeal isn't your forte," *Behavior Today* continues, "be consoled with the knowledge that the nitty gritty of grantsmanship consists at least as much of practical strategy as of charisma and inner fire." "Grantsmanship boils down to common sense," it quotes former NIH Research Chief Ronald Havens as saying, "In the world of federal funding, common sense extends beyond a researcher's scientific know-how. It embraces real knowledge of the grantor's program." How does one find out about grantors' programs? The following material will tell you, first discussing the federal scene and then the foundation. The federal picture has its counterpart in state programs, so many of the same mechanisms of procurement and announcement may, with modification, be transferable.

13.

Finding Federal Funding

STEP 1--LOCATE RELEVANT PROGRAMS

One of the significant causes of the rejection of proposals is that the request does not fall within the grantor's program. No federal agency can legally help you if its legislative authority does not encompass what you wish to do. Therefore, the first task is to locate an agency with legislatively authorized power to commit funds in your area of interest.

General Listings of Programs

Assuming you do not know either the relevant legislation or the appropriate federal agencies, a good place to start is the *Catalog of Federal Domestic Assistance (CFDA)* (available from Superintendent of Documents, Government Printing Office, Washington, D.C. 20202), a sourcebook of the federal programs that provide any kind of aid (fellowships, training grants, formula grants as well as research, demonstration, development grants, and so on). The *CFDA* is regularly updated; its loose-leaf format facilitates this. Programs are arranged by agency within federal departments. But the *CFDA* is thoroughly indexed. For example:

1. Agency Program Index--Lists all the programs under each agency heading, e.g., Appalachian Commission, Department of Education, National Institute of Mental Health.
2. Functional Purposes Index--The headings are broad purposes, e.g., Education, Information and Statistics, Science and Technology. Research is a subhead under these headings.
3. Deadlines Index--Programs are listed by deadline date.
4. Applicant Eligibility Listings Index--Separate listings of programs open to application from 1) individuals, 2) local agencies, 3) nonprofit organizations, and 4) states, etc.
5. Subject Index--A thorough listing of the topics of programs, e.g., alcoholism; education, research; education, early childhood; mental health, research; narcotics and drug abuse.

The program descriptions themselves are ordered by agency within each department and are quite complete. Each contains a statement of objectives, types of assistance, use restrictions, eligibility requirements, applications and award processes, deadlines, appropriations and current funding requests, program accomplishments, regulations and guideline references, information contacts, and related programs. Look for the very useful flow chart that appears in the introductory material that describes how to use the *Catalog*.

The Annual Register of Grant Support (Marquis Academic Media, Marquis Who's Who Inc., 200 E. Ohio St., Chicago, Ill. 60611) covers both federal and foundation sources. Its entries are categorized under subheads of ten broad subject headings (e.g., Education: "Education Projects and Research," "Higher Education Subjects and Research." Social

Sciences: "Business and Economics," "Communications," "Labor," "Political Science," "Sociology and Anthropology"). Individual entries give a contact address, major fields of interest, types of support, statement of purpose, the federal authorizing legislation, eligibility requirements, fiscal nature of grants, average amount or range of grants, total funding available, cost-sharing stipulations, total number of applicants, total recipients (the ratio of the last two gives an idea of the competition one faces), application requirements and deadlines, and names of principal personnel and staff. Relevant indexes include an excellent subject index, an organization and program index, and a personnel index.

The *Register* includes information on the number of applicants, which the *CFDA* lacks. The *CFDA* includes more programs and gives more information on each; its subject index is larger and therefore more detailed; and its references to the *Federal Register* and other information sources are quite useful.

Targeted Listings of Programs

Recently attention is being given to providing more targeted information for social and behavioral science researchers. The *American Psychological Association's Guide to Research Support*, second edition (see Dusek et al., 1984, in references), is an especially relevant source; it describes about 200 federal sources and 55 nonfederal sources and programs of funding. An addendum to the *Guide* was published in 1986 that updated half the programs (Burke, 1986). A new edition is due in 1987. A companion volume, *Guide to Federal Funding for Social Scientists* (Quarles, 1986), prepared by the Consortium of Social Science Associations (COSSA), describes 300 programs in the social and behavioral sciences and related areas of the humanities.

Both COSSA's and APA's guides are less expensive than the other sources, and though published less often than the *CFDA*, they provide information that will be sufficient to locate the programs of interest to you, except for the most recently established programs. Both are based on interviews and correspondence with agency directors.

APA's Guide . A sample entry from APA's *Guide* appears in figure 22. Programs are arranged by agency within departments. For each program, the areas of research supported are described in key words, terms from the *Thesaurus of Psychological Index Terms*. This is also the source of indexing terms for *Psychological Abstracts*, with which many researchers will already be familiar. The "funds available" section gives actual, budgeted, and appropriated amounts; amount of funds supporting behavioral science research; and, where possible, the proportion of funds available for new and competing projects. It states the longest possible project period and the time from submission of proposal to award of funds and describes the application and review procedures as well as giving other sources of information. Like the *Register*, it includes information on the number of applicants as well as awards, but it also gives information on the proportion of awards to universities, nonprofit organi-

Figure 22. Sample entry from APA's *Guide*
(Copyright 1984 by the American Psychologial Association.
Reprinted by permission of the publisher.)

Office of Special Education
400 Maryland Avenue, S.W. • Washington, DC 20202

Division of Innovation and Development

Research Projects Section
Contact: Dr. James Hamilton (202) 732-1110

Areas of Research Supported

The Division of Innovation and Development supports applied research on the topics
listed here only as they apply to the education of handicapped individuals. Three
types of research are supported: field-initiated, student, and directed research.
Field-initiated research projects may address any applied issue pertaining to education of the handicapped. Student research projects support research conducted by
either master's or doctoral candidates. Support is provided for research costs
only, not for student stipends. Directed research supports projects conducted on
one of the special priority areas published in the Federal Register. Directed
research contracts may also support research institutes at which investigators study
several aspects of a given issue.

In the past, directed research topics have included research integration (state-of-
the-art reviews in selected areas to interpret research needs); assessment (instrument and systems); youth employment (the role of the school in increasing employ-
ability, and the transition from school to work); unique educational problems of
handicapped and other special populations; nonvocal communication (severely handicapped individuals who can not talk); provision of related and facilitative services
to complement educational programs; specific handicapping conditions; post-secondary
and continuing education; and parent roles (the role of parents and the family in
educating the handicapped). One or several of these priority areas are selected
each year for separate competitions. Application review and funding is separate for
each competition. In addition, the field-initiated research competition is held
once every year, and the student-initiated research competition is held twice per
year.

For this program a handicap is defined as mental retardation, hearing impairment,
speech impairment, visual impairment, serious emotional disturbance, orthopedic
impairment, deaf-blind, multi-handicap, or specific learning disabilities, when
those impairments result in the need for special education and related services.

> Key Words: aurally handicapped, blind, deaf, early experience, educable men-
> tally retarded, education, educational measurement, educational
> psychology, emotionally disturbed, employability, ethnic groups,
> handicapped, health impaired, instructional media, learning dis-
> abilities, mentally retarded, physically handicapped, preschool age
> children, special education, speech handicapped, technology, visu-
> ally handicapped, vocational education

Funds Available

The Division of Innovation and Development spent approximately $12 million for
research in FY 1983. The FY 1984 budget for research and demonstration projects is
approximately $15 million.

Longest Possible Project Period: Directed research, 5 years; field-initiated re-
search, 5 years; student research, 1.5 years.

Time From Submission of Proposal to Award of Funds: 6 months

Application and Review Procedures

A program announcement is published in the Federal Register in late spring for the
competitions to be run the following year. Application packets may be requested
from the Section staff. The packet outlines the priority topics of research and the
amount of funding expected to be available for each competition and contains pertinent regulations, forms, and instructions for application.

zations, profit-making corporations, and "other units" (which includes
state and local governments). It summarizes award data separately for
contracts and grants: their number, average size, range, and whether they
were new applications, noncompeting renewals, or competing renewals.
Obviously this answers many questions about one's chances with a
particular agency, such as whether it mainly has grant competitions with
many awards or concentrates on contracts, where each competition
usually has only one winner; whether its money is largely locked up in
noncompeting renewals or there is new money; and the grant or contract
range.

The APA *Guide* has three indexes: a federal agency personnel
directory, a federal and nonfederal program index (the second edition also
contains information on foundations supporting behavioral science
research), and a subject index, which goes beyond the key words used in
the description of programs. Confined to the behavioral sciences, the
subject index is much more detailed than that in $CFDA$ which covers all
federal programs. Although the federal personnel information gets out of
date rapidly, nonetheless it provides a contact point. (As we go to press,
the third edition, edited by Kenneth Lee Herring, 1987, has just been
published. Apparently a new edition is published every three years with
an addendum in interim years.)

There is useful discussion of the trends in federal funding as well as
information on how to influence federal policy. A primer on proposal
writing, a glossary, and a list of sources of information complete the aids
in this very valuable addition to the fund seeker's armamentarium.

In addition to the *Guide,* the American Psychological Association runs
a Research Support Network out of its Science Directorate. It publishes a
regular newsletter describing budget and legislation activities for those
interested in monitoring and affecting research policies, and it includes a
section on research funding opportunities. Because the staff gathers
much more information than it publishes and because the newsletter is
currently quarterly and therefore cannot handle short deadlines, the staff
is reevaluating ways of getting information disseminated. They have
maintained a computer bulletin board. For up-to-date information
contact the Science Research Directorate at 1200 Seventeenth St. NW,
Washington, D.C. 20036.

COSSA's Guide. Like the APA's guide, COSSA's is arranged by agency
within departments and general information on the department or agency
precedes that for programs within agencies. Although information about
who gets awards, typical size, and so on is less detailed, COSSA's guide
does contain information on the budget and review process. There are
sample awards, with their dates and titles. COSSA's coverage is broader
than APA's, including areas of interest to historians, economists, and
anthropologists that, if included in APA's, are more cursorily treated. Its
section on independent executive agencies includes many not covered in
APA, for instance. It also has a section on federal statistical agencies.
The first few chapters describe the structure of federal social science

Figure 23. Sample institute and program entry from COSSA's *Guide* (used by permission of Russell Sage Foundation).

National Institute of Child Health and Human Development

The mission of the National Institute of Child Health and Human Development (NICHD) is to conduct and support research in the reproductive, developmental, and behavioral processes that determine the health of children, adults, families, and populations. NICHD administers a multidisciplinary program of research, research training, and public information. The Institute has four major components: the Center for Population Research and the Center for Research for Mothers and Children, both extramural programs supporting research through grants and contracts; the Intramural Research Program; and the Epidemiology and Biometry Research Program.

The Center for Population Research (CPR) conducts the federal government's central effort in population research. Because population research is inherently interdisciplinary in nature, CPR was created to treat the subject in a systematic manner and to fill in the gaps left by other federal agencies. CPR supports basic research, while other agencies support primarily applied population research or data-gathering activities.

CPR comprises four branches: Reproductive Sciences, Contraceptive Development, Contraceptive Evaluation, and Demographic and Behavioral Sciences. Most social and behavioral science research is supported by the Demographic and Behavioral Sciences Branch.

The Center for Research for Mothers and Children (CRMC) is the primary extramural program supporting research and research training on the special health problems of mothers and children at NICHD. The CRMC was reorganized in 1984. Five branches now administer the CRMC research program: (1) Human Learning and Behavior, (2) Mental Retardation and Developmental Disabilities, (3) Endocrinology, Nutrition and Growth, (4) Pregnancy and Perinatology, and (5) Genetics and Teratology Branch. The first three branches support research in a variety of topics in the social and behavioral sciences; the latter two are largely biomedical in nature.

The National Advisory Child Health and Human Development Council serves as an advisory body for NICHD on matters of policy and funding. This council is unique among NIH advisory councils in that among its 15 members are three behavioral scientists and one social scientist.

CENTER FOR RESEARCH FOR MOTHERS AND CHILDREN

HUMAN LEARNING AND BEHAVIOR BRANCH

Norman Krasnegor, Chief
7C18 Landow Building
7910 Woodmont Avenue
Bethesda, MD 2089 '
(301/496-6591)

Program: The Human Learning and Behavior Branch (HLB) has as its primary mission the development and support of research that maximizes knowledge of child health. The HLB research portfolio in the aggregate is designed to determine how the interaction of biological, psychological, and socio-environmental factors result in normative development. Processes and behaviors from the prenatal period to the beginning of adulthood are investigated across a wide diversity of research. A major focus of the HLB Branch will continue to be descriptive and experimental studies in developmental psychology. Special consideration will be given to research on children born at biological risk for a variety of behavioral disabilities and to investigations of accidental injuries and risk-taking behavior.

The Human Learning and Behavior Branch is divided into five programmatic areas:

1) behavioral pediatrics (applying principles of human learning to health and illness behaviors of children);

2) developmental behavioral biology (studies of brain/behavior relationships, the biochemical, physiological, and hormonal bases of behavior, sensory motor processes, and comparative animal behavior);

3) learning and perception (research on basic learning mechanisms necessary for optimal behavior development, studies of perception, cognition, and memory—primary emphasis on infants, secondary emphasis on children and adolescents);

4) communication (research on the acquisition and development of speech, language, and reading ability in children—special emphasis on factors involved in dyslexia);

5) social and affective development (understanding basic behavioral, psychological, and genetic mechanisms involved in normal social and emotional development).

A limited number of requests for applications (RFAs) are issued by the HLB Branch. The FY 1986 research program will focus on learning and cognition, prenatal behavioral development, and behavioral pediatrics.

Budget: The HLB Branch spent approximately $16 million in support of research grants and research training in FY 1985.

Application/Review Process: See the general description of NIH in chapter 4.

Funding Mechanisms: See the general description of NIH in chapter 4.

Examples of Funded Research:
1) "Processes of Learning and Memory in Infancy" (awarded $48,432 in FY 1984; 1-year project).

2) "Development and Maintenance of Creativity in Children" (awarded $54,983 in FY 1984; 2-year project).

3) "Marriage, Parenting and Infant Development" (awarded $115,508 in FY 1984; 1-year project).

4) "Teen Social Behavior and the Prevention of Smoking" (awarded $129,778 in FY 1984; 1-year project).

5) "Adolescent Social Networks as Predictors of Development" (awarded $54,488 in FY 1984; 1-year project).

6) "Early Computer Access: Social and Psychological Effects" (awarded $198,121 in FY 1984; 3-year project).

7) "Cross-Linguistic Development Studies of Language" (awarded $57,117 in FY 1984; 2-year project).

8) "Effects of Mother's Education on Offspring Achievement" (awarded $53,664 in FY 1984; 1-year project).

funding, some of the problems of academics and contract research, and insider views of the award processes of the National Science Foundation (NSF), the National Institutes of Health (NIH), and the Alcohol, Drug Abuse and Mental Health Administration (ADAMHA). There is an index to fellowships and other individual research awards and a subject index. A sample entry from COSSA's guide is shown as figure 23. COSSA also publishes a newsletter, which has had a column giving sources of research support.

Other Information Sources on Federal Programs

Numerous individuals in Washington make a living communicating hot new items on the funding scene. Some produce private subscription newsletters, some a regular column for a periodical, and some are sponsored by professional associations. The private subscription people must merchandise information as though it were exclusively yours, yet send it to a large enough audience to economically justify their existence. If their audience is small, the price must be very high; thus, some of the subscription services are very expensive. Professional associations deal with the question by giving all their members an equal chance, making the information widely available. This is, also, the intended government strategy, which is why the government publishes announcements of grants in the *Federal Register* and of contracts in *Commerce Business Daily* (more on these in Step 2, below) and issue *CFDA.*

Appendix B contains a list of other reliable sources of information. Many such sources have stable funding bases and have been around for years, but there are always newly established ones. The *American Psychological Association's Guide to Research Support* mentioned earlier has a section titled "Additional Reading" with sections on federal research funding information, foundation and corporate funding information, and science policy/regulatory information, as well as a list of general references. Since APA intends to keep the *Guide* up to date, this is a good place to look. COSSA's *Guide* also has such a directory, though it is less comprehensive.

Up-to-date information is maintained on-line by the Office of Management and Budget in the Federal Assistance Programs Retrieval System (FAPRS). Each state has certain access points from which the material may be searched, and it also can be accessed by microcomputer with a modem through commercial time-sharing companies. For more information write to: General Services Administration, Federal Program Assistance Center Staff, Reporter's Building, 300 Seventh Street, SW, Washington, D.C. 20407.

Computer searching of federal programs is also available for those with a modem through a number of information services. Consult a current issue of *Commerce Business Daily* for a listing. Data bases include *Commerce Business Daily,* the *Federal Register,* and the *Congressional Record.*

STEP 2--THOROUGHLY UNDERSTAND THE PROGRAM

When you have found one or more federal programs that seem likely possibilities, the next task is to become sufficiently acquainted with them through printed material or conversations with their staff to ensure that your proposal would be of interest. For most agencies this is largely a matter of knowing how your proposal fits their goals and mission. All federal agencies are established with a mission; even the National Science Foundation, which supports basic research, is to spend its money in ways most advantageous to gaining new scientific knowledge. But as Lowman and Dusek (1984) indicate, whereas the National Science Foundation can support basic research with no applied payoff in sight, that is not true of other agencies. These more typically support applied research with some rather immediate relation to the problems in the area of their responsibility. When they support basic research, they do so in order to advance the day when that research will be useful in the solution of those same problems. So one of the tasks of researchers is to determine how their research relates to and advances the agency's mission. But how to find that out?

A general statement of the agency's mission is found in the legislation that established the agency and/or its program, but that is usually too broad to be helpful. The agency typically cannot support all possible approaches to the solution of problems in its area of responsibility, so its plans for attacking those problems and the priorities that it is assigning to them are formalized in regulations under which the program is administered and are published in the *Federal Register*. Changes are also published there.

The *Federal Register* is a daily publication of the Office of the Superintendent of Documents, Government Printing Office, Washington, D.C. 20202, which prints official notices of many kinds. Offprints of these regulations or brochures that include them are available from each program office and are usually included in the application package. But, if not, the correct reference to the *Register* can be obtained from the agency. The *Catalog of Federal Domestic Assistance (CFDA)* and the *APA's Guide* will have references to such regulations, but be sure that they are the current ones. Some programs or agencies, such as NSF, publish newsletters to keep researchers abreast of deadlines, staff changes, new programs, and program changes. If an agency of interest to you publishes one, get on its mailing list.

Knowing the history of legislation sometimes helps one understand the various stands an agency may take. It may also aid in predicting which ideas will interest an agency and what may be its next stage of change and growth. A currently active program must have received two Congressional approvals: once when it was authorized, again when funds were appropriated.

Program Authorization

How does a program determine its goals and directions?   Directions
come to a federal agency from several sources.   Depending on whether
the idea for the legislation originated with the administration or the
Congress, there is usually a concept or position paper somewhere that lays
out the intent of the legislation's authors.   Congress, through the
mechanism of hearings on authorizing legislation, frequently describes
what it wants the legislation to emphasize and accomplish. The results of
such hearings may modify, sometimes markedly, the original legislative
proposal. Reading recent reports of the committees may be instructive.

Once the legislation is passed and approved by the president, the
agency entrusted with implementing it begins to prepare regulations
describing how it will proceed if funded (see below). Such regulations are
developed and reviewed in-house before being published in the *Federal
Register* for public comment. The regulations may also be tried out in
prepublication draft form on advisory committees or selected external
consultants. After *Federal Register* publication, depending on the public
response, they are revised (or the original draft defended) as deemed
appropriate and published a second time, but now in final form, in the
Federal Register. Competitions for funds are also typically announced in
the final regulations, giving the deadlines, the criteria for judgment, and
the form of application.

Program Appropriations

Even though Congress has authorized the spending of funds and the
president has approved, no funds can be committed (nor a grant contest
announced) until these same bodies approve appropriations. Sometimes
appropriations hearings influence program directions as well.   Approval
via the Congressional appropriations route makes funds available for the
current fiscal year (October 1 through September 30). The fiscal year is
named for the year with the nine-month segment--for example, October
1986 through September 1987 is fiscal 87. The past year's appropriation,
as well as current administration budget plans, is noted in the *CFDA,* and
sometimes the typical grant size is also given.

Program staff can tell you whether funds have been appropriated for
the program in question and whether they are largely or entirely committed to projects already approved in past competitions or whether your
request for new funds will have to compete with projects requesting
continuing funding.

Getting Information from Program Staff

The printed material such as APA's *Guide, CFDA,* and regulations has
enough information to winnow the programs that might be possibilities,
but there is no substitute for calling or visiting a responsible staff person.
In particular this allows you to try out your idea to be sure that what is of
interest to you is of interest to the agency as well. Make a phone call

using the personnel listings in *CFDA* or APA's or COSSA's guide and briefly describe your idea. Find out whether it is appropriate for the agency's competition and whether the intended dollar request is feasible with its present funding--indeed, are there sufficient uncommitted funds to make applying worthwhile? Inquire about the next deadline, the form the application should take, whether any restrictions apply to the project as described (limitations on consultants, travel, purchase of equipment, and so on). Finally, don't forget to ask for an application kit or a copy of the proposal guidelines. The reaction of the staff officer to your proposal and any suggestions she may make give you some idea of the agency's interest in your proposal. When you receive its material, you should be able to decide whether to consider that agency as one to which to submit a full proposal.

Many agencies will discuss your proposal with you in some detail and may even be willing to react to a preliminary draft. The preliminary proposal should be briefer than the full proposal but should contain all the essential elements of the design as well as a realistic, though not necessarily detailed, budget. Listen to the reactions carefully and be guided by them. Staff can help this way in grant competitions and with requests for proposals (RFPs) before they are issued. After an RFP is publicly announced, staff are legally barred from helping you in ways that might favor your proposal. In some instances after a grant competition has been announced, staff also may feel that helping you shows favoritism, but this is more likely with one-time competitions than with continuing ones with regular deadlines. If they are able and willing to react to your proposal, staff can be very, very helpful.

If it is convenient, visit the agency. The staff are acquainted with past legislative and appropriations history, as well as the legislation's current status, and are willing to help one understand them. Frequently, they may also be willing to show, or let one take, in-house position papers that reveal the thinking of the agency staff with respect to new directions. Such papers are invaluable in anticipating future funding priorities and competitions. Sometimes one can get on a mailing list for such papers.

In contacting agency staff, it is important to remember, as pointed out in Chapter 2, that they achieve their goals through other people. It is in their interest to locate the best possible personnel across the widest spectrum of institutions who will submit proposals that aid in accomplishing the agency's objectives. They are interested, therefore, in meeting and encouraging those who can be of help to them. They will try to direct project efforts toward the agency's goals, possibly helping you redefine your project toward their ends. Do not mistake their friendliness and encouragement for promise of actual funding, however. This mistake leads to disappointment. Understanding the staff's role and what they are trying to achieve avoids this.

Some staff members will be very bureaucratically "proper" and give you only the forms and instructions. Seek out those who have enough experience to know their way around and who like to help people succeed.

STEP 3—GRANTS OR RFPS: WHICH IS FOR YOU?

Suppose that the program that appears most interested in your idea achieves its mission through both grant and request for proposal (RFP) competitions. Which is for you? The basic answer is, the one that is more likely to allow you to do what you want to do, but it may help if we describe the different forms of agreement used to support projects and then compare grants and RFPs. There are definite differences.

Forms of Agreement between the Government and the Awardee

The form of agreement between the government and the award winner for grants is a cost-reimbursable contract. Under its conditions, costs are reimbursed up to an agreed-upon limit. Grants are usually paid to the institution in quarterly installments, the unused funds to be returned when the project ends. Usually the final payment is withheld until the agency considers the project complete and the institution submits a final accounting of costs. Since your institution doesn't get paid until you finish the project, your fiscal officer and administration may be unhappy if your project is late. Getting them to pressure you to finish on time is part of the government's reason for holding up the final payment. Excess costs must be absorbed by the grantee unless the agency can be persuaded to amend the contract to change the scope of work or to provide additional funds for unforeseen contingencies. Neither is easy to negotiate, but if an unexpected contingency has arisen, ask about some kind of adjustment. It hurts to ask only if the request reveals bad management or inept planning by the grantee. Remember, one builds one's reputation with the agency with each piece of work performed.

Many RFPs are also on a cost-reimbursable basis, but contractors are reimbursed on the submission of invoices, usually submitted on an agreed-upon periodic basis. Fixed-price contracts are also frequently issued; the agreed-upon product or work must be completed for the contract price, but if the contractor can do it for less, the balance may be retained. In addition, there are cost-plus-fixed fee contracts for private contractors where the fee is their profit.

Cooperative agreements are a relatively rare form of support in the behavioral sciences. They involve researchers outside the federal government working collaboratively with those employed by it; funding is provided for those parts of the research carried on by the nongovernmental researcher. Both are involved in the design and development of the project, however, and presumably both would be involved in the final report as well.

A Comparison of Grants and RFPs

When programs describe their plans and goals in the *Federal Register*, they may announce grant competitions or they may wait and issue an

RFP; RFPs are announced in *Commerce Business Daily*. This is but one of the differences. A grant program is used to encourage the growth of knowledge in an area of government interest. It does this through supporting projects that are devised and planned by nongovernment researchers in the field. Thus, the area of interest or problem to be solved is announced, but the method of pursuing it is left to you to develop. The government holds a competition to see who has the best ideas with costs within available funding limits.

The request for proposal, or RFP, is used where the government knows what product or task it wants and is seeking someone to develop that product or perform that task (which can be a research task). It holds a competition to find who can do it satisfactorily for the least cost. The description of the product or task is developed by the government staff, sometimes with the assistance of consultants, and this becomes the RFP. Consultants are typically forbidden to bid on an RFP that they helped prepare.

The following table compares grant with RFP competitions:

	Grants	RFPs
Purpose	To support the development of an area of governmental interest	To accomplish a specifically described task (e.g., evaluation of a particular program) or procure a product (e.g., development of equipment or a curriculum) built to specifications
Development of idea is done by	Researcher	Government
Development of specifics of plan's procedures is done by	Researcher	Researcher
Time from announcement to proposal submission deadline	Unlimited for program with regular deadlines throughout the year	Short, typically 45 to 90 days or less

	Grants	RFP's
Places a premium on	Creative and important research idea, well developed and reasonably priced	Quick development of creative procedures that meet specified criteria least expensively and anticipate problems well
Number of winners of each competition	As many approved projects as the available money will support	Usually only one
Announcement appears in	*Federal Register*	*Commerce Business Daily*
Announcement sent to	Anyone asking to be on mailing list plus copies to institutions and organizations that would typically get information to researchers who might be interested	Researchers selected by government as competent and competitive bidders; copies available to others on request as long as supply lasts; one may ask to be on mailing list for certain RFPs announced as forthcoming
Advantage of early receipt of information	Some for one-time competition, less for regular ones	Considerable because of short deadlines
Agency staff's freedom to give assistance in preparation of proposals	Not highly restricted	Highly restricted, especially once RFP is published
Much monitoring of progress?	Variable; more likely if the agency is small and grant is fairly large	Typically, only for the largest contracts
Usual competitors	University faculty and graduate students and large nonprofit research organizations	Research organizations, both profit and nonprofit, that can respond

quickly and
efficiently to the
announcements

Note the marked differences between grant and RFP competitions
that appear in the table:

- A grant will support *your* idea, an RFP the government's. That is
  great if they are the same, but some people get trapped into doing
  the government's work just to get the money. That can be a
  problem, especially if the job is a chore and therefore gets done
  with a "let's get it over with" attitude.
- In grant competitions, there are as many "winners" as the
  appropriated funds will support;[1] in most RFP competitions only
  one contract is awarded--one winner.
- The turnaround time from announcement to deadline is short for
  RFPs; 45 days or less is not unusual, more than 60 days is atypical.
  The assumption is that if this line of work is appropriate for you,
  you'll be able to respond to the request quickly. This may be true
  of organizations largely devoted to research and development.
  Academics, however, teach, advise, work on committees, and, in
  addition, do research. They often do not have the support staff to
  produce and submit a proposal quickly even if they were able to
  prepare it. Further, most universities do not subscribe to the
  expensive services that, by keeping in touch with federal staff,
  learn ahead of time what RFPs are to be issued in the future so one
  can get a head start on them. Thus, the university's share of RFP
  competition awards has typically been small.
- In grant competitions, staff often will react to a preliminary
  proposal and make helpful suggestions; with RFPs you are on your
  own except as you raise questions at a bidders' conference (see p.
  205).

From these comparisons it should be clear why the section on
preparation of the proposal is aimed most directly at grant proposals.
Most of the remaining material on finding federal funds will discuss
additional specifics you need to know to respond to RFPs. Don't forget to
read the section "Other Useful Information" (p. 207), and if your proposal
doesn't seem to fit current funding priorities, the subsection "Unsolicited
Proposal Programs."

---

[1]There are nearly always more approved projects than there are funds
to support them. It must be a form of Parkinson's law that the total cost
of approved projects always expands to exceed available funds. In some
competitions unfunded approved projects are carried over to the next
competition; in most they must be resubmitted. If revised in accordance
with reviewer comments, they typically have a better chance of being
funded next time through.

STEP 4—GET INFORMATION ON THE CHOSEN COMPETITION

Grants

Remember, notices of grant competitions are announced in the *Federal Register*. The notice will include, at least, the deadline dates, application format, criteria for judging proposals, and amount available for making awards. Usually, such an announcement will accompany the publication of final regulations for a program, a restatement of program priorities, or similar communications. Write for the application package. It will contain the application form or format, rules and regulations, criteria for selection, and often the authorizing legislation.

RFPs

The use of RFPs results in part from the administrative requirements of the Office of Management and Budget, which, through the program planning and evaluation staffs in each department, office, and bureau, asks what each program plans to accomplish, how it expects to get there, and how much it will all cost. Therefore, much of the initial (and sometimes surprisingly specific) planning of research and evaluation is done in the agency's offices at budget time. These plans are then further refined and issued as an RFP (occasionally in such detail that little initiative is left to the contractor).

A synopsis of each RFP is published in *Commerce Business Daily*, published each government workday and available from Superintendent of Documents, Government Printing Office, Washington, D.C. 20202, Catalog #C41.9. It announces government procurement requests and awards, printing them in a form equivalent to newspaper classified ads. A complete listing of the classification headings is currently given on the back of the subscription form. Two relevant major procurement categories are "Services" and "Supplies, Equipment and Material." Basic and applied research RFPs are published under the subhead "Services: "A--Experimental, Developmental, Test and Research Work." Other "Services" subheads of possible interest are "H--Expert and Consultant Services"; "U--Training Services". Under "Supplies, Equipment and Material," the relevant subhead is "69--Training Aids and Devices." In addition to requests for proposals (or quotations--RFQs), it announces sole-source contracts, contract awards, surplus property for sale, and research and development sources sought. This last is a request for statements about specific capabilities. It is used to compile a mailing list for RFPs. As a space-saver, the issue for the first working day of each week contains a definition for each of a series of numbered notes that are used in subsequent issues. It takes some experience to screen through the many notices and headings to find what is relevant; the tremendous variety of items is a bit bewildering at first.

Obtaining the RFP. The *Commerce Business Daily* synopsis will give the title of the RFP, from which one must judge whether it may be of interest, and the deadlines for proposal submission. If the RFP appears to be of interest, phone or send for a copy at the source indicated. Remember, early response is often important! Only enough copies are printed to meet expected demand. If the copies are gone when a request arrives, the applicant is typically referred to the nearest federal deposi- tory where a copy was filed. Such regional or local offices can be most inconvenient, especially for those not living in a large city with a depository handy.

Having located an agency that supports work in your area, ask whether and when it intends to issue RFPs that might be relevant to your interest. Request that a copy be sent when available. This will save considerable time over watching for the notice in *Commerce Business Daily* and then requesting a copy. Discuss your capabilities and interests with program officers so they have an idea of what competitions you would like to enter. If they are impressed with your capabilities, they will seek you out, sending an RFP copy at their initiative. Some program officers will accept requests for routine inclusion in mailing lists for RFPs of a specified kind and size. Occasionally a "Sources Sought" entry in *Commerce Business Daily* will provide an opportunity to get on such a list.

How to read an RFP.   Currently RFPs are quite bulky and cumber- some, since each contains restatements of the variety of constraints (sometimes referred to by title and reference number to save space) to which the contract is subject. This legalese, commonly known as "boilerplate," often constitutes the initial pages, so that one has to hunt for the "meat" of the document. This is contained in the "scope of work" or "statement of work" section, often placed at the back as one of the "attachments." Somewhere in the early pages, most often on the cover, there will be a statement of the deadline for proposal acceptance and the number of copies of the proposal required.

If an RFP is of interest, scan the boilerplate, reading carefully the section titled something like "Preparation of Proposals--Instructions" or "Format and Content of Proposals." Although many of the paragraphs of this section will be standard, there are likely to be changed ones as well, frequently designed to facilitate the proposal evaluation process (e.g., a request for separate "technical" and "business" proposals on a large RFP). Be sure to note also the section that describes the proposal review process and evaluation criteria. Response time for RFPs is almost always too short. Use the statement of evaluation criteria to determine where to put emphasis--what section of the proposal gets the most points?   This problem is discussed in Chapter 2 under the heading "Where Should Precious Proposal Preparation Time Be Concentrated?" (p. 33).

A careful reading of an RFP will frequently reveal the agency's analysis of the problem, its perspective, and the expected approximate level of funding. The latter is inferred from the number of person-months or person-years of work that certain major tasks or the job as a whole is predicted to require. A "person-month" is the working time available to a professional person over a typical calendar month and includes the costs of support for that work such as secretarial help. (See also "Budget," p.

92.)

RFPs may look quite forbidding to the neophyte, but as with any complex situation, a little familiarity changes one's perspective radically. One gets quite accustomed to the standard sections and jargon. In any RFP, however, first find the work statement; even the neophyte will feel at home there!

Beware of RFPs that call for bids on the second or later phases of a study that was previously carried out by another contractor. If that contractor is interested in bidding on the new phase, his depth of experience and familiarity with the problem may give him a commanding lead in the competition. Discuss suspect RFPs with the program staff. Remember, it is usually in the staff's interest to ensure an open competition, so they will be unlikely to volunteer information that would discourage other bidders. But they are supposed to answer your questions fairly and honestly.

Characteristics of the RFP procedure. The RFP has the weaknesses of any bidding procedure, one of which is the difficulty of so specifying the work that those contractors not competent to bid on it are excluded. If an unqualified contractor submits the low bid, the program staff must be confident that they can demonstrate that the contractor is indeed incompetent should he or she appeal the decision to go with the next-lowest bidder. Incompetence may be difficult to prove. Yet, to let the bid go to an incompetent contractor may cost more than letting it to a higher bidder. Extra cost will be incurred if the program staff are compelled to bolster the incompetent contractor with additional funds midway through the work in order to save their investment. Either way the program staff may be accused of poor management. Hence, writing the RFP carefully to ensure that the contract will go only to contractors who can competently complete the task is a prime staff responsibility.

Such carefully prescribed RFPs may run the risk, however, of seeming to be written to fit only a particular bidder. Unless the RFP is a sole-source procurement, this is, of course, illegal. Sole-source procurements are legal and are used when only one contractor has the equipment or know-how to properly fulfill the contract. Such contracts are announced in *Commerce Business Daily.* If program staff choose this route, they must justify it to top administration, who also listen to the financial staff, who, as watchers of the purse strings, typically oppose it as more costly than competitive procurement.

It would be naive to assume that some favoritism may not on occasion occur, and one should be wary of this possibility. Yet, if one understands the problem of the staff, one can put in better perspective the perennial rumors that a particular RFP is "wired" or "locked up" for a certain bidder. To avoid this, both program staff and bidders must continually seek a middle road. Explorations with the program staff before the RFP is written are important in finding that middle ground so that a competent contractor is not unintentionally excluded. Such discussions are particularly in the interest of new bidders.

Bidders' conferences for RFPs. The *Commerce Business Daily* notice may announce that a bidders' conference will be held (usually not more than a few days after the RFP is issued) at a specified time and place. Such conferences can be useful in several ways:

1. They provide an opportunity for program staff to explain in detail the background of the request and to answer questions to clarify obscure points.
2. You can size up the competition who were interested enough to attend. This may help to determine whether it is worth the effort to apply. But do not be too easily discouraged--some of those attending are also checking the competition and may not follow through with a proposal.
3. The bidders' conference may help you decide whether your capabilities need to be strengthened by joining forces with a potential competitor through subcontracting arrangements or with several competitors in a consortium arrangement. Those attending may be potential partners or remind one of others who could be. A joint proposal may be stronger than any one competitor could have submitted.
4. Answers to competitors' questions may clarify ambiguities not previously noted.

Digests of these conferences are sometimes for sale from private Washington consultants. Transcripts are sometimes available from the agency.

As may be inferred from the four points above, the bidders' conference has an element of gamesmanship about it. The answers to questions asked by competitors may help others than themselves. Therefore, consider your questions from the standpoint of how much you will gain from them and how much they will aid the competition.

When questions are asked to which there are not ready answers, replies may be sent by mail. Be sure to get on the mailing list.

On some occasions, the RFP due date may be absolutely impossible to meet. In rare instances an extension may be sought and given. This will not give any competitive advantage, however, since the same extension will be given to all competitors.

Responding to RFPs. Time is of the essence in responding to most RFPs; a great deal must be done in a short time. Some RFPs, particularly those issued toward the end of the fiscal year to use up unspent funds, carry deadlines so short that only persons in institutions geared for fast response are able to reply in time. Colleges and universities typically have been ill equipped for these contests. (See Plotkin in Appendix A for how a commercial firm organizes to respond to an RFP. See also the reference there for Engelbret for another method of organizing.)

Deadlines must be scrupulously observed for RFP responses as well as grants. Most air express services will hand-deliver proposals. Some RFPs specify that to be eligible, mailed proposals must be sent by registered or certified mail at least five full days before deadline date and arrive before the award is made. Express Mail may be the least expensive quick option if you live near a pick-up point.

Remember, only one contractor wins the typical RFP competition. A few RFPs specify that more than one award may be made. Competitive pricing is important for RFPs, although it is not the sole determining factor (see "Determining the RFP Winner," below). Gross underbidding is more likely to backfire than to win the contract, since the bidder is likely to be rejected as having asked for inadequate funds to satisfactorily complete the work. It suggests the contractor didn't understand what was expected. Similarly, too high a price may exclude one.

Remember when responding that the RFP's "scope of work" is the controlling statement. Proposals, otherwise satisfactory, have been rejected because parts of the RFP were not responded to. Be sure your proposal is *completely* responsive.

Giving specifications for your intended products provides a measure of self-protection, creates realistic budgets (cost goes up as greater technical perfection is expected), and provides for common expectations of outcomes by proposer and program staff. Stating specifications for products to be delivered can prevent misunderstandings and save time, money, and effort (e.g., for a paper-and-pencil test: level of readability, number of test items, item format, administration time, and so forth).

Despite the care with which RFPs are usually formulated, one can sometimes propose a much better approach than the one requested. The typical "boilerplate" accompanying the RFP states that alternatives deemed in the best interest of the government will be considered. Develop and present the alternative, carefully labeling it as such and describing its advantages. Just in case the program staff find the alternative unacceptable, it may be well to develop what the RFP requested as well, if there is time.

Determining the RFP winner. RFPs are more likely to be judged by program staff than by external experts. After all, it is usually the staff who wrote the RFP, and they know what is wanted. Sometimes even writing the RFP is contracted, and in these instances external reviewers, possibly the same ones who were asked to write the RFP, are used.

With cost-reimbursable RFPs the programming and contracting officers look for the combination of "most responsive" and "most responsible" contractor. As the "boilerplate" puts it, the award will be made to "that firm whose proposal demonstrates that the firm would be most advantageous to the government, price and other factors considered. The Government reserves the right to award the contract to other than the low offerer or not to make the award if that is deemed its best interest."

The technical part of RFPs is often judged separately from the financial part. The former is judged on its adequacy as a response by the program officer. Large contracts may require the aid of outside readers. The financial proposal for large RFPs is often read and judged by a contracting staff officer. Together they make a judgment of what is in the government's "best interest." Other things being approximately equal, that "best interest" is sometimes served by employing a minority-controlled firm or a "small business." Prior experience with an individual or a firm is also frequently an important consideration in determining who is "most responsible." Price, especially if there are big differences between nearly equally acceptable proposals, is also an important consideration.

If one's price is competitive, the technical proposal may be the determining factor. However, one must be prepared to negotiate. Legally, the scope of work may not be changed without rebidding, but specifications, such as number of subjects or percentage of questionnaire return required, may be negotiated. Often, the writers of the few top-ranked proposals are contacted and adjustments discussed. They are then asked to submit a new and final bid, which is used in choosing the winner. Price is the determining factor for fixed-price contract RFPs if the contractor is deemed responsible and the response is acceptable. Most RFPs are cost-reimbursable, however.

The material from *Grantsmanship Center News* reprinted on the next two pages indicates some of the questions the program officer may ask about a proposal. Though developed for judging evaluation proposals, it has much wider applicability.

The first inkling that one may be among those in the finalist group usually comes in the form of questions about the budget. Sometimes there are requests that it be reworked or reestimated in certain parts. Don't start spending until written notification is received; such adjustments may be requested of all the top contenders.

OTHER USEFUL INFORMATION

Unsolicited proposal programs. Your idea doesn't fit any of the announced priorities of the current grants and contract programs? Many programs run an unsolicited proposal program just to get a chance to see ideas like yours. Good staff are always concerned that the best ideas not get lost even if outside the current priority targets. The unsolicited proposal program provides the opportunity to screen for these. The existence of such a competition may not be well advertised, so you may have to seek it out, but ask! You may be surprised to find how many fellow researchers have entered this relatively unannounced competition.

Another approach is to find an agency that ought to be interested in your idea and try to find a staff member in that agency whom you can bring around to your point of view. Sometimes there are unprogrammed funds that can be used for consultant service or to authorize studies for

An Inside Look at How HEW Evaluates Proposals.
(Excerpted from The Grantsmanship Center News,
Vol 2, No. 7, March–April 1976, pp. 57–59. Copyright.
Used by Permission.)

The NEWS has obtained a copy of a guide that provides unusual insight into the process the government goes through in awarding contracts. The guide was prepared for the Office of the Assistant Secretary for Planning and Evaluation in HEW and it is distributed internally to department personnel involved in managing evaluation contracts. One section of the book is particularly interesting: a checklist to instruct HEW personnel in how to evaluate proposals received in response to an RFP. The checklist provides invaluable information about the way the government evaluates proposals. Most of the concerns expressed in the checklist apply not only to proposals for evaluation contracts, the specific focus of the book, but to nearly all proposals for government contracts.

When evaluating proposals, the panel considers the following factors: (a) demonstrated understanding and approach to the scope of work; (b) capability and resource allocation of specific personnel; (c) availability and access of necessary facilities; and (d) organizational capability and experience in the field. Specific evaluation criteria relative to the project should be stated in the RFP.

Upon receipt of the proposal package, individual evaluators may begin their independent evaluation of the proposals. When the panel meets, each proposal will be discussed, and each evaluator will finalize his/her ratings and comments for each proposal on a separate score sheet. At this point, proposals are evaluated. The following guidelines may be used to examine each proposal during evaluations by individual panel members, as well as during the panel discussions. Although the evaluation criteria appear in the RFP and have been distributed to the panel prior to the initiation of the review, these questions about *major components of a proposal* should assist in the evaluation process.

Scope of Work

This section of the proposal should be the most comprehensive because it reveals the offeror's knowledge of the field and contains the suggested approach for performing the requirements of the evaluation study. In most instances, the heaviest weight will be given to this section of the proposal.

Has the offeror demonstrated adequate knowledge about the background, operations, and status of the program to be evaluated?

Has the offeror presented an approach which will achieve the stated objectives of the RFP?

Is the proposed approach supported with justification of why it should achieve the evaluation objectives?

Do you think the suggested approach will work?

Has the offeror introduced unanticipated events which may result in a project overrun or an expanded scope of work?

Has a specific management plan by task for period of performance been included?

Has the offeror demonstrated efficient use of time and resources, especially if special services such as computer time are required only for a short duration of the study?

Has the offeror been realistic in the amount of time allotted for the performance of each task?

Has the offeror demonstrated competence in a highly specialized area, such as statistical analysis, which is required for the evaluation study?

Has the offeror allowed for slippage in the preparation of questionnaires, test instruments, test administration, data process, etc.?

If appropriate, have site visits been adequately provided for throughout the period of performance?

Are reports keyed to major milestones/events of the study.

If appropriate, has the offeror provided for use of community resources?

If data collection is required for a comparative study, has the offeror allowed for an adequate sample of an experimental or control group?

Does the offeror specify the products which will result from the evaluation study?

Has the offeror allowed for OMB clearance on the development of measurement instruments?

Has the offeror demonstrated knowledge about evaluation techniques and procedures?

If appropriate, has the offeror indicated that an adequate representative of all levels of program personnel will be included in the evaluation?

These questions are not all inclusive, and items specifically related to the proposed study should be added.

Personnel

Proposed personnel should be examined critically because they are critical to the successful completion of a study. The capabilities, experience, and training of the personnel relative to their specific assignment on the study should be explicitly reviewed. If the RFP also requested references for projects on which personnel worked, then these references should be at least spot-checked.

Is it clear to which tasks in the study specific personnel will be assigned and for what amount of time?

Are the personnel assigned to specific tasks qualified by training and experience to successfully perform the tasks?

Has enough information been provided about personnel to allow adequate judgments to be made about their proposed roles in the study?

Is the apportionment of personnel level and time to specific tasks realistic?

What assurances are made concerning the availability of personnel proposed? Was a contingency plan requested if certain personnel become unavailable?

Have enough time and personnel been included to provide adequate administrative management of the study?

Are consultants to be utilized; if so, to what extent? Is the proposed use appropriate?

Is the author of the proposal one of the key personnel?

Does the success of the project depend, to a large degree, upon personnel not directly associated with the prospective firm?

Facilities

On-site availability of special facilities or easy access to required facilities must be indicated in the proposal. The source of facilities and equipment necessary for successful completion of the study, but which is not on site, should be stated, as well as the expected provision for use.

Are the facilities and equipment needed for successful completion of the study specified in the proposal?

How does the offeror intend to access facilities not at the contractor's site?

Does the use of facilities outside of the contractor's firm require a subcontract?

If subcontracting is necessary, is the proposed subcontractor specifically mentioned, along with an explanation of its required qualifications?

Is the planned use of facilities, such as printing, data processing, etc., realistic in terms of the planned evaluation?

Is a realistic time schedule planned if some services are to be performed at facilities located apart from the contractor?

If computer services are required, are there controls built into the processing so corrective action can be taken at intermittent points if necessary?

Past Performance

An organization's "track record" supplies some insight into the firm's capability to perform activities within specialized areas. Reference to past experience establishes a frame of reference from which to judge organizational capability. However, it can also be misleading in terms of the specific requirements of a study. Keep this in mind during the evaluation process. Glossy, vaguely worded statements with little support provide meaningless information. If the proposer has been asked to provide references regarding work performance, then the contracting officer should spot-check those given.

Do the references to past experience include activities specifically related to the requirements of the proposed study?

What reputation does the firm hold in the area of the proposed study?

Has the proposer been honored by professional societies because of the performance in a specific professional area?

Are the statements of past performance worded in a meaningful way so you can identify what work was actually performed?

Has the offeror bid for a contract in an area where the performance has not yet been demonstrated?

As mentioned earlier, one or more meetings of the evaluation panel is held to determine the acceptibility, unacceptability or potential acceptability of the technical proposals. Each proposal must receive an absolute, rather than a relative, judgement; a pre-determined cut-off score must not be used. A proposal is considered acceptable if, without qualification or revision, the panel judges that the offeror can perform the work competently. An unacceptable proposal might be made acceptable with the submission of clarifying data and therefore be included in the zone of consideration. This may delay the final award for a few weeks. An unacceptable proposal requiring major revision would not receive a rating worthy of selection for the competitive zone.

The contract file must contain documentation of how and why certain decisions were made in the evaluation of proposals. The responsibility for this justification rests with the technical representatives on the panel. These representatives rate and rank each proposal on a separate score sheet, then state why those ratings and rankings were given. This is especially critical if a debriefing is requested by contractors who want an explanation of their proposal's deficiencies. Rarely will contractors pursue this issue beyond the normal debriefing unless they feel unfairly treated, discriminated against, etc. Evaluations of proposals should be carefully thought out and recorded if the unhappy occasion should require presentation of this evidence in court.

Cost Information

(Ed. note: The evaluation panel reviews cost information after considering the technical aspects of the proposals. The responsibility for evaluation of costs often rests primarily with the contracting officer, who relies on inputs from other members of the evaluation panel.)

Is the overall cost within range of your (the contracting agency's) budget?

What is the relationship between the cost figures and equivalent items in the technical proposal?

Are the personnel costs reasonable according to the tasks to be performed?

Are the appropriate personnel assigned to perform the appropriate tasks?

Have expenditures been set aside for subcontracting requirements, such as data processing?

If a large-scale questionnaire must be mailed, has an adequate sum been set aside for postage?

Have costs for development of instruments, purchase of materials, such as scoring sheets, etc., been included?

Does the travel seem reasonable when compared to the tasks to be accomplished?

If consultants or experts are included, is their daily rate reasonable and within the proper financial range for your agency? Is the proposed time reasonable?

If appropriate, have costs for local personnel been included?

the agency, position papers, surveys, and so forth. It may be possible to authorize what you want to do, or at least support the development of your idea, out of such funds. If they find your idea of enough worth, they may offer a sole-source contract to give you time to develop it. This has happened! It eliminates any competition, which is only appropriate, since it was your idea. There must be justification that the "sole source" is uniquely fitted to do the task, but who is better equipped than the person who proposed it? Usually nobody!

Phased competitions.   It is becoming increasingly common for grant and sometimes RFP competitions to be phased. Phased competitions are used when a large number of applications are expected and there are few available awards. They reduce the time required of both agency and proposers. Usually, the first phase is a request for a brief prospectus, which, if it survives the initial competition, describes the idea that would form the basis for a fully developed proposal. Since the turnaround time following first-phase notification is usually short, it is important to continue some efforts in the interim so that second-phase work can be accomplished in the time available.

Sometimes at a preproposal stage an agency seeks information on persons, firms, and institutions with certain specialized competencies and/or interests as possible entrants in a later competition. Requests for this information are published in *Commerce Business Daily.*

Site visits.   Site visits are usually reserved for large projects, research centers, and laboratories. That you are being subjected to a site visit is a good sign since, because of its expense, it is reserved for those who are the finalists in a grant or RFP competition. The site visit has two purposes: to confirm the information presented in the proposal and to gather other information that may assist in making a complex decision. Your proposal indicates that you have the support of the various community organizations helping the handicapped; well, have you, really?   Do those letters of support stand up under site visit scrutiny?   You indicated that your research space was easily accessible to the handicapped;, how accessible is it?   What are the working conditions?   How much administrative support does the project have?   The proposal was well written, but did the principal investigator do it?   Is she really as "savvy" as the proposal suggests?   Is her load such that she really can put in the time she has promised?   How competent are her colleagues who will be working with her?   How well do they appear to get along?   These questions suggest the kind of issues that may be probed by a site visit. Some questions are fairly standard, such as the capabilities of the investigators, their ability to work as a team, the adequacy of support for the project, the sufficiency and appropriateness of the facilities and equipment.   But every project raises unique questions that will be investigated on the site visit. You'll have to predict what they will be as best you can, but try to do so.

You will typically be called by the program staff person to arrange for the visit and often will be asked to arrange for certain persons to be available.   The nature of the persons asked to be available begins to suggest the questions the site visit team wishes to answer. Many times the staff person will specify his areas of concern when he calls for the visit.

Site visits are usually made by all or part of the team of reviewers and one or more staff persons. They are usually short, sometimes too short to really present one's case or to recover from a bad gaffe.

Inevitably the question arises of how much to prepare for the visitors. It is to be hoped that your group is a cohesive team by this time, but if not, *you'd best use the time between the submission of the proposal and any notice of a site visit to mold it into one.* It doesn't hurt to have a rehearsal of what you expect, provided it doesn't put your staff on edge. It is best if everyone is alert but as relaxed as possible under the circumstances; you want to be on top of the project but have nothing to hide.

Preparing for the visitors also raises the question of how much and how lavishly to entertain them. That is one you will have to decide in your particular circumstances; certainly the team should be made at least adequately comfortable but not go away thinking you are a wastrel.

Relations with Congress. Announcement of the winner of any kind of award always includes a notification of the relevant House members and senators. In fact, federal offices are quite careful to be sure there is no public announcement until *after* such notification is given. One often receives a letter of congratulations from one's Congressional representative and sometimes from one's senators, too.

It is well to remember that all federal funding depends on Congress's good will. They like to know that the money they are appropriating is well spent. One does oneself and one's colleagues a favor by responding to the letter, indicating the potential for good that the project can achieve. When the project is finished, write these same public representatives, and in language devoid of jargon, describe what good has been concretely achieved. If possible, enclose brief statements or letters from constituents affected; this will help to make it clear that you are not just "tooting your own horn." Send copies of the letters to the sponsoring agency's staff; they will appreciate knowing of your correspondence. It provides a point of leverage when they testify about the program during hearings. Since Congress and agency staff accomplish their good works through you, it is appropriate that you, as their "agent," report to them.

Speaking of Congress, should one try to use political influence to be sure one's proposal is given the attention that is its due? In general, the answer is "No!" In the first place, consider what a mess it would be if everyone believed that only by political intervention could justice for his or her proposal be gained! Should this indeed be the situation, the remedy lies in measures other than everyone using the political process. Second, agency personnel are likely to wonder how much faith is being placed in their judgment and fairness if one must ask one's legislator for protection. Seeking the intervention of one's member of Congress "goes over their heads" and takes the decision out of their hands. Remember, if this is a relevant source of funds for this project, it may be for other projects, too. You are building a relationship with program staff.

In general, Congress is better saved as a court of last resort. It is wasted when routinely used as a source of pressure on administrative operations that are being accomplished to most applicants' satisfaction. But when one has been done an injustice and cannot receive satisfaction following the channels of the regular administrative machinery, *then* it is very helpful to ask that "inquiries from the Hill" be instituted. Be sure you have exhausted your options for appeal first. As indicated in Chapter 6 (p. 129), one can find out specifically why a proposal was rejected. Some agencies hold postaward briefings on the problems of a recent competition's proposals as well as offer comment on individual ones. Seek this information first. Then if an injustice appears to have been done, follow the formal appeals procedure that each agency has developed. If you do not follow that procedure, Congressional staff may feel that if you are unwilling to try to help yourself, why should they take on the burden? But if you have tried, they can often move the decision into different channels or open up new possibilities.

14.

Finding Foundation Funding

Some researchers prefer to seek foundation funding even though government funding might be available. As noted earlier, there is much less bureaucratic "red tape," there is less reporting, and the proposal is much simpler. Further, good ideas do not necessarily fall into the government's priority categories! If no state or federal program seems likely as a possibility, there may be a philanthropic foundation that can be interested. Sometimes one will want to seek funds from both sources to complement each other (the creators of *Sesame Street* did this). Foundations, like government, have their own priorities, and some seek out individuals to do what they want done. But not all foundations do the latter, and even among those that do, there is usually still room within their categories for proposer-initiated studies. Further, each foundation is seeking to make a mark in this world, to find a niche in society in which its resources are adequate to make a memorable contribution. Frequently cited examples are the Carnegie Library movement and the Flexner Report, which revolutionized medical education. Foundations seeking such niches may be found in some highly unusual fields; the problem is to match foundation and proposer interests.

Large foundations are usually much easier to work with than government agencies and have far fewer constraints, certifications, and the like. Most will need to know that they are dealing with a nonprofit organization and will ask that this be certified to them. They can make grants to individuals only with IRS permission, and there are certain restrictions. But they are generally much less formal in their application instructions and, certainly in the opening discussions, prefer brief proposals. Further, there is less interim reporting; much greater budgetary flexibility; less monitoring of progress; and freedom to report the project as seems appropriate without clearances. It is easy to see why some investigators prefer foundation funding even if government funds can be obtained.

With fewer constraints, foundation officers are free to make exceptions to their guidelines if one can convince them that a project ought to be supported. But few want to. If they are to have impact, the foundation must limit the scope of its interest; it can't support everything. Besieged with projects, a foundation sets guidelines and priorities to provide protection against things that lie outside the target areas it hopes to affect. The most common reason for rejection is that the project falls outside the foundation's scope of interest. Foundation officers have boards and benefactors to whom they are responsible and who usually define the fields of interest. They will usually resharpen the target area's definition should the foundation's staff blur it too badly. Still, when the officer has the confidence of his board or benefactor, there exists the possibility of finding ways to fit a project within the foundation's guidelines, particularly if the gap is not too great, and occasionally even when it is. Don't bank on this possibility unless you receive encouragement, however. The bulk of one's effort should be

devoted to finding a foundation where there is mutuality in the prime
interests of proposer and sponsor.

STEP 1--SCREEN FOR FOUNDATION PROSPECTS

Anyone interested in foundation information soon turns to the Foundation Center for help, either directly or to one of its publications or
services. This nonprofit organization, with a main office in New York (79
Fifth Ave., New York, N.Y. 10003; toll-free phone is 800-424-9836 for
ordering publications), has established Foundation Center Reference
Collections in four cities: New York, Washington, D.C., Cleveland, and
San Francisco. It has one or more cooperating collections in each of the
50 states.   These collections contain a wealth of information about
foundations, their grants, and the application process.   The cooperating
collections typically concentrate on the foundations within their state but
may request information or records from the New York collection or
others. For a listing of the Foundation Center addresses as well as those
of cooperating collections, see Appendix C.

Perhaps even more widely used than the center's library are its
publications, which have increasingly turned the search for foundation
funds from a "hit or miss" process into a reasoned procedure. They
publish information on specific foundations, program interests, fiscal
data, and personnel. They also provide indexes to grants and information
on funding research, proposal writing, and sources of information.

An excellent source of information about the center's services and
about finding and approaching foundations is the center's *Foundation
Fundamentals: A Guide for Grantseekers*, third edition (Read, 1986). It
contains detailed directions for subject, geographic, and types of support
searches using both the center and other sources.

The starting point of your search will depend on both the nature of
your project and the amount of funds you plan to request. Each of these
limits potential sponsors--the former where your project falls outside a
foundation's field of interest, the latter if it is beyond the foundation's
resources. The accompanying table is a synopsis of the different starting
points for seeking sponsors and the resources used. The four entry points
given there and their special usefulness organize the discussion of
information sources that follows. The entry points are these:

   A. Especially if yours is an unusual subject matter, but even if it is
      not, it is always useful to see who has made grants for similar
      projects.   This provides a more targeted search.   Use the
      Foundation Grants Index Annual (its bimonthly edition for the
      latest information), and/or if a relevant one is available, start with
      a *COMSEARCH: Subject* printout derived from the *Index* . In
      addition, there are specialized directories of agencies that make
      grants in certain topical areas.
   B. If yours is a large proposal, you are confined to foundations with
      the largest resources.   The Foundation Center's *Source Book*

Figure 24. A compact guide to foundation funding.

| | Entry | | Point | |
	A	B	C	D
Especially useful in support for project when	Prefer targeted to broad search Subject matter has unique aspects	Project requires substantial funding	Prefer broad subject search	Project is within resources of small foundations and/or has local impact
Also use to enlarge sponsor pool when search started at points			A and B	A and C
Basic data base	*Foundation rants Index* (annual or bimonthly) Grants of $5000 or more from about 500 reporting foundations*	*Source Book Profiles* 1000 largest foundations covered in 2-year cycle	*Foundation Directory* 4400 foundations with assets of 1 million and yearly grants of $100,000+	*National Data Book* 24,000 foundations giving at least a dollar a year
Arranged	Alphabetically within states	Alphabetically in quarterly issues	Alphabetically within states	By state in descending order of annual grant total
Relevant entry point index	Key word index and/or subject/ geographical (lists foundations by state under 150 broad heads)	Subject/geographical (same as Grants); national and regional foundations in bold type	Subject/geographical (same as Grants)	No subject index
Other indexes	Recipient/category (cross-lists type of recipient with type of support) Recipient index	Alphabetical Type of support Geographical by city and state	Alphabetical Type of support Geographical by city and state Donors, trustees, officers	Alphabetical
Other sources of information to consult	*COMSEARCH: Subject* printout Specialized topic directories (Appendixes A and C of Read, 1986) Organizations and associations serving grantseekers (Appendix E of Read, 1986)		*COMSEARCH: Broad Topic* printout *Annual Register of Grant Support* Foundation and federal programs, detailed subject index Various directories to corporate foundations: *Corporate Foundations Profiles, Corporate Fund Raising Directory, Corporate Giving Yellow Pages, Taft Corporate Giving Directory* See also Appendix D of Read (1986)	*COMSEARCH: Geographic* printout State and local directories (Appendix B of Read, 1986)

*Start with *COMSEARCH* printout
if a relevant one is available.

Profiles covers the 1000 largest foundations on a two-year cycle.

C. If yours is a large proposal but you didn't find a potential sponsor among the 1000 largest, if you wish to enlarge your pool of potential sponsors, or if you wish to do a broad search, use the Foundation Center's *Foundation Directory*. It includes about 5000 large and intermediate-size foundations, listing all those with assets of more than a million dollars and annual awards of over $100,000. *COMSEARCH: Broad Topics* also facilitates a wide search if one of the topics covered fits your interest.

D. For a small request or one with largely local impact, use the Foundation Center's *National Data Book,* which lists all currently active grantmaking foundations (approximately 24,000). *COMSEARCH: Geographic* may be helpful in finding a local foundation, and if there is one, be sure to consult the local geographically based directory.

Since the indexes to foundation programs tend to be broad descriptors, rather than fine-grain indexes, a more precise match to one's interests can usually be made using grant titles and their accompanying key word indexing, so entry point A is the best for a focused subject search.

Starting Point A—Indexes to Foundation Grants

One of the best guides to what a foundation will do is what it has done. If your search is related to any of the 60 specific subjects or 20 broad fields included in *COMSEARCH* printouts, you are in luck. This is the best place to begin. These lists are regularly accumulated by computer from the *Foundation Grants Index*. The cost is small, and it saves looking up each separate topic in the listings of the *Index*.

For a list of current *COMSEARCH: Subjects*, write the Foundation Center, 79 Fifth Ave. New York, N.Y. 10003, or call 800-424-9836 toll-free. In addition to subject searches, there are also *COMSEARCHES: Geographic* and *COMSEARCHES: Broad Topics* (art and cultural programs, children and youth, higher education, hospital and medical care programs, science programs, social science programs, public health, public policy and political science, community and urban development, elementary and secondary education, and others).

If there is no *COMSEARCH* printout near your area of interest, or you wish to check the key-word index itself for relevant grants, consult the base from which the printouts were drawn, the *Foundation Grants Index*, the annual or its bimonthly edition. It gives information reported by the foundations for all grants of $5000 or more to a nonprofit organization. For each state, grants are listed by foundation. Each entry gives the amount, recipient's name and location, date, a sentence about the grant, and the source of information. For the most recent information see the bimonthly *Foundation Grants Index*. Each issue also includes information about grantmakers--changes in address, personnel, and so on--and their publications.

The most valuable index is the subject index based on key-word descriptors, there usually being several key words descriptive of each grant. An index by organizational type (e.g., graduate school, private university or college, public university or college, research institute) lists for each type the grant reference number by state for eight categories of support (e.g., fellowships and scholarships, program development, research). In case one knows of similar grants or similar agencies who might have received grants, there is also an index of recipients and one by geographic location. The grants indexed represent 47% of all foundation giving.

As an important adjunct, *Foundation News* (published by the Council on Foundations, Inc., 1828 L St. NW, Washington, D.C. 20036) is a journal aimed at foundation officers and personnel. For those who want to better understand the foundation world, it is a very useful source of information on trends, legislation, and regulations affecting foundations. It has occasional articles on how grantseekers look from the other side of the desk, which provide useful insights.

Those involved in international projects or in communities where a non-U.S.-based corporation has invested may find H. V. Dodson (Ed.), *The International Foundation Directory*, third edition (Gale Research Co., Book Tower, Detroit, Mich. 48226, 1983), of use. It lists 705 foundations by country. They are indexed by name and under 11 broad headings (e.g., arts and humanities, education, international affairs, medicine and health, science and technology, social welfare and studies).

The sources of targeted information are surprising. For example, one targeted to research grants is compiled by Betty and William Wilson: *Directory of Research Grants* (Oryx Press, Phoenix, Ariz.). Here is a sampling of specialized compilations:

- *Foundation Guide for Religious Grantseekers.* Peter S. Robinson (Ed.). (Scholars Press, Missoula, Mont., 1979)
- *Funding in Aging: Public, Private, and Voluntary.* Lilly Cohen (Ed.). (Adelphi University Press, Garden City, N.Y., 1979)
- *Handicapped Funding Directory.* Burton J. Eckstein (Ed.). (Research Grant Guides, Oceanside, N.Y., 1980)
- *National Directory of Arts Supported by Business Corporations.* Daniel Millsaps (Ed.). (Washington International Arts Letter, 1979)
- *Private Funds for Mental Health Research.* U.S. Dept. of Health, Education and Welfare. (National Institute of Mental Health, Rockville, Md.)

Read (1986) lists a wide range of additional such sources of information in her Appendixes A and C, and her Appendix E lists associations and organizations, many in specialized fields, that serve grantseekers. The American Psychological Association's *Guide* describes foundations that have shown interest in psychological projects.

Starting Point B--*Source Book Profiles:*The Largest Foundations

If one is looking for large amounts of money, only those with adequate resources are potential sponsors. But remember, you don't have to get your support from only one sponsor; foundations frequently cooperate to jointly support a worthy project. So consider joint sponsorship among the largest, joining smaller ones (entry point C or D), or some combination.

The *Source Book Profiles* annually provide updated information on 500 of the largest 1000 foundations so that over a two-year period all are profiled. Its indexes, however, refer to all 1000 foundations. The book gives information in greater depth than the *Foundation Directory*. A typical entry includes addresses, phone numbers, and contact points; a list of officers; financial data including the number and total amount of grants, the largest and smallest grants, and their general range; some background on the foundation, its publications, and its statement of purpose; and an analysis of the grants and the kinds of support and recipients involved.

Starting Point C—The Foundation Directory, Annual Register of Grant Support, and Corporate Foundation Directories

Just as the CFDA maps the federal programs, so *The Foundation Directory*, published by the Foundation Center, is a sourcebook of foundations and their programs. The current eleventh edition, just being published in 1987, lists about 5000 foundations. Although it contains about 1000 new entries, like the previous, it probably includes less than a fifth of the active foundations. Those listed in the tenth edition had 97% of the assets and awarded 92% of the total grant dollars in 1983 and 1984; this is also probably still true. To be listed in the *Directory*, a foundation must have assets of $1 million or more and give $100,000 annually in grants. More than half the small foundations hold assets of less than $50,000, so they generally confine their interests to local needs.

The *Foundation Directory* has five indexes: (1) broad fields of interest (e.g., anthropology, educational research, sociology, psychology); (2) foundation names listed alphabetically; (3) foundations by city within state; (4) donors, officers, and trustees (in case one should happen to know any); and (5) types of support awarded (e.g., equipment, grants to individuals, research, seed money). Foundation entries are ordered alphabetically for each state. Each entry gives information about a foundation, including its purpose and activity; assets and expenditures; high and low grants and number of grants; its officers, donors and trustees; its address.

The *Annual Register of Grant Support* is another source of information, one already described in the previous chapter since it combines federal with foundation funding. The *Register* is issued annually. Whereas the *Directory* arranges entries state by state, the *Register* categorizes its entries under ten broad subject headings, each of which is subdivided. See the description in the previous chapter for details of headings and entries, p. 189.

For foundation programs, the *Register's* information is similar to that in *The Foundation Directory.* Since the *Register* is updated annually, its information may be more recent. The *Directory* appears to be more inclusive of foundations, so that both references might well be checked. The subject index in the *Register* is considerably better in that it contains a much more detailed listing. For most research grantseekers, the *Register's* clustering of programs by primary area of interest is more helpful than the *Directory's* listings by state. A listing by state is also available in the *Register* in a separate index.

Corporate giving has increased and along with it the means to gain access to it. Corporate foundations are included in the *Directory* and the *Register,* but if you have a special interest in them, the Foundation Center's *Corporate Foundations Profiles,* like its *Source Book Profiles,* gives detailed data on over 250 of the largest corporate foundations and brief descriptions of nearly 470 smaller ones. In addition, there is *The Corporate Fund Raising Directory* published by the Public Service Materials Center, 111 N. Central Ave., Hartsdale, N.Y. 10530. Read (1986), in her Appendix D, addresses the general problem of finding corporate funding sources and lists a number of directories, some of which are targeted to specific states. A prime object of corporate philanthropy is public relations. Therefore, many give only in geographic areas where they have operations, information that is included in the directories.

Taft Corporation (5125 MacArthur Blvd. NW, Washington, D.C. 20016), which has been providing information on foundations to fund raisers for many years, has a Corporate Information System that includes the *Corporate Giving Yellow Pages* (names and addresses of 1300 programs and foundations) and the *Taft Corporate Giving Directory,* seventh edition (1985). This directory is extensively indexed, showing states the corporation operates in as well as the headquarters state. It even provides indexes to the places of birth and alma maters of important corporation individuals. Like other privately produced fund-raising materials, this is priced primarily for an institution, rather than for the individual. Its information is quite useful for nonprofit organizations dependent on gifts, so you can probably find a nonprofit organization near you that subscribes.

Starting Point D—Locating the Smaller and Local Foundations

For smaller projects or ones with largely local impact, the smaller foundations may be potential sponsors. Probably not many small foundations are interested in research, but one never knows unless one asks. The Foundation Center's *National Data Book* describes all 24,000 currently active grantmaking foundations and 200+ community foundations. It gives their address, principal officer, assets, grants paid, gifts received, fiscal period, and whether they publish an annual report. Foundations are listed by state in order of descending total grant size. There is also an alphabetical index but no subject index. *COMSEARCH: Geographic* may be helpful in locating local foundations.

In addition to the national directories, there are a number of state directories. These vary in the information they give, but many pattern their entries after *The Foundation Directory.* They are a likely source of information on small foundations. Appendix D of Read (1986) gives a state-by-state list of state and local directories. Bauer (1984) has a list of state and local grantmakers. Your closest Foundation Center cooperating collection has material on local foundations and information sources. (See Appendix C)

Computer-Accessible Foundation Information.

Individuals with a computer and modem who wish to run their own searches will find that up-to-date files of *The Foundation Directory,* he *Foundations Grants Index,* and the *National Data Book* (under the title "National Foundations") are available on-line through DIALOG Information Services. Information about access can be obtained from the Foundation Center or from DIALOG. Searchers can get such information as the names and addresses of smaller foundations in a given Zip code area, which foundations have given grants in excess of a specified amount for a particular topic, and which foundations would be likely to fund a research project at a given location on a particular topic. The Foundation Center will also do a custom search for a fee if you become a member of its Associates Program--a program that also permits you to get information by toll-free phone.

STEP 2--WINNOW THE PROSPECTS

You probably have been winnowing prospects as you located them in the various references, but if you haven't already, your next step is to narrow them to a few worthy of concentrated effort. Use the *Source Book Profiles,* the *Directory,* and the *Register* for information that will permit you to reduce your list. Read (1986) has an excellent set of questions to bear in mind in screening prospects. The following questions are adapted from that list:

- Is the foundation interested in what you propose to do? Prior grant statements of policy are the best clues. (Beware of grants given because of ties to institutions, rather than interest in your topic. These are hard to spot but do occur.)
- Is the foundation bound to a geographic region? Look for geographical patterns of giving. To increase their impact or because of the benefactor's specific direction, many foundations limit their giving geographically.
- Are they likely to grant money in the amount you are seeking? Will they continue support as long as you will need it? Some may not have the resources you need or, if they do, may not be likely to make grants of that magnitude. Some may make one-time grants only; few take on long-term commitments.
- Will they make grants for what you intend to do? Some won't fund building or equipment costs; others, operating costs.
- Will they cover full costs, or do they always look for cost sharing?
- Are you eligible? What types of organizations do they support?

Some will not support individuals, others prefer only established institutions, most deal only with nonprofit agencies.

● Is review continuous, or are there deadlines?   Review and processing often takes at least three months and sometimes longer. Most foundations review continuously with approvals given at the next executive or board meeting after the staff recommends approval. The established dates for these meetings indicate how long your project may require for approval.

STEP 3 -- LEARN ALL YOU CAN ABOUT THE BEST PROSPECT(S); DO YOUR HOMEWORK!

The sources above have led you to the one best prospect or perhaps a few of the best. Now find out all you can about them before you approach them. From the various directories you can tell which publish annual reports; about 600 currently do. About 700 publish a brochure describing their programs; send for those of interest. Some, like the Rockefeller Foundation *(RF Illustrated)* and the Ford Foundation *(Ford Foundation Letter)*, publish newsletters. Write for the reports and newsletters or look them up in your nearest Foundation Center Library.

There is another advantage in going to the Foundation Center Library. It subscribes to a clipping service that sends copies of news stories about foundation activities. This provides information about the individuals involved and their interests as well as the foundation's activities. *Foundation Grants Index Bimonthly* in its "Updates on Grantsmakers" gives up-to-date information on changes in personnel and programs of major foundations.

The Foundation Center Library will have copies of the Internal Revenue Service reports (IRS-990PF and IRS-990AR) for some foundations, usually those in-state. Most of this information is abstracted by the various directories; but for the small foundations, these are the best records if there is no state or local directory. These reports, which foundations are required to file yearly, give the foundation's name and address, its officers and trustees, receipts over $5000, assets, and grants (often, unfortunately, only the recipient and amount). The Internal Revenue Service will let you inspect these records in its district offices at no charge.   To order copies of the individual returns of particular foundations, send orders to Philadelphia Service Center, Internal Revenue Service, P.O. Box 245, Bensalem, Pa. 19020, Attn. Photocopy Special Processing Unit-A, Drop 536. Copies are currently $1.00 for the first page and ten cents per page thereafter. In addition to the usual name and address and year of return, the IRS would like the employer identification number, found in *The National Data Book*. The various foundation directories will usually, however, have the information you need.

If you can, talk with persons who have had experience with the foundation and its staff. Your own or a nearby institution may have a development office with personnel who have had such experience. They can often give very useful insights not available in print.

Learn as much as you can about the people you are contacting. Foundation executives are sometimes concerned that you are not interested in them as persons.   Nils Wessell (1975), a foundation executive, notes that a number of college presidents have lectured him on the elementary facts of academic administration "in total ignorance that I spent 27 years in that vineyard." This need not occur. Many foundation staff members appear in *Who's Who* and similar directories, and the clippings in the Foundation Center Library may add additional information.

STEP 4--CONTACT THE FOUNDATION

Foundations are generally much more informal in their proposal requirements than governments. If you are sure that your proposal should be of interest to them and you have good interpersonal skills, call for an appointment and visit them. If you have really done your homework, you should be able to call a particular person for an appointment and know enough about her to start a conversation on a topic of common interest.

If you are still trying to find a good prospect, or if a visit is out of the question, a brief letter of inquiry of one or, at most, three pages should start the ball rolling. Address the letter to an individual, if possible, and indicate how the project furthers the goals of the foundation, how it is unique, and why that foundation's help is needed. If you are enclosing a brief proposal, describe it very briefly--a sentence or two that will catch the officer's eye and motivate her to read it. Cite persons known to both you and the funder to establish a personal relationship if possible, or cite information that might provide a common bond (e.g., you graduated from the same college or university--look up the funder in *Who's Who* to find possible points in common). Offer to discuss the project by phone, saying in your letter that you will call in a couple of weeks to chat with her about it. Give a number where you can be called earlier if she wishes.

Some foundations, besieged by proposals, do not meet with (or send replies to) a proposer unless that individual is known to them or to one of their trustees or in some way vouched for as having a possibly legitimate claim on the foundation. If it is possible to find this out beforehand, it is obviously a timesaver.

Some small foundations list an address but no phone number. Since whoever serves as executive of the foundation is nearly always also a trustee--usually a lawyer--compare the foundation address with those of the trustees. When there is a match, one knows the likely foundation executive and how he can be reached.

Institutions, particularly colleges and universities, usually have an office whose function is to maintain contact with foundations for purposes of general fund raising. They can be useful in helping get information and in gaining access. Such offices also like to keep track of persons who are approaching foundations so as to be sure that the institution's top priorities are given adequate foundation attention. If you have such an office, contact it!

Sometimes it is desirable to approach a corporation through a local contact. This is particularly true of corporate foundations, where the local plant manager usually has direct foundation access and often must approve any local grant before it is awarded.

FOUNDATION PROPOSAL EVALUATION

How is your proposal evaluated in a foundation? There are as many ways as there are foundations, but in general there is much less use of outside consultants. Most commonly the staff make the evaluation. They typically do their first screening by deciding when you call whether to encourage submission of a one- or two-page prospectus. If, judging from the prospectus, they believe that it is worth going further, they will typically help you prepare the proposal by saying rather specifically what they see of interest, what kind of information they want in the longer proposal, how long it is to be, and what kind of limits the budget should observe. Development of the proposal is much more likely to be a collaborative process in foundations, since you are working with the staff officer to prepare something that he can feel comfortable in recommending to the chief executive officer of the foundation. Or, if you are dealing with the foundation executive, then it is a matter of preparing something that can be recommended to the board of trustees.

Some foundation boards include specialists who serve the role of outside consultants to staff on technical matters. But, typically, they are laypersons, often lawyers. Therefore the proposal needs to communicate to them. Your foundation staff person will usually explain all this to you and tell you the kind of background the persons reading the proposal will have. If he doesn't, be sure to ask. Knowing your audience is critical to communicating well and accurately.

"What a foundation will look for...." on the next page are the questions one foundation asked regarding applications. Be prepared to answer such questions before foundation contact is made. Once the contact is made, you are your own salesperson; that's part of the *art* of proposal development.

*What a foundation will look for in a proposal is often an enigma for people seeking grants. This guide
developed by the Cleveland Foundation succinctly communicates many of the things
on which foundations (particularly those with professional staff) may base their evaluation.
(The Cleveland Foundation is a community foundation, meaning that it can fund only
projects based in the Cleveland area.)*

The form of an application is much less important than the content. All grant applications, however, should start with a summary letter outlining purpose, background, amount requested and time limits. Detail may be included in attachments.

1. Purpose and Definition of Project:
• What is the basic purpose of the project?
• How long will the project last?
• Is this a new activity? Has the field been researched to find similar projects? Has a similar project failed? Succeeded? What has been learned from previous projects of this nature?
• Is this a continuation of a program or project? How well has it succeeded? Is it a modification? Why?
• What provision has been made for client participation, if applicable? If the proposal is to do a study, what plans, if any, have been made to implement the findings? Will the results be made available to others? What new methods and techniques will be tested?

2. Priority of Project:
• How serious is the need and necessity for immediate action?
• Why does this project deserve aid more than others competing for funds in the same field?
• Is this request in effect competing with other requests from the same organization? If so, what priorities would the organization establish among these requests?
• What is the target population? How large is it? How and to what extent will the program benefit the target population?

• What immediate and long-range results are expected? Will these results help other organizations?

3. Financial Information:
• What is the current operating budget of the organization? Itemize income and expenses.
• What is the anticipated budget for this program? Is the budget large enough? Is it too large for the results anticipated? Give a complete budget breakdown. What provisions have been made for independent audit of budget expenditures?
• Will the project continue beyond the funding period? If so, who will provide the funding? How firm a commitment for this future funding has been made? Will this ensure ongoing funding?
• Have requests for financial support of this project been submitted to other foundations, governmental agencies or other funding sources? Has the project secured funding commitments from any of these sources? If so, for how much and from which source(s)?
• Are requests by this organization for other projects currently pending before other funding organizations? How are they related to this proposal?

4. Background of Request:
• How long has the requesting organization or agency been in existence? What has been the performance to date of the requesting organization? List previous foundation-support projects.
• Is the organization tax exempt [501 (c) (3)]? Attach exemption form if it is a new organization.

• What other organizations are active in the same or similar activities? What are the cooperating organizations, if any?
• Has this project been approved by the proper personnel in the requesting organization? Does it have their full support? Is there professional support for or other evidence of the validity of this project? What is the relationship of this project to the overall goals and services of the requesting organization?

5. Personnel:
• Who are the trustees and officers of the requesting organization? What financial support do the trustees give to the organization? What part do they take in policy formation and program direction? How, and to what extent, do the trustees participate in the programs of the organization?
• Who are the staff personnel? What are their professional qualifications for doing the proposed work?
• Will additional staff be required for this project? Are these persons readily available? To whom will they be responsible?

6. Evaluation:
• By what criteria will the success or failure of this project be measured?
• Has adequate provision been made for the preparation of a final report? What type of progress reports are planned? How often will they be prepared? Who will get them?
• What provision has been made for objective evaluation of the results, short and long range? What techniques will be used in making evaluations? Who will do the evaluating?

Excerpted from the The Grantsmanship Center
News, Vol. 3, No. 1, August-October 1976. Copyright.
Used by permission.

Section V

Suggestions and Insights

For Beginners and Doctoral Students

Because those most at a disadvantage in preparing a proposal are beginners and doctoral students, this last section of the book provides special assistance to them. References to the special problems of the beginner appear in prior discussions, but Chapter 15 goes beyond that advice, reemphasizing some of the important points.

Though originally intended for postdoctoral researchers, previous editions of this book have been widely used by doctoral students preparing their dissertation proposals. I decided this edition would be even more useful to them if material were added to help the student understand the dissertation process as a whole. Thus, Chapter 16 develops a perspective on doctoral dissertation development, discussing how it is differently perceived by faculty and by students and the resulting implications for faculty/student interaction and for student self-development. It also deals with the problems of writing. This latter material may be useful to beginners as well as doctoral students. Chapter 17 deals with each of the steps of the dissertation process and how to master them.

15.

Suggestions for Beginners

You are considering submitting your first proposal for funding. What advice can I give you? If you have read this far, you have already noted the fact that the proposal itself is used as a basis for·judging the kind of work that you will do, so careful preparation of the proposal is clearly one of the messages that you should have heard by now.

A second is that there are several places in the proposal itself where you have a special opportunity to show your skills:

- The conceptualization of your problem is the first of these. Your ability to conceptualize your problem in a framework that places it in a position of importance in its field is the first sign that you have a good understanding of your field and what you intend to do in it.
- Your handling of the review of the literature is the second place where you can demonstrate your command of your field. When you present your project in appropriate perspective in relation to the other relevant work, your ability shows. Appropriately critique that work and show how your study will not repeat those mistakes but will move beyond them. If you are able to include as yet unpublished as well as the already published and cited work, it shows you are well connected with the "invisible college" of researchers already working on your problem, a very positive sign. In particular, your ability to select only the appropriate literature and weave it into the fabric of your proposal, rather than citing everything but doing little other than citing it, is critical.
- Your ability shows when you present a study design and procedure which appropriately eliminates alternative explanations of the relationship you wish to demonstrate, which explicitly recognizes those explanations that were not eliminated and tells why a compromise was made and the basis for it.

Handling well those three aspects of the proposal will go a long way toward making yours one that will be funded. But what else can you do?

- Make a test of the work plan and budget to see whether, if one knows the prices of things, the work plan translates easily into budget figures. You may not know the prices, but you will be able to tell whether you could make the translation if you did. If the translation is difficult, you need to revise your work plan, design, and/or procedure. Get help on the budget from someone who knows the prices of things and the implications for your project of whatever procurement restrictions exist at your institution.
- Have one or two persons read the draft proposal whose criticism you can accept and who will be as honest as possible in their appraisal of the material. Preferably the critics should have had experience writing proposals. Then listen *very carefully* to what

they say. *Listen for the meaning behind the words* as well as the overt meaning, particularly if the critics are friends of yours or persons below you in an academic or other hierarchy. They may prefer to tell you something indirectly, rather than hurt your feelings. Subordinates may think "I don't understand this but I'm sure she knows what she is talking about."

Don't necessarily immediately do everything that is suggested. Ponder a bit; try to figure out what caused them to say what they did. The impulsive action you take in presumably understanding the prescription may be wrong and leave the flaw unscathed. They may be correct in their diagnosis of where the problem lies, but their remedy may not be the best one. Indeed, it could even be wrong. Use your carefully-arrived-at best judgment about what to change and how to do it; it is your proposal and your reputation you are building, not theirs.

- Ask an experienced proposal writer to prepare your first proposal with you. Possibly include her as co-investigator or as a consultant on the proposal. See expansion of this point in Chapter 5, p. 85.
- Look at some accepted proposals. Brodsky (1973, 1976), Ezell (1981, listed under Brodsky), and White (1983) in Appendix A present good models. Remember, too, that under the Freedom of Information Act, you may request copies of funded proposals. Find a program to which you may wish to submit. Call the staff person listed in the *CFDA*, Dusek et al. (1984), or Quarles (1986) for that program and ask how you can get copies of approved proposals.
- If your institution has a grants administration office, ask for its help. Personnel there may be able to provide several things:

1. A person who is familiar with the nature of proposals in your field, either on their staff or in the organization. If the latter, they will probably be willing to make the contact with that person for you.
2. A file of previously successful proposals from your institution that you can examine for ideas.
3. A library of other helpful materials on writing proposals and getting funding for them such as some of the materials listed in Appendix A. Some institutions also have internal publications that describe the procedures to follow to make grant submission and administration go smoothly in their bureaucracy.
4. Information on where to find funding, both governmental and foundation. Many do subscribe to some of the information services that are too expensive for an individual, such as Taft for foundations or Oryx for federal funding. When many people use them, they can be cost effective in an institutional budget. (See Appendix B)
5. Funds to travel to Washington, D.C. so you can visit the appropriate agencies, or to a foundation to try out your ideas in person. Knowing that office budgets rarely have extra money for travel, some institutions have an incentive fund to help individuals get started. Nothing is so reinforcing as finding a sponsor interested in one's ideas, and that comes from making

personal contacts.

6. Contacts with persons in foundations, either from their own personal knowledge or from knowledge of who has such contacts in the institution, so you don't go in "cold."

7. Help with the budget. What is brand new to you is the daily responsibility of these offices. This is the one area where you should be able to count with certainty on their help; it is in their interest to get you funded adequately.

8. Representatives in Washington. Some institutions, particularly universities and large research organizations, maintain representatives in Washington, D.C. Such representatives may have lobbying responsibilities but usually also are willing to help the institution's staff find their way in the bureaucracy. They will usually be able to tell you which offices to contact for funds and also will often be able to provide an introduction. Make use of them; that is part of what they are paid for.

9. Set-up grants to get research started. Usually such grants are for equipment, but sometimes they can be used for personnel and supplies as well. Such a grant can get your research underway so you have something to show an agency. Alternatively, it may pick up the cost of an expensive piece of equipment or personnel time. These investments show an institutional commitment to your work and indicate the institution's confidence in you. This display of confidence is not lost on potential sponsors. And sometimes, by funding a significant portion of your project, an institution can make it feasible for the sponsor to pick up the remaining expenses.

- Make use of your professional organization, especially if it has a grants or governmental affairs person. Few large professional organizations are without someone who serves in a government relations role. Some of the smaller ones that don't have their own belong to the Consortium of Social Science Associations, which published Quarles's (1986) *Guide to Federal Funding for Social Scientists*; they may be helpful. As with institutional representatives, their main responsibility is often lobbying; but they have learned the bureaucracy and know the nature of programs as well as the personnel. Unlike the institutional representative who is expected to cover all academic fields, these individuals are targeted to your own and closely related ones; they nearly always personally know the people you want to see. Their information and advice can be invaluable, but obviously they can't favor you over persons from other organizations, so they will not give the personal attention your institutional representative should be able to give.

- Some professional organizations have grant-writing workshops. These can be helpful not only in giving advice, but also in getting you started writing. The leaders usually expect you to bring in a draft of a proposal to critique. Some, like ones I have run, include a follow-up session in Washington. Appointments are made ahead of time with appropriate agency personnel so individuals go right over to see them while the workshop's assistance in providing a strengthened formulation is still freshly articulated in their minds.

- One of the real hurdles is getting started, beginning to put your ideas on paper. Part of the problem is likely to be the pressure of other duties; more of it is likely to be procrastination and giving proposal preparation too low a priority. Time management specialists agree that your making the decision to give the highest time priority to getting started is critical. Set aside a time and don't let anything else interfere with it. Make the time a large enough block that you can get something done and find a place where you can hide out until you get a draft completed. Revising a draft is always easier. You may also find the advice given near the end of the next chapter with regard to writing useful. Writing problems are not unique to doctoral students.

It is when people turn in sloppy work that they get into trouble. Both staff and reviewers feel that you believed you could put one over on them. It shows disrespect for them and implies your time is more important than theirs. It also shows that you were unwilling to spend the time to take seriously the proposal you were submitting; why, then, should they?

But you need never be ashamed of a proposal that you worked through carefully and prepared as well as you could. Even when we do our best, some of us fail. But even that has its positive aspects: one is that we learn from our failures. A second is that it shows we weren't afraid to try. People respect that; they know that those who don't try, don't learn. Everyone respects a best effort. A best effort is apparent, and staff will typically be most helpful to you. Your having made that kind of effort contributes to the reputation you are building with that agency; they know you will try again, and they want you to succeed. There is advice on what to do with a rejected proposal in Chapter 6; follow it if that should be your fate. But here's hoping that you succeed the first time!

16.
Suggestions and Insights for the Doctoral Student:
1. Dissertation Perspectives

These last two chapters of the book are for those who are or will be facing the doctoral dissertation. This material goes beyond the proposal to include a discussion of all the various dissertation phases and to give practical advice. The first chapter examines differing perspectives on the dissertation among faculty members and between faculty and students. The chapter then explores their consequences for student-faculty interaction and for the graduate student's self-development. The chapter also deals with the most common problems of writing and explores ways of taking advantage of some of the opportunities offered by the dissertation experience.

The next chapter embeds advice within the description of each of the successive steps of the process: choice of problem, choice of adviser and committee, working with adviser and committee, the proposal and its defense, doing the study, writing it up, and the oral examination.

These chapters create an awareness of the dissertation process, so that one can make it a positive experience. If one understands a situation, one is in a much better position to be successful. Professor Harold Hill repeatedly cautions, in the opening song of Meredith Willson's Broadway hit *The Music Man*: "You've got to know the territory; you've got to know the territory." As a professor, you will recall, Hill turns out to be an impostor. But his advice is right on target!

THE FACULTY PERSPECTIVE

Traditions are slow to die. Sometimes they keep their form but change their purpose. To some extent this has happened to the doctoral dissertation. In centuries past, few degrees were awarded; as a capstone, the candidate developed and defended a piece of original thinking before a faculty assembly. The present dissertation is a modified version of this tradition. Indeed, for many faculty and institutions the core idea remains: the dissertation is an original piece of work that demonstrates your capability to contribute significantly to the literature of your field. But approval authority is now vested in a committee that supervises the student's work and in examining committees that in some institutions must approve the dissertation proposal as well as the final dissertation document and in nearly all institutions must give a final oral examination. As a surrogate for the faculty assembly, the final oral examination committee usually includes individuals from outside the student's department, school, or college and occasionally from another university. Further, as a contribution to knowledge, the final manuscript is filed in the university's library and referenced in *University Dissertation Abstracts International* .

These characteristics affirm that very real vestiges of the original view are still preserved. This is particularly true in fields where few degrees are awarded and most of the students intend to become faculty. The product emphasis is also much more likely where the dissertation is part of a larger research study, often an externally funded one. Then, so far as the sponsoring agency is concerned, responsibility for the quality of the dissertation is the project director's, and the dissertation must match in quality the project as a whole.

In fields where large numbers of students take the doctorate, possibly as part of the requirements for some kind of certification, the dissertation tends to be viewed, at least by some faculty, as more of a learning experience. No doubt all faculty would agree that any dissertation has an element of learning in it, but a few faculty and departments see it mainly as a learning process. In a few instances this extends to allowing a dissertation to pass with weaknesses provided the student's write-up makes clear that the problems are recognized and their remedies understood. At the opposite of the process extreme, an occasional faculty member is highly product-oriented and will require that all problems be remedied, even if it means repeating part of the data gathering. By far the majority of faculty are between these extremes, combining emphasis on product and process, especially in accepting unanticipated problems as part of the learning process.

Whether process- or product-oriented, a professor dreams of having a coterie of doctoral students, each working on a part of a problem that is central to his own research. But few students in the behavioral and social sciences and related professions work on projects given them by their major professors. In contrast to the natural sciences, no doubt this is in part due to the paucity of funds and therefore the small likelihood that a student will be employed as research assistant on a funded project from which he might quite naturally derive his dissertation. For whatever reasons, a tradition seems to have grown up that students try to find a problem they can call their own, one that represents some original thought on their part, one they have personally selected, not a topic someone else has chosen for them.

This view has a number of consequences. It puts the problem more on the student's "turf" than the professor's. That does not mean the faculty are uninterested. But they do have less investment in the problem, and it is less likely to contribute directly to their current thinking and research. It also means that some students are likely to come to know more about their problems than the professor, who learns from them as the project proceeds. These characteristics of the process have consequences themselves.

Basically faculty live in a marketplace of ideas where new knowledge is competing for attention with the propagation of the established view of things. One might think that a cooperative stance, in which everyone contributes what he or she can, might result in the fastest growth of new knowledge. But the competitive aspect of the marketplace for ideas tends to cast its pattern on social relationships as well. Broadly speaking, competition, rather than cooperation, is the rule. One may find groups of researchers cooperating as teams, but they are competing with other teams to advance a knowledge claim and to attract the field's thought to their discoveries. (See, for example, J. Watson, *The Double Helix*, New York: Atheneum, 1968.) There is a subtle, usually friendly, competition among faculty to see who can come up with the best ideas, can extend someone else's contribution, is the brightest and most original.

Students doing a dissertation unwittingly enter this arena, in most cases without realizing it, only vaguely understanding the rules of the game and the criteria by which findings become knowledge; many want mainly to complete a requirement and get through rather than enter the competition. As we shall see in the next section, for many students, this is a period of extreme growth, of self-testing, of maturing, of becoming self-assertive. Implicitly, it means entering this competition with the faculty, especially if the student is the expert in a problem. For some students, this is exactly what they want, a chance to show their ability. For a few, it is anxiety-producing, self-threatening, uncomfortable, and conducive to avoidance behaviors--even to the point of not finishing. Most students are between these extremes.

THE STUDENT'S PERSPECTIVE

Just like faculty, students differ in their views of the dissertation. But although both see the learning experience aspects, they tend to emphasize different things. Consider these excerpts from interviews with past and recent graduates:

- It is your first big piece of research that is really *you*!
- Sometimes it is a test of one's intelligence, but it is always a test of one's *endurance*. It is the person *who stays with it* who makes it.
- The dissertation isn't the "be-all and end-all"; keep it in its perspective as a stepping stone and allocate time and energy to it accordingly.
- It's a sensitive time! Your assumptions about yourself are challenged. You learn a lot about yourself and your self-concept. Advisers who understand this are helpful.
- Choose a theme that will speak well for you in the future--one you'll be glad to talk about at job interviews, one you can build on.
- The dissertation process is a radical departure from the courses of the regular curriculum. Those tend to create student dependence on the instructor. Now you must be independent! It is sometimes hard to shift gears. Some of us who are good at the dependent role are uncomfortable in the new one.
- We have chafed under the required course requirements and the paternalistic stance of faculty. This is our opportunity to show we can do it, and do it our way. It can even be like a *second adolescent* declaration of independence!
- Some of us perceive the faculty as though we were paranoid, as though faculty wanted to "wash us out," to make things hard for us.

Fearful of every negative comment, we take every innocent suggestion as evidence of a personal shortcoming. Without a supportive adviser, the dissertation becomes a high hurdle indeed! But, surprisingly, some of those whom you perceive to be the "toughest" faculty may sometimes actually be of the most help.

- This time of your life can be very stressful! It is easy to forget to take care of yourself. Keep your health; pace yourself. You can't make your target dates if pressing too hard causes you to fall ill.

- You feel tremendously *empowered* in handling a problem especially with a solution that your adviser has been dubious about. You feel great when you carry the day!

- This is your last big hurdle; large numbers of us will never do research again. You have to jump it before they will certify you, so grit your teeth and do it. If you have to get your "union card," get it done as quickly as possible and get in the job market. *Bastardis non carborundum!* [sic] Maintain your equanimity!

- I told my professor, Dr. Ray Kuhlen, that I hoped my dissertation would be a searchlight that would brilliantly illumine some long-sought item of knowledge. He countered with "Whoa! You are more likely to light a little candle to stick out there on an island at the dark boundary of what is now known." I would add, "Don't go too far; knowledge is the illumination of lots of small candles."

IMPLICATIONS OF DIFFERING FACULTY AND STUDENT VIEWS

As we have seen, there are differences in perception of the dissertation experience among faculty as well as between students and faculty. In addition, there are environmental pressures that modulate the behavior of each group. All this has implications both for the interaction between student and faculty and for the nature of the dissertation itself. Let us examine some of these.

Implications for the Nature of the Dissertation

Since faculty differ in their views of the dissertation, how am I to know what constitutes a dissertation, when it is a contribution to knowledge? How far out must be that island on which I stick my little candle? How close to the other candles? And, by the way, how big is a "little candle"?

Every graduate student reads prior dissertations with an eye to "What is going to be expected of me? How much is enough?" And sometimes when the committee or adviser requests you to do more or change something, there is the query "Why me? You didn't require it of Chris Anderson last year!!"

Put yourself in the faculty's shoes. You are working with students individually, trying to ensure that their problem is appropriate for them and is a good learning experience. Would you hold the same standards for each one? Would you let your best students go unstretched? Would you require your least able to do a study they are sure to be unable to complete? Certainly not! And neither, typically, do faculty! If you find yourself being stretched, that is probably a compliment to you--although it may be of little comfort at the time.

As must be apparent from the section on faculty views of the dissertation, standards vary. Let there be no mystery about this--the variance is a combination of perceived student ability and faculty expectation. Some dissertation committee chairs routinely demand more from their students than others. Sometimes new faculty have difficulty calibrating their demands to what is reasonable, requiring either too much or too little until they gain experience. Some, *but not all,* faculty will change standards under pressing circumstances, as when a student must finish to start a new position. But to make it a meaningfully individualized experience, standards must vary; and they do.

So, what constitutes a dissertation? The nature, methodology, and size are strictly matters for negotiation between you and your committee, the chair of the committee usually taking the most active role. You must work with them to make sure your project meets whatever standards are perceived to apply as well as your personal expectations of what it will do for you. (More about the latter later.) To the extent that existing norms are embodied in past dissertations, in the minds of outside readers, and in the graduate school,[1] it is up to your chair and committee to interpret these as they apply to you and your project.

Must the dissertation have positive results to be acceptable? A proposal ought to have a reasonable chance of showing positive results. But if it doesn't work out as expected, must you start over? Despite rumors to the contrary, both Steinberg (1981) and I know of no instance where this has been required. Instead, students are asked to explain as best they can why negative results appeared and what can be learned from the apparent blind alley.

Which is the better choice, faculty who emphasize the dissertation learning process or those who emphasize a quality product? This is a trade-off. As the question suggests, it is best if one can make mistakes, learn from them, and have a quality product too; that is the ideal and many dissertation experiences approach it. The choice may have been made for you by selection of your initial graduate adviser or by departmental or institutional policy. But if not, and given a Hobson's choice, what are the implications each way?

Emphasis on the process aspect can result in a faster track; one may get more faculty attention if that is what one desires (many don't; see

---

[1]Some institutions have graduate schools responsible for facilitating graduate work and maintaining standards. In some of these, only those designated as graduate faculty can supervise dissertations and serve on committees. Typically institutions with the oldest graduate programs (not necessarily the strongest, however) do not so differentiate faculty, and some have no graduate school.

"Implications for Student Self-Development," below), and in truth, once one is employed, what one does after the dissertation is more important than the dissertation itself. Faculty emphasizing process are often not researchers themselves. In fact, they frequently have more than their share of advisees, so that they have little time for their own research. Clearly this is a popular path, especially for those for whom the doctorate is essentially a route to some kind of professional certification. Further, since these faculty see many students seeking that certification, they are in a good position to give comparative recommendations for appropriate positions and are often queried. Giving them a chance to know you through your dissertation helps them write an appropriate recommendation.

However, faculty who emphasize a quality product are equally concerned that you learn as well. They are more likely to be experienced researchers themselves, and they can be excellent models of how to do research as they work with you on your problem. Apprenticing is a great way to learn an art, and there is much about research that is art as well as science. Many such faculty will have national reputations based on their publications and thus will be visible on the national scene. A recommendation from them for academic and research positions may be very valuable, and they are also likely to be queried about suitable candidates for such positions.

If research is part of the responsibility of the entry-level position you seek, a well-done dissertation can be an important competitive factor. Candidates seeking a faculty position are often asked to present a colloquium based on their dissertation; a good dissertation is a harbinger of their work if hired.

So there are things to be said for both approaches--the best of both being probably the most desirable. But your choice may be slanted toward one end or the other by the importance of research in the position you seek and by the available faculty.

Implications for Student-Faculty Interaction

Obviously I am building my reputation by doing my dissertation, but sometimes I get the feeling that my professor's is on the line too. Is this true? Universities' reputations are typically little changed by the quality of their dissertations. In part that is because there is very little communication among universities about the run-of-the-mill dissertations and few behavioral science dissertations are published. But within universities with dissertation committee meetings and oral examinations that are group affairs, there is much more communication about dissertations among the faculty of a school or college. We've already noted that faculty operate in a competitive marketplace of ideas and there is a subtle competition among them. The situation is ripe for judgments to be made. Indeed, since the outside members of an oral examination committee are charged with deciding whether the product is acceptable, judgments cannot be avoided. Further, although the dissertation may be perceived as a demonstration of your competence, that competence is presumably built on the training you have received from faculty as a doctoral student. Therefore, it is a demonstration that can be perceived as reflecting on the faculty, your adviser, and your dissertation committee.

If you sit in on dissertation oral examinations, you will occasionally see the dissertation committee chair become defensive at the criticism implied in the questions of outsiders who were not on the committee. I have seen the discussion become a "free for all" in which the chair of the examination must remind everyone that the candidate, not the faculty, is being examined. Clearly when this occurs the dissertation committee chair perceived that an injustice was being done to the student, the dissertation committee, its chair, and maybe all of them. Their reputations in the eyes of their colleagues were involved.

So, although you knew your reputation was at stake, you probably had not thought about the fact that, to a considerably lesser extent but not entirely trivially, what you do reflects on your major adviser and on your committee. You may justifiably reject this notion, arguing, "This is my degree, not anyone else's." And of course from one standpoint you are perfectly right; perhaps faculty egos shouldn't be involved. Nonetheless, we have not found a way to prevent it; and unfortunately, in some cases, the negative judgments are entirely justified--chair and committee may not have provided adequate or appropriate guidance.

It helps to understand situations if you stand in the other person's shoes (just as you'll often want your adviser and committee to stand in yours as the process proceeds!).[2] So if you can sense when your adviser and committee feel uncomfortable, you will better understand their advice. Their discomfort is usually signaled by requests to change your plans or the dissertation itself. Such changes are usually to satisfy their own criteria of a satisfactory study but on occasion are requested with an eye on those shadowy figures looking over their shoulder who will later judge the study in the oral or when it is made publicly available. For both your sake and theirs, your chair and committee want it to be acceptable.

Dissertation chairs are almost universally supportive of their candidates both in committee meetings and in oral examinations. But occasionally students are surprised to find themselves criticized by their chair in those situations. What happened? The student "went through a red light!" Only rarely does such criticism occur without prior warning, but some students pay it no heed; they insist on having their way. The adviser tries to make them see the light--cut the study down, try another problem, run a pilot test, use a different method of analysis, add a needed explanation, defer the oral examinations for more changes, or whatever

---

[2]It is to be hoped that they will, but whether they do is in part up to you. The graduate student who educates the adviser and committee about her situation and problems has a much better time of it!

else is needed. If the student still insists, the adviser may reluctantly assent; but rather than lose her reputation, she joins the fray, especially when the problem is found by others. If this happens to you early in the process, it tells you that you have not been adequately alert to "red lights." Later in the process, when you are hurrying to finish, try not to let your frenzy blind you to warning signals.

What else is going on in this process that I as a student should be aware of?   Dissertation work helps develop and refine the faculty's own notions about what is good research and research practice. Since it is the student's project rather than the faculty member's that is the focus of discussion at dissertation committee meetings, faculty are less personally threatened and considerable learning can take place. Ideas can be tried out in this small collegial group that might result in uncomfortable criticism if ventured in a larger and more public one. This is especially true of new faculty who are still making their reputation and being socialized to faculty ways.

In a larger sense, the doctoral process serves to help operationalize, to reinforce, and to provide a forum for modifying the social norms within which science proceeds for all faculty. This applies especially to the social and behavioral sciences, where team research is rare and each faculty member usually pursues a research niche in an individual way. Under these circumstances, the proposal defense and the oral examination provide especially important arenas in which notions about what is good, or at least acceptable, science can be discussed.

Consider the final doctoral dissertation and defense: The committee has indicated its provisional approval of the dissertation when it lets the oral be scheduled--the dissertation meets its operational definition of acceptable research. The outside reviewers or readers operationalize their idea of what is acceptable research in their critique of what the candidate has done. Often the committee may agree that it has missed something the outside reviewer caught. Occasionally, however, the outside reviewer's idea of what is acceptable research may operationalize as something different from the committee's. This may break out overtly as argument. More often, each side gives a little to provide grounds for agreement. But it is in these exchanges that the norms of science are made real for faculty, are reinforced as they agree on remedial actions, or are modified for a faculty member as he comes to see things in a different light. These examinations serve a very important and continuing inservice training role for faculty--especially as they work with students who are using new methods and new instruments and are venturing into new areas.

What are the implications for students? There is little that students can do about this except to recognize that it may be occurring when there are disagreements among faculty. This often explains substantial changes in faculty opinion. Faculty themselves realize that this occurs but rarely conceptualize the doctoral process in these terms and do little to maximize this aspect of the process. But they usually protect the student from the consequences of changed opinions, recognizing they were at fault in the first place. The relatively few instances where they don't, however, represent a small, but potential, hazard the student has to negotiate his way through.

   Since the topic I chose is off-target from my chair's research focus, it might help me to know what motivates her to work with me. You may need to work harder to find someone who will chair your committee if your work is so distinctly your own that none of the faculty feel competent to work with you. But such cases are rare; more often your work is in the same field, it just is not on their particular research target. That has its advantages, since it helps faculty to keep abreast of their field more broadly than they might do with their own reading. Faculty learn from you when you tell them about new material. You will read more widely than they have time to and will digest and evaluate recent literature they haven't yet got to--a real favor.

   Further, most faculty genuinely enjoy being involved in the unstructured problem-solving dissertation process. They like what Blanton (1983) calls "the stimulation of finding creative solutions to problems, and an empathic sense of adventure" (p. 74). They share the joy of the successful student. The deeply satisfying development of someone who may take their place someday, someone who may exceed their own accomplishments, is an ever-present possibility. (Granted there are exceptions, faculty who have grown tired and jaded, but those probably are not faculty to invite for your committee.)

   Students need to recognize, however, that there is also a downside to faculty taking on dissertation responsibilities in the social and behavioral sciences. In contrast to the natural and biological sciences, such responsibility is usually in addition to their other duties, rather than there being any load adjustment. Most faculty accept this situation, and it creates no problems except when certain faculty are overloaded and the department has no mechanism for spreading the burden. Sometimes everyone tries to finish at once; this semester, I am on the committees of six students who hope to finish--a lot of reading. When the faculty member's load is heavy and a student can adjust his schedule to relieve it, he will probably get not only a more careful reading but also more help from the faculty member. When faculty have too many committee assignments, there is less incentive for them to work with the student who has no intrinsic motivation to work on the dissertation. An increased premium is placed on the student's finding a problem that results in the mutual attraction of student and faculty on a problem of common interest.

   For most faculty, however, seeing students successfully through the dissertation is one of the most important things they do. A student who successfully completes the requirements reflects favorably on faculty and gives them a sense of having contributed to the student, their university, their field of study, and, ultimately, society.

Implications for Student Self-Development

Student comments indicate that doing one's dissertation is a growth experience, possibly a second adolescence. What are the implications? After many highly structured graduate courses, most students are suddenly thrust into an independent role, and it's a new feeling. You can discern that in the students' view of the dissertation: "It is really *you!*" "It's a sensitive time! You learn a lot about yourself." "Now you must be independent! It is sometimes hard to shift gears." "It becomes a self-test: I have to make it!" "You feel tremendously empowered."

The dissertation can be a real growth experience. As Blanton (1983) notes: "Many students seem to mature as persons as well as scholars during this phase. . . . Their abilities to set priorities, organize time, and manage conflict often improve. Rather than having to please a single instructor, they must learn to juggle the expectations of an entire committee and, at an even higher level, to take responsibility for and evaluate their own work" (p. 74). Most grasp this opportunity and grow greatly as they meet these challenges.

In the quotations earlier in the chapter, one student suggests that attaining independence at this level is somewhat analogous to an earlier developmental stage: "It can even be like a *second adolescent* declaration of independence!" Consider this comment by a completed student: "Many colleagues found it convenient and rewarding to carve out dissertation topics from their major professor's larger research projects, but something inside me actively resisted. I still feel good about my own thesis work, not just because it was done well, but because it was conceived and completed independently."

This fits what a number of faculty members said when I asked how they had done their dissertations. With only one exception, these men and women said that once they had their proposal approved, *they went off on their own and did it.* They had very little help from their committee or adviser and wanted it that way. This was *their* study, and they wanted to prove to themselves and others that they could do it!

"Second adolescence" isn't quite the right name for this phenomenon, which combines an assertion of independence and a need to demonstrate one's capability. Graduate students are mature adults. "Second adolescence" could imply regression to an earlier stage; that is clearly *not* intended. But there are useful and analogous parallels between the switch from the structured life of the child to the freedom and testing of youth and the change from the professor's course-structured demands to the self-developed structure of the dissertation; between the instructor's setting problems within students' ability limits to provide success and the students' choice of problems that test their limits. Further, just as adolescents' problems are lessened by their gaining perspective on their development, so giving graduate students perspective is intended to result in greater comfort with their situation and the ability to better adjust their actions appropriately.

For example, when one realizes that graduate students' actions result from this desire to stand on their own and show what they can do, then two of their most common problems are quite understandable: 1) rejecting suitable dissertation topics suggested by the adviser and 2) proposing too grandiose a project. In the first instance they are implicitly saying, "I don't need your help, I can find a topic on my own!" In the second, they want to show they can do something "significant." They dislike reducing the size because their professor is perceived as saying, "You can't do it! You are less capable than you thought you were. You have to be protected from yourself just as when you were a child!"

With such a perspective students can understand why they rejected certain help that was offered, why they attempted as much as they did, and why they mentally resisted their adviser's suggestion to make certain changes in the study, especially simplifying it or cutting it down. This perspective can be freeing by helping one realize that really mature problem solvers take the best of what is offered, integrate it with their own thinking, and develop a teamwork or partnership relationship where "two heads are better than one."

We noted earlier that faculty work in a marketplace of ideas and that there is a subtle competition to be the best and brightest. Graduate students experiencing a need to prove themselves may become increasingly self-assertive with their chair and committee. One can sense that this can implicitly merge them into the competition. Faculty who do not realize what the student is experiencing may react overenthusiastically and automatically rise to the challenge, overpowering the neophyte and perhaps improperly instilling self-doubt, maybe even resentment, in the student. Faculty often recognize what is happening too late and apologize or try to retreat, but the damage is often done. So faculty, too, can benefit from this perspective by recognizing the desire for independence when it appears, trying to help students in ways that facilitate their feelings of accomplishment and self-esteem, and to the extent possible, modulating their own ways of working to better fit the independence needs of the student.

Though apparently experienced by a great many, the need for freedom and to prove oneself is not experienced by all. Indeed, the amount of independence sought varies with the student, as, incidentally, the amount given depends on the faculty member. Most give a great deal of freedom; some hold a tighter rein. Like so many other aspects of this process, it is a matter of exploration and negotiation to arrive at a level satisfactory to both parties. Open communication about one's dependence or independence needs helps. A faculty member may take the lead in opening such a discussion, but if she doesn't, then the student, particularly if feeling these needs, will have to tactfully initiate it.

This is a sensitive time when it is easy to take criticism personally. Is it really meant that way? Because this is such a sensitive time--one is venturing where one is unsure--it is easy to take criticism as though it signaled personal deficiency. "You didn't include the basic theory in your literature review!" isn't meant to suggest you were too dumb or too lazy to do so. It indicates a deficiency that, for whatever reason it occurred, needs to be remedied and possibly learned from. Don't take criticism of your work at any stage personally.

Faculty occasionally get so enthusiastic about making a point that they do so tactlessly. Some few, I hope none on your committee, build themselves up by cutting others down. Among faculty widely chosen for committees this is rare, but if you encounter it, try not to take it as a threat to your competence. After all, you've put more time on this than they have, and you know a great deal about it--no doubt more than they think you do. It is tough, possibly the toughest of the things you'll have to do; but detach yourself and look at the criticism as impersonally as possible. If it hurts, go to a movie with a good friend. Then tomorrow reexamine it and take from the criticism whatever seems appropriate.

Quite frankly, unless you live and work as a hermit, this won't be the last time your work will be criticized. The more research you do, the more likely you are to run into someone whose threshold for what is knowledge is different from yours (as per the definition of "knowledge" in Chapter 11) or who views your design choices as less valid than you judged them to be. Whenever one publishes work, even in *Dissertation Abstracts,* one opens oneself to public criticism. Most of us can expect that not all will go smoothly, and some of the criticism may border on invective if we touch a sensitive spot. Rise above it and try to understand where they are coming from; it's tough, but do it. When you look back later, you'll realize this is one of the best pieces of advice you ever took.

If you find it difficult to follow this advice and find the interaction with faculty undermining your self-confidence, take a friend with you to these meetings. Find one who can be honest with you, whom you trust, and who can look reasonably objectively at what is being suggested. This in itself may moderate the comments. But, more important, discussions with your friend following such sessions will most likely lead to better handling of the sessions on your own.

Is working on a dissertation really like a roller coaster ride from jubilation to the slough of despond? People vary in the pattern they experience, but few go through without some high and low points; periods of growth seldom proceed smoothly. Grant (1986, p. 65), a recent graduate, writes: "Expect to have periods of black despair over the whole thing. One Christmas I was home working while others were travelling and partying, and I had just hit a particularly difficult obstacle with the thesis. I was speaking to a friend long distance who had just recently finished his dissertation. 'How are you?' he asked. I told him. 'Terrible, I'll never do it. I thought this part was fine and now there seem to be insurmountable problems. I can't even think about it anymore.' 'Good,' he said, 'You must be almost done with that part.' He was right. When you hit the low points, give yourself a break. It will pass."

Steinberg (1981) notes that problems seem to fall in three areas:

"negative and gloomy feelings about the dissertation . . . ; a diminishment of self-esteem; a real or believed deterioration in relationships with significant others" (p. 159). If you feel you need help, Steinberg gives very good advice in his chapter "Down in the Dissertation Dumps: How to Get Out" as well as in his final chapter. Here is a sampling:[3]

Feelings about the dissertation:

> *"I picked the wrong topic."*--"Almost all ABD's believe at one time o r another . . . . that their particular topic was 'wrong' " (p. 216). With "so much groundwork and prior committee approval and validation . . . there is no such thing as the wrong topic" (p. 160).

> *"I'm ruined. The data aren't panning out."*--"Almost invariably some of the data do not pan out" (p. 160). "In the real work of dissertation writing everybody has to use a range of . . .after the fact adjustments . . . to (the initial) plans"(p. 217).

> *"Nothing comes; I can't write another word; the well's gone dry."*-- "Periods of blockage are inevitable . . . The only way out here . . . is to put in the daily time . . . whether the juices are running or not. Immersion . . . will--a few days sooner or later--prime the pump once more. The absolutely worst possible path is to lay off. Upon return from a three-week break, in my experience, the trail will be colder than ever" (pp. 160-161). I'm not sure Steinberg is entirely right about the latter. I'd agree that "sticking with it" is important; indeed, sometimes the prospect of taking a break can unconsciously reinforce a blockage. Further, this is consistent with most advice to professional writers. But if, after sticking with it, one is still blocked, sometimes taking a break is helpful. True, it does take extra time to get back into it, but a fresh perspective and the renewal of enthusiasm that often occurs after a restful break can be very helpful, particularly if one has been fixated on the wrong perspective. Another alternative is to work on another part that is better structured and then come back to the blocked section. Often one's unconscious will have reorganized things so they now flow.

Feelings about oneself:

> *"What have I gotten myself into? I must have been crazy to take such a job on."*--"It is common for candidates . . . to suffer second thoughts. When a candidate is in mid-dissertation doldrums, he has to 'get back to basics,' remind himself that a whole history of dissertation development--involving countless days of proposal writing, negotiations . . . field work . . . chapter drafting--preceded today's urge to rip up Chapter Three" (pp. 162-163). No point in giving up all that previous

---

[3]The quotations in this section from David Steinberg's How to Complete and Survive a Dissertation are used with permission of St. Martin's Press, Inc., Copyright©1981, David Steinberg.

investment now; every journey is completed just one step at a time;
keep taking steps and you'll get there.

"Bob and Carol finished, and I'm the dummy who's left behind."--
"Dissertation writing is not really a 'group sport,' but much more like
an individual one. If the dissertation is any kind of competition at all,
it is one with yourself, on the order of a marathon, where . . . the goal
is simply to finish" (p. 163).

Feelings about relations with others:

"I'm selling my soul to the committee."--"The faculty-demanded
accommodations . . . that one makes with so much pain . . . during
dissertation days will appear trivial upon five-years-hence reflection
(if, indeed, one remembers them at all)" (p. 163).

"It's coming between me and Jack/Jill."--"Dissertation times are
trying ones for family and love relationships. In certain serious
respects, living with an ABD wrapped up in his thesis is like living
with a handicapped or 'problem' person (e.g., an alcoholic). Support
and information groups" for candidates' partners similar to those for
the candidates themselves may be helpful (p. 167).

The course of writing a dissertation, like true love, seldom runs
smoothly. One's major adviser, a supportive committee member, support
groups (see below), or an advanced graduate student who has gone through
the same thing can often be helpful. But sometimes it is enough to know
that such feelings and concerns are quite normal and that substantial
numbers have overcome problems exactly parallel to yours and run the
course successfully; so can you.

Do support groups really help?   There is considerable evidence that
support groups are a great help to persons under stress, and certainly
periods of growth are typically such times. Some of the group are
experiencing periods of self-doubt, while others have got past that point
and are feeling empowered for a change. There can be considerable
opportunity for catharsis as well as gaining insight in sharing experiences.
Further, unless you are one of those rare individuals who plan their time
and need no help in keeping on task, prioritizing use of time, and keeping
things in perspective, a support group can be of tremendous help.

Get together a group of individuals who are all going through the
process at about the same time, if possible from roughly the same area of
study. Often such groups are already underway and you can join one.
Support group members can react to one another's ideas at the problem-
finding stage, critique one another's proposals, make suggestions about
finding a suitable adviser and committee, facilitate the organization of
material (the literature, data, and so on), see hidden faults in the design
of a study, suggest how to get the data, provide an expanded network of
contacts for data collection as well as assistance in its collection, see
things in the data one may have missed, critique one's analysis plans, and

react to one's conclusions. Best of all, having a group that expects you to perform and to do so on the dates that you promised markedly facilitates living up to the schedule you have set.

In addition to such direct help on the dissertation, a group can help put faculty criticism in perspective, overcoming the initial emotional response, focusing on its content, and helping to formulate an appropriate next action. Indeed, the support, help, and friendly competition that a support group provides can mean the difference for some individuals between getting through and being an ABD. Steinberg (1981, pp. 180-187) has additional useful suggestions for such groups.

WRITING THE DISSERTATION

Writing the dissertation is quite a different experience from writing a term paper. A term paper is of such a size that one can think it through before sitting down to write, and then write it. Listen to Donald Chisholm (1986), just graduated and writing advice to those who follow:

> Usually the dissertation is the largest and most complex work any of us will have attempted by that stage of our careers. It cannot be held in our heads as a complete entity, and must be decomposed into smaller, more manageable problems, which of course are themselves never discrete or simple. Dissertations have to be done piecemeal, relying on notes, outlines and other memory aids to help us along the way p. 66 .

For term papers, as Becker (1986) notes, the process of writing consists in taking one's first writing and polishing it into final draft. With the dissertation, by contrast, for many (but not all) of us, the first step is a matter of getting the material out of our heads and onto paper. Our thoughts come faster than our fingers can translate them into words; the trick is to capture them and get them down. Then they can be organized into a coherent analytical pattern and one can construct the first real draft. Here is Chisholm again:

> It came to me only in the midst of the dissertation that the logic of presentation in academic work rarely resembles the logic of discovery or creation. Writing turned out to be messier and more roundabout than I had ever imagined. When my mind refused to work in . . . linear fashion . . . I initially despaired, and then surrendered, writing on the problem my mind wished to entertain at the time. Nothing I wrote was ever thrown away; instead I filed it so I would stumble over it when I reached a point where it might fit p. 67 .

In addition to giving good advice, note that here is a person who has learned his writing style. That is very important. It is surprising how many students have not experimented with different writing patterns to find out which works best for them. If possible, do so before you begin your dissertation work. There are a number of approaches; here are some possible patterns and my reactions to them for your consideration:

- *Progressive Outline.* Make a rough outline of all the major sections; then as you begin each section, outline it in detail before writing it. No doubt you were taught to outline your writing when you were in elementary and secondary school. If you can make this work for you, great! Your work will be well organized, and you can probably pick it up as you wish, working on it a piece at a time. This is a big advantage if you can't find large blocks of time--and most of us can't. Although nearly all of us were taught to outline, it doesn't work well for all of us; other methods may fit us better.

- *Detailed Outlining.* Outline the whole project in detail before you begin. This is even harder than progressive outlining, since it means that you need to think through the whole study from the very first and then keep material in its place as you write it (otherwise adjustments may be extensive and time-consuming). Excellent work can be done this way. A friend of mine wrote a 35-page outline for his study and had it approved by his chair. The study was so good it was later published by a university press. This method is even better for picking up and laying down, as most of us have to, since the detailed outline holds everything in place. But outlining the study from the beginning is a formidable and time-consuming job.

- *Letting It Flow.* Sit down with an idea of what you plan to write, and let it flow. When you pick it up again, read what you have previously written, *leave it alone* (or you'll spend all your time revising it), and proceed with the next section. You can always revise later once you have all the major pieces. This method reminds me of Rosner and Abt's (1970) interview with Neil Simon, the playwright, in their book on creativity. Simon said his friends had encouraged him to outline on the assumption that it would improve his plays. He tried it but couldn't make the characters fit the outline; it just wouldn't work. He found that he needed to get the characters well in mind and let them interact. As he described these interactions, the plays wrote themselves.

Writing dissertations is not exactly like writing plays, yet there are a number of characteristics that do demand treatment on their own terms and could be thought to act like characters in a play. Sitting down and deciding which "characters" enter when will allow you to let the dissertation evolve.

But Simon, like most writers, likes to work continuously when in the midst of a project, hardly stopping to eat. You can understand this when you discover the problem of reentering a piece of writing after a layoff. That is a weakness of the "go with the flow" method. One is likely to rewrite the first chapter forty times and never get to the rest of the dissertation. One has to resist this, difficult as it may be. Chisholm (1986) says: "I also tried never quite to finish a thought as I closed the day, so that I would be provided with priming of the pump on the following day" (p. 68).

● *Starting Where It's "Hot"*. Write the section you are ready to write, no matter where it is in the study. You do your best work writing the section that you have thought about and feel motivated to take on. This is an interesting method if you do your best writing where it is "hot"; many of us do. But it then means that all the pieces have to be fitted together, and this can be a formidable task. Probably this method is best practiced in conjunction with some form of crude outlining.

The list by no means exhausts the possibilities. It is merely intended to illustrate them and to get *you* thinking about *your* pattern. Try to find your best one; it will help considerably.

Make a work space.   Where you do your writing can have quite an effect on your ability to persist and, especially, to concentrate. Although there may be differences in innate ability, some research suggests that it is the capacity to concentrate whatever ability we have that enables us to be effective. For most of us, having a place to work that is *completely dedicated* to the dissertation task and keeping it *free from interruption and distraction* will markedly facilitate that concentration and, therefore, the speed and effectiveness of our work. Indeed, it can mean the difference between finishing and being an ABD.

The space need not be fancy, but having a separate room helps. Steinberg (1981) notes that research shows children with their own room perform better in school and concludes, "There is every reason to believe such . . . effects stretch into adult performance" (p. 43). If the space is only a corner of a room, try to fence it off with file cabinets and bookshelves. Lack of a phone, unless it is needed for the dissertation, is an asset. The Center for Advanced Study in the Social and Behavioral Sciences intentionally provides phoneless studies. Some university libraries make carrels available to dissertation students; they are superb work spaces. Check out their availability.

The space should be yours for the dissertation work only, and family members should respect your privacy when it is being so used. Keep it free of other tasks that might cause your attention to wander--bills to pay, letters to answer, phone messages to return. A colleague of mine has a checklist that he suggests his students use to prepare for each writing session. It includes anything one could think of that might provide an excuse for leaving the writing area: before you start, provide candy, gum, soft drinks; sharpen pencils; get markers as well as pens; use the bathroom; take a drink; and so on.

Schedule your writing time.   Use the space regularly; most people find it helps to set a schedule and *stay with it* even if nothing happens. Sometimes in the last few minutes a block will clear and one can really start to write. The very productive psychologist B. F. Skinner is said to have a desk he reserves for his professional writing with a light attached to a timer that ensures that he puts in at least two hours a day. Steinberg notes that Hemingway kept a chart of his word output, which averaged 500 words a day, and when he played hooky one day, he made it up the next (1981, p. 56).

How long should the time blocks be? Two things need to be optimized: a minimum of time spent in getting back to where you left off, and a long enough time so that when you do get into the swing of it, you are able to make some progress. Just what is the best length needed to accommodate these two functions will vary with the problem, your memory, and your freedom to get large blocks of free time. Some problems can be kept fresh by putting in small amounts of work on them daily. Others require large blocks of time to get into them and make progress, so setting aside a whole day once a week or more works best. Find your optimum, but be sure to minimize going back and rewriting until you get a complete draft. It is difficult; I must have rewritten my first chapter twenty times to get back into the swing of working on it after long lay-offs. Too often that took most of the available time until after the next lay-off. You get nowhere that way!

Word processing. If you already can type well enough to compose at the keyboard and can get access to a word processing system, it is worth learning how to use it. It will save you a great deal of time in revisions, and once an error or typo is corrected, it stays corrected; one doesn't have new ones introduced, as often happens in retyping. The use of good spelling software catches most of the typographic errors. My style is to do a draft on the word processor, print it out, and revise the draft by hand. Nearly everyone agrees that it is difficult to catch all your errors rereading copy on the screen. Having someone else make the corrections is the most efficient use of my time; even with word processing's ease of making corrections, I spend too much time trying to attain "perfect" copy.

Every microcomputer has a variety of word processing programs that will work on it. The easiest one to learn may not be sophisticated enough to handle footnotes and other complexities. It may be worthwhile to learn a more complex one.

Investigate what form of computer output is acceptable as final dissertation form at your university. Most require letter-quality printing and will not accept a dot-matrix product, although that may change as the printers improve. There are usually ways of getting a letter-quality printout, but it may require more than you think, considering software mismatch problems. Try a sample all the way through the process before you commit yourself to a given combination of word processor and equipment. Alternatively, your word-processed draft can be used as copy for a typist. Even it that seems a waste of time and resources, it can be the way to go, especially if you need the help a good typist provides in cleaning up spelling and punctuation. Don't assume, however, that because the work was done by a professional typist it will be errorless. Check the typist's work; proofread your manuscript.

Hiring a typist. If you cannot compose at the keyboard, consider hiring a typist. Even if it seems a waste of time and resources, it can be the way to go, especially if you need the help a good typist provides in cleaning up spelling and punctuation.   Don't assume, however, that because the work was done by a professional typist that it will be errorless.   Check the typist's work; proofread your manuscript.   If the university's format regulations are stringently enforced, you can save considerable time and agony by employing a typist who is familiar with the system.   The graduate school or college office usually maintains a list of such persons, and they can be worth their weight in gold, especially for the final copy.

In my own case, dissertations were reviewed by Ms. Turabian, the author of the most widely used style guide.   She would flip the pages, spotting errors as they went by; she would then circle the error with a grease pencil to ensure that the page had to be retyped to correct the error! Needless to say, candidates were scared to death of this process. I worked with a lady on the graduate office's recommended list; and when all was in order, she asked me to meet her at Ms. Turabian's office. When I arrived, she told me to stand near the door and let her do the talking. It was spring, and she carried a big bunch of daffodils she had picked from her backyard.   She bounded into the office, proceeded to greet Ms. Turabian enthusiastically and to arrange the flowers on her desk, meanwhile, presenting the dissertation for her sign-off, but chatting with her all the while as she perused it. Needless to say, she got off with no pages to redo. It is possible there were none that needed to be redone; I'll never know. But I do know that it was well worth the extra cost to have her on my side. Ask around and find such a typist!

Protect your copy. Be sure to put a copy of your draft where it will be safe from loss or other disaster. *Freezer compartments around the country are protecting thousands of manuscripts*--to the distress of spouses who assumed that space was available for food. You may wish to make copies of your drafts. Nothing is more disheartening than to lose the text and have to start over! Students often have nightmares about losing their drafts. It is highly unlikely, but take no chances.

If you are using word processing, back up your discs, even if you have a hard disc storage. At some institutions you can send your copy via modem to the mainframe storage.   Mainframes routinely back up their storage, but find out how long they keep their back-ups.

The value of prior experience. For the experienced person, doing research presents difficulties enough; for the graduate student, having to simultaneously "learn while doing" the first time through clearly complicates an already complex situation.   There are a variety of possibilities for gaining prior experience: doing a master's thesis, participating in a research internship, taking a course or seminar built around doing a research project, or having a research assistantship. Some close association with the research process helps a great deal in knowing how to carry out a dissertation.   There is, of course, some practice value in the research one does for the numerous course papers, but few of these are sufficiently extensive pieces of research, and few go beyond the library phase. The more extensive the experience, the better.

The master's thesis is ideal in this respect, since it requires the same kind of problem identification, methodological selection ("methodological homesteading"), and follow-through to completion as the doctoral dissertation. Indeed, the master's thesis is often the preliminary or pilot phase of the dissertation and thus gives directly parallel experience. Even if you change topics, the experience is very valuable. So, if at all possible, *gain some prior experience with the combination of research and carefully organized writing before taking on the dissertation.*

OPPORTUNITIES PROVIDED BY THE DISSERTATION

Fulfilling the dissertation requirement can be turned into very special opportunities for your benefit; it requires some forethought and planning. Among other possibilities, you can use it to:

o   Learn or practice particular research, political, and communication skills.
o   Become acquainted with a particular faculty member who knows something you would like to learn.
o   Become acquainted with one who, later, might be able to help place you in a good job.
o   Get a start on a publication.

Learning a Skill

By the time you get to this level of the doctorate, you are getting personal supervision by a faculty member. This is an excellent time to pick up special skills and to have the personal help of a skilled expert in doing so. Such a person isn't usually going to be able to take the time to teach you from the beginning, but if you have an entry-level competence, she can take you a good bit further. In my own case, I wanted to learn the Rorschach and the IBM equipment of the day. I found a topic that combined these and got great training in both; the IBM skill later helped me understand computer programming. You can often find a topic that allows you to master a skill you wish to learn at the same time you investigate an interesting area.

Of special value is the opportunity to get to know someone whose work habits, conceptual skill, understanding of a particular phenomenon, administrative or social skill, or research technique you admire. Much can be learned in the informal and usually numerous meetings that occur over the development of the dissertation.

Becoming Acquainted with Faculty

In large departments, students may have difficulty getting faculty to know them well enough to give them meaningful recommendations for employment. The dissertation experience is particularly useful in this regard, since you generally come to know your committee quite well. In informal meetings where you can express yourself freely just as faculty are doing, everyone gets a better idea of what the others are like. The opportunity to get a valuable reference for your placement file is there and possibly some help in calling your attention to employment possibilities in addition. Faculty tend to feel more responsibility to place in good positions those students they have worked with and come to know well.

Remembering the "second adolescence" phenomenon, you may wish to have a situation with freedom to make mistakes and benefit from them so long as they don't get you into serious trouble. Exploration is half the fun of research. Other researchers know that, and most committees would like you to have that fun. Remember, the nature of your dissertation and the relationship with your faculty are matters of negotiation between you, your chair, and your committee. Let them know what you would like to do and how you'd like to do it. If they think your project is feasible, they will likely cheer you on and help.

By contrast, if you seem to lack direction, they will most likely try to provide it; that is their way of assisting you. If that is the way you want it, fine; if not, decide to take responsibility for the direction of your work and negotiate with your committee toward that end.

What are the symptoms of not "being in the driver's seat"? Steinberg (1981, p. 36) notes how students complain that every time they see a committee member he will "find something else wrong, or something else for me to add." One professor suggests adding another variable to the study, another a change in design, yet another additional cases and data collection sites. What is going on? The faculty are trying to be helpful; but like the blind men with the elephant, they are viewing your dissertation from whatever part is most salient for them. (They may also have different ideas of what is good research--see the end of Chapter 11.)

While this piecemeal problem solving adds to the student's confusion, the situation is compounded by the fact that the student is still not on top of his problem. "To do a dissertation one has to . . . have in mind the big picture; if you fail to have the grand design blocked out, then you are constantly at the compartmentalizing mercies of faculty and various advice-givers, since they can capriciously change the shakily charted direction of your thought and inquiries" (Steinberg, p. 36). You must take an active, not a reactive, role with respect to the faculty's suggestions, molding them to what *you* want to do as *you* perceive it. Of course, that doesn't mean being completely rigid, but you must actively hold up your end in the negotiating relationship.

Facilitating Publication—Format for the Dissertation

Most students don't realize it, but the dissertation can be molded in such a way that it gives them an opportunity for easy publication. The typical form of a doctoral dissertation, though pedagogically useful, is an anachronism. Unless you write a research report on a funded project for the government, you will never again be accorded the space to supply so much detail; publication is just too costly. If you wish to publish the findings of your study, you must cut it down to fit either into a single article or into a series of articles that cover the major features. Often one attempts this on one's first job while also mastering the details of that job, learning how to teach at the college level, developing new courses, and getting acquainted with new colleagues and the community. This is hardly the most propitious time to try to cut the dissertation into articles and rewrite it.

There is another way. Most universities will accept a single article or a set of articles as the dissertation. These articles are of the kind that one would write after completing the dissertation in order to fit it to a journal format. University regulations usually specify such format details as page size and bibliographic style but are silent on form, leaving this to the chair and committee. Thus, even when substituting articles for typical dissertation form has not been done before, there is usually no regulation that stands in the way, only custom. That can be formidable if one does not have a strong committee, so talk thoroughly with your committee about this. Also check the dissertations in the natural sciences at your university; more departments in those areas have picked up this idea than in the behavioral sciences. The natural sciences may have broken the path on your campus.

The material that the chair, committee, and outside readers require to ensure the study was done correctly (or to provide detail so it can be easily replicated) can be put in an appendix. With luck, the appendix will be considerably shorter than traditional dissertation format, but it may not be if you are the first to use this procedure. Still, you will have developed the articles to publish your study immediately. Further, you will have done so under the tutelage of your adviser and committee; their help will give you a much better idea of how to conform to correct publication form, style, and content than if you were doing this on your own after graduating. There is, therefore, a greater likelihood that your submissions will be accepted for publication. (See Derbort, 1987, for an example. John's two articles are still a bit too long and still a bit dissertation-like but close enough that he can trim them easily to fit the journals in his field. He starts with a big advantage over traditional form.)

The publishable article dissertation format is very desirable, since it means that one leaves with articles in hand to submit. That can be impressive to those examining your credentials for possible employment. Send the articles off immediately so your vita can at least show "submitted for publication" and maybe "accepted." You will probably be putting more resources, time, and effort into your dissertation than any activity you have previously attempted. This opportunity can help maximize that investment.

17.

Suggestions and Insights for the Doctoral Student:
2. The Dissertation Process

The following sections deal more directly with the process of doing the dissertation. They follow a generic pattern, noting when practices vary widely among universities. Find out about the process that is *prescribed* at your university. It is usually written in a graduate handbook, the university catalog or bulletin, the graduate school bulletin, or some similar source. Find the pattern *actually in use* by asking other graduate students and also faculty. Their versions may differ from that prescribed. You will then need to find out whether the informal rules are at real variance from the formal ones; they may not be.

If the informal and formal processes are not congruent, the formal statement is the legal one if "push comes to shove," and every so often an administrator will feel the informal way things are being done should be brought back in line with what was intended. You can get caught if you have deviated. If your adviser and committee assure you that a deviation from the formal statements is appropriate, reflect that fact in a written memo that you send to them indicating this is your understanding of appropriate procedure, and keep a copy. You may feel odd doing that, but it's good protection; if necessary, just ask them to put up with your little eccentricities. You won't feel at all silly when it protects your right to a degree if the rules are suddenly enforced.

CHOICE OF PROBLEM

As Steinberg (1981) points out, one factor you generally do control is your choice of problem. The earlier you focus on a field of interest and begin to think about dissertation research possibilities, the better you can integrate your course work and faculty contacts so as to facilitate the process. Some universities have courses that, early in your program, help you begin to develop a tentative research proposal. This not only gives you experience, it also gives a feel for what it is like to narrow a problem within the conceptual limits that make it practical to carry out. Even if that first project is not what you eventually choose to work on, having once gone through the process makes the next easier and faster. If you have the opportunity to take such a course, do so early in your program.

Nicholas Smith, a professor at Syracuse University, gives this advice to his students: "With what do you bore people at cocktail parties? Put aside the idea of trying to find a dissertation topic. Ask yourself what you are interested in, what turns you on. That's what your dissertation topic ought to be." See how you can shape it into a feasible project.

If you want to learn a particular technique or skill, you may find it desirable to work with a faculty member on one of her projects and then find a part of that project that you can call your own for the dissertation.

Typically, faculty welcome such expressions of interest and are happy to have you share with them the development of the research topic.

When choosing a topic, consider the competencies and interests of the current faculty. If theirs match yours, that can be the start of a very fruitful relationship. But you need not be limited by them. Remember, in most institutions you can invite committee members from other parts of the university, and they will usually agree to serve if they are not too busy with their own students. Sometimes, by arrangement, even the chair may come from another part of campus or another university as long as there is representation of one's program on the committee; but that is more unusual. At most universities, even individuals with no university affiliation can serve as dissertation committee members provided they are willing to volunteer their time, are perceived as suitably qualified, and have knowledge, skill, or interest not currently represented on the faculty.

The two major problems students often create for themselves are 1) hunting for a completely unique problem and 2) attempting too grandiose a project.

Owning the Problem

It is natural for you to seek a topic you can live with for the substantial period of time that the dissertation requires; you want it to be a problem that you can own. As Grant (1986), a recent graduate, puts it, "This is your baby; you are going to be the one who will be up walking with it in the middle of the night; so it better be a baby you can love" (p. 65). For some individuals, this means that they must think it up themselves, that it must absolutely be original with them--they want to devise *their own* problem, not accept one their professor hands them! There may be a touch of the "second adolescence" phenomenon in this, but whatever it is, it causes problems, since they feel inwardly compelled to find a reason for rejecting the suggestions made to them by their professor and others trying to help them. In this connection, I am reminded of my own major professor, Dr. Benjamin Bloom, who, during a symposium honoring him at his retirement, was listening to a recounting of persons who had built on his work. Some work of mine was mentioned, and the speaker noted that I had not properly credited Ben as the source of the idea! I was mortified. But Ben leaned over and whispered in my ear, "That's all right, I stole it from _____ " (a distinguished psychologist like himself who shall be nameless). So we all stand on the shoulders of others, sometimes acknowledging it, sometimes carelessly forgetting to, maybe other times unconsciously suppressing the fact. It helps, however, to accept the ideas of others if one realizes *it is not only all right, it is essential to use and build on others' ideas.* Nobody starts "from scratch," and we all know it.

Cutting the Problem to Feasible Proportions

Students want to do something that will have some impact, make a difference, not just gather dust on the shelves. Fine! But this shouldn't be your last such effort, and just maybe that is a lot to expect of your first one. Topics are often "scaled down" several times before they are feasible. Spending time on a less than significant project may be undesirable, but taking on too much and not finishing the degree is worse! It may deny your opportunity later to make the difference you desire.

Setting Boundaries

Many dissertations have no natural stopping point as an experiment does; with an experiment, when one has gathered data on the intended number of cases, one can draw the project to a close with the analysis of those data. But if one is building a theoretical model, developing or critiquing a point of view, or describing a situation, when has one done enough? Presumably when the model is adequately described, the point of view appropriately presented, and so forth. But such words as "adequate" or "appropriate" don't help one to know when to let go. They describe judgments that may be made by oneself but must also be made by one's chair and committee members. Thus they are not entirely under one's control; one may make the judgment only to be overruled. It is probably no coincidence that students in the humanities take a lot longer to complete their dissertations than students in the natural sciences. The former's studies are typically without an easily determined stopping point; the latter are often experiments where the end is reasonably clear. There are, no doubt, many other reasons, but surely one is the difficulty of obtaining agreement on closure. What to do?

The time to face this with your committee is *not* when you are winding up your dissertation but at the time the proposal is being written and accepted. The shape of some problems simply must emerge as one works; their final nature is extremely difficult to predict early in the process. But anything you can do to shape your own and your committee's expectations will help both of you recognize closure conditions when they are reached. This can take many forms; some possibilities are:

- A specified period of observations or number of persons to be interviewed.
- Certain books to be read, digested, and brought to bear on the development or critique of a point of view.
- Identification of a certain dissertation length as generally appropriate to present a position or model.
- If your professor is working closely with you, she may even agree to a certain period of concentrated work, using the end of the time period as an approximate stopping point.

As early as it is feasible to do so, try to find some kind of boundary that seems reasonable for your study. Setting such tentative markers is not a guaranteed fix. Not only have faculty been known to change their minds as the problem develops, no doubt you will as well. But the salience of closure conditions is always greater once the issue is raised. Raise the question and make a provisional try at answering it; this will go a long way toward making it possible to find reasonable closure conditions.

Reformulating the Problem

In addition to cutting the problem to an appropriate size, a key question is "When is the problem reformulation finished?" Is spending additional time likely to yield a better one? Is this one good enough? You will recognize this as one of the conditions to be optimized if you have read Chapter 11; there are no easy or general answers to these questions. But the fact that they are asked points to the importance of problem formulation. Getzels (1982), in a chapter well worth reading, "The Problem of the Problem," quotes Einstein: "The formulation of the problem is often more essential than its solution. . . . To raise new questions, new possibilities, to regard old questions from a new angle, requires creative imagination and marks real advance in science" (Einstein and Infeld, 1938, p. 92).

Zimbardo, Andersen, and Kabat (1981), for example, noted that older people are often paranoid. They also tend to lose their hearing gradually, often unawares. Zimbardo thought these might be related. Growing deaf without knowing it while becoming increasingly socially isolated might lead older persons to view the world as a hostile place and lead to paranoia. How to study this relationship? He could hardly test repeatedly for deafness and measure the paranoia of a group of individuals but then do nothing about either. No ethics committee would stand for that!

Zimbardo reformulated the problem to an oblique attack. If he could not demonstrate a correlation between deafness and paranoia in older people, could he do so in younger ones, somehow artificially inducing deafness? This is what he did, using hypnosis to induce deafness as a posthypnotic suggestion of which the subject was not aware and then measuring paranoia development. The reformulation of the problem made it amenable to solution.

Problem reformulation is important. You'll know when you are there, but it is often difficult to judge what it will take to get there. Use your best judgment.

Helpful Techniques

Much research has been done on problem choice, problem solving, and creativity (Getzels, 1982; Rosner and Abt, 1970). The following suggestions may be helpful.

Work the conscious and unconscious. Make your conscious mind work for you; keep a written log. Talk to yourself *in writing* about your ideas, elaborate on them, see where they lead you. From Getzels again, here's another useful quotation, this time about art from Henry Moore: "I sometimes begin drawing with no preconceived problem to solve, with only a desire to use pencil on paper and only make lines, tones, and styles with no conscious aim. But as my mind takes in what is so produced, a point arrives where some idea becomes conscious and crystallizes, and then control and ordering begin to take place" (p. 77). Writing things down on paper has an effect on patternmaking in itself. There is a latency between the time an idea is formed and the time it gets on paper, a period when important things can happen.

Make your unconscious mind work for you. It is especially good at patternseeking; it has a wondrous way of silently processing and organizing material. The unconscious mind grinds away at your problem even when you are concentrating on something entirely different! Reviewing your ideas from time to time loads the hopper. Engaging in periods of concentrated reading, thinking, and trying to find patterns as you write your log fills your mind for the unconscious to digest. Then relax, go to a movie, play tennis, take a nap. Alternate your periods of concentration with off-target activities that allow the mind to ruminate at will. Then out of the blue may come a new idea that builds on the previous one--thanks to your unconscious! Be prepared with paper and pencil to record it; keep them even on your nightstand.

Read actively the seminal minds in your field. Active reading in which you anticipate, argue with, and go beyond the author's ideas is very conducive to discovery. Some of the best ideas come when, in active anticipation of the logic, you find the author zigs when you zag! If, on further consideration, the "zagging" proves to be a reasonable path, there it is; a new idea has been born!

Many times such ideas will come from reading the seminal writers in one's field. These people seem to have an intuitive grasp of their subject matter beyond what they can fully articulate. Careful reading sometimes allows one to grasp something they foresaw but did not develop. Coming at their material in the light of today's knowledge may illuminate something they only dimly understand, on which they provide a new perspective. Cronbach told me once that he found that R. A. Fisher had intuitively grasped information theory before it was invented. The best researchers seem to seek out such authors.

While you are in the library, read and benefit from critiques of studies similar to what you are planning; don't repeat others' mistakes. This should be a part of the literature review you would do anyway.

Use the excellent guides to libraries that have been prepared to help you: Marda L. Woodbury's (1982) *Guide to Sources of Educational Information*, second edition, is a superb guide to locating material in many of the behavioral sciences. Ask your reference librarian for other sources if Woodbury doesn't help you.

Get some perspective on the perceptual set induced by the problem's context and the way it is stated. Tversky and Kahneman (1982) and Slovic, Fischhoff, and Lichtenstein (1982) note that formulating the chances of a disfiguring auto injury as once in every 100,000 miles was not especially persuasive of seat belt use. But the information that over a 50-year lifetime of driving the chances rise to 33% made seat belts very attractive. The context in which one frames a question can have considerable impact; be aware of this and look for alternative frames.

Find a problem with optimum breadth. Architects will tell you that the breadth of a public hallway is a problem: only so many people can traverse it at a time. Similarly, a communication channel can carry only so much information, and as Cronbach (1982, 1984) has noted, the bandwidth-fidelity problem is characteristic of research. One alternative is to try to cram the channel with a wide spectrum of messages (wide bandwidth in electronic terms) with little redundancy and take the risk that the noise of the circuits will mask some of the messages. Put another way, there are messengers with so many different messages trying to traverse the hallway that some lose theirs, others get torn or crumpled. Alternatively, one can concentrate on getting few messages through with considerable redundancy and therefore considerable accuracy (fidelity in electronic terms) even if parts get masked, lost, or scrambled--many messengers carry duplicates rather than original messages. Similarly, in research studies we can opt for wide bandwidth (study lots of things, but without very certain answers) or concentrate on a few things and obtain dependable answers. Finding the optimum point in the bandwidth-fidelity trade-off is part of the problem formulation task.

Stuck? Break the set! Sometimes one seems to be unable to get beyond a certain point or to be going in circles around an issue. Break the set by discussing your thinking with a friend. Sometimes it helps if the person has some knowledge of what you are doing; other times, having to explain where you are in simple terms is better. Studies of problem solving show that observers are much better at finding the solution to a problem than those actively engaged in seeking it!

Choose a topic that can be investigated with research methods consistent with the direction you want to take as a professional (unless, of course, you want to use this opportunity to broaden your methodology repertoire). Here is a peculiar phenomenon: Student clinicians and administrators frequently choose topics requiring extensive experimental design and statistical knowledge. They have little or no prior study of the topics, are very unlikely to use knowledge of them professionally, and often have an intense aversion to the subjects. If one were to write a recipe for a stressful and unpleasant experience, one likely to result in an unsatisfying product for all concerned, one could hardly do better. Choice of topic is yours; make it one you can live with comfortably.

Start wherever you wish: Concrete versus conceptual styles of problem finding. Advice on problem finding resembles advice to writers. Teachers recognize that good writing is well organized and assume, therefore, that everyone should organize (outline) what he is going to say before he writes it. But some research problems often start somewhere in the middle or at the end with the rest fleshed in. The reports of good studies begin with a highly credible explanation or conceptualization that guides the study. From that, the operationalization and implementation of the study flow logically. It is natural, therefore, that those teaching research methods assume, as do English teachers who teach outlining, that everyone should start with the conceptualizations and explanations: "Develop those first and the study will almost write itself." They are right if that is how one can work. Indeed, many extremely strong studies do seem to have been developed "from the top down." There is, however, often as much creativity, and therefore developmental work, involved in the operationalization of a problem as in the initial conceptualization. Indeed, it is possible that even the Zimbardo study of paranoia, cited earlier, began with some interesting things that might be done with hypnosis and the investigators worked backward to the problem, explanation, and significance.

Some persons clearly find it more comfortable to start with the design of an interesting operational study and then work back to the conceptualization that would undergird it. Others may start with the conceptualization and then operationalize it. Working through the undeveloped aspect usually informs one about the starting point and often requires one to go back and possibly reformulate it. An interactive process of successively working back and forth between the conceptualization and its operational translation ultimately develops a stronger conceptualization that neatly fits the study's design and measures. That permits one to present the results as a strong chain of reasoning (as per pp. 27, Chapter 2; also Chapter 11), marking the study as one of distinction.

So start where you feel comfortable: with the conceptualization, or with something you would like to do or investigate, or with certain people. Whether you start abstractly or concretely, work back and forth, so that both sides are adequately developed when you are finished. Not only will you develop a better study this way, but you will also find it exciting to see the problem emerge and grow.

Avoid constructing measuring instruments, curricula, training programs, and other complex treatments as merely a part of your problem. Most good measuring or observation instruments are so difficult and time-consuming to construct that if you can use someone else's and improve or modify it, do so--unless, of course, the construction of the instrument is your dissertation topic. Constructing a needed instrument as only one part of a study that is also a substantial piece of work can mean you are taking on too much. The ERIC Clearinghouse on Tests, Measurements and Evaluation, Educational Testing Service, Princeton, N.J. 05841, has an excellent bibliography on sources of instruments that may be your salvation (current version is Backer, 1977). The same advice applies to treatments, training programs, and curricula.

Keep it as simple as is feasible. Some individuals tend to make too much of their studies, feeling that if it is to be worth anything, it must be almost too complex to handle. Don't feel that if you can do it, it must be too easy. The best studies are often the simple ones. It is a matter of balance; try out your ideas with others to see when you have found the correct "range."

An interdisciplinary topic? Consult your chair. Depending on the problem and the circumstances, topics that are interdisciplinary may be encouraged or discouraged by faculty. Some campuses have extensive arrangements such as interdisciplinary committees to support such work. Sad to say, on other campuses, it is better to avoid them. Disciplines have different research traditions, and even their criteria of what constitutes good research may differ. The socialization of committee members to these differences may be more than you want to take on if those before you have not already begun it. Consult your chair carefully on this matter.

CHOICE OF ADVISER AND COMMITTEE

Although dissertation practices differ from university to university, one common theme is that you have a major adviser or chair who works with you on the dissertation. At most universities, you will have a dissertation committee as well, composed of persons from the same or a closely related area and, sometimes, someone from outside the area as well. The research adviser chairs the dissertation committee in most universities. The committee constitutes the core of the final examining committee or oral. Selection of your research adviser is one of the most critical decisions of your graduate career, since he is usually the person with whom you will work most closely in developing your dissertation.

In some institutions, you have no choice: you are assigned to an adviser at admission and this person carries you through the whole program, including dissertation. In other institutions choice is restricted by the fact that faculty members prefer advisees whose topics fit their research programs. An adviser may suggest possible next steps in his long range plan for your consideration or expect you to indicate what aspect of that research program you would like to work on. Such arrangements have advantages. One is more likely to have the interested supervision of the adviser. Where outside funds are available, one's resource problems may be solved. Because the project must measure up to the rest of the research program, it is likely to result in a high-quality research product with increased chances of being published. But students may feel constrained to develop the study in accord with the adviser's ideas rather than their own; they may feel less ownership of the study. There are pros and cons.

Students who are already into the dissertation stage are often knowledgeable sources of information on prior students' dissertation experiences with faculty. After all, they had to do this research when they were at the chair-and-committee-choice stage. Since they have finished their class work, they are often not conveniently around. Make it a point to seek them out; for example, attend social affairs where they might be present.

The dissertation chair is your choice in most universities. Some distinguish between the adviser who guides you through appropriate course work and your dissertation chair. This leaves you free to choose a dissertation chair appropriate to your topic. Some departments assign all new students for course advisement to one person until they are ready to make a choice of a dissertation adviser. In other instances, students have a temporary adviser who may or may not serve as dissertation adviser, depending on the student's decision. In some instances, in order to apportion the workload, the department chair appoints the dissertation chair and may also approve committee members. But even in these circumstances, the student's interests are usually taken into account. Common to nearly all these options is the deferral of choice of dissertation chair until you are familiar enough with the faculty to make an appropriate selection.

Which comes first, the adviser and committee or the topic? The committee is usually chosen *after* the topic is chosen, but the adviser or topic may come in either order. If you know what you wish to work on, you will want to choose an adviser who can help you with that topic. If you don't and you want an adviser's help in finding your topic, you may wish to choose the adviser and search for a topic with her. Should you then, as a result of that search, choose a topic outside the expertise of that faculty member, in most institutions you can and should change advisers to someone who can be of more help to you.

Be sure to discuss your committee choices with your chair. She will be working with them as well as you, so they should be persons acceptable to her. It goes without saying that there are usually regulations to be observed on the size and composition of the committee; they are usually codified in some official publication, such as a graduate handbook.

It is a courtesy to let the potential committee choices who do not know you well (and you may not know them well either) first view a brief write-up of what you plan to do and discuss it with you before you ask them to be committee members. Go to them in the role of a student seeking advice. Keep your proposal summary to no more than five pages (preferably two if you can). Drop it off ahead of your appointment time, indicating that this is what you wish to see them about. Leave the description somewhat open, so that there is the opportunity for them to contribute to it. This provides the opportunity to get acquainted in a problem-oriented situation, and you can both get some idea of whether this is a relationship in which you would feel comfortable. If the discussion goes well and you would like to work with the person, then you can ask whether she would be a member of your committee.

Criteria for Choosing Committee Members

There are a variety of criteria for choosing committee members, some of which were discussed in the previous chapter. Others are discussed below, but the main ones are to choose persons who add to the knowledge of your chair on some aspect of your topic or who add skill in research methodology. In addition, you may want to get one or more nurturers on your committee, persons who like to help graduate students grow and learn, as well as those who see the dissertation as a demonstration of your competence. You will find the former will help you gain access to others when you need special expertise. Some faculty have idiosyncrasies that can be annoying--peculiarities in working or writing styles. Other students (and faculty) usually know them well enough to permit you to judge how critical these are for you. Availability and stability of committee membership are also important criteria.

Availability. Be sure to ask faculty about their availability during the period when you will need them. Availability during summers may be part of the problem, but even more serious is the faculty member who is on leave just when you want to make the grand dash to the finish. If there is a sabbatical system, most faculty will be glad to tell you when they are next eligible for leave and what they are planning to do.

Stability of committee membership. It is difficult to predict whether a faculty member will leave the institution for another position. Often your chair will know about job-seeking activity and may share this information if you raise the question in the context of needing committee stability. Negative tenure decisions can also be disruptive. Although the outcome cannot always be predicted with certainty, usually the date for consideration of this matter is available. It may seem embarrassing to ask about these sensitive issues, but it is your education. You are the one who can get hurt, so be tactfully assertive.

Typically, it is easier and less disruptive to find committee replacements than to change one's chair. Because of the seriousness of the loss of a chairperson, faculty usually rally around the "orphaned" students and do their best to help them. Some institutions encourage faculty members to continue as chair even after leaving the institution; in fact, they have been known to pick up the expenses of bringing the faculty member back to campus for the oral examination. If you are so affected, it pays to ask whoever oversees graduate programs about this possibility (assistant dean for graduate programs, or secretary of the department, for example).

Size of committee. When putting together a committee, the smaller the better, all other things being equal. Don't forget that you must obtain a consensus decision, not a majority of your committee, for all the phases of your project. In general, it is easier to get agreement among few members than among many. Besides, there are fewer people to have to please with changes in drafts, fewer copies to have to produce, and so on. Three is typically the minimum committee size on most campuses. Add more sparingly and with good reason--to get a certain competency, to balance points of view on the committee, and the like.

Advice from Faculty and Student Interviews on the Choice of a Chair and Committee

Here is some useful advice from faculty and graduate student interviews on a variety of aspects of choosing a chair and committee members:

- Getting human research subjects to participate in a research study is tough and often touchy. Find someone who can help you get them. A faculty member who will go to the school or institution with you to make the request is to be treasured.

- Find someone who wants to run the first subjects with you in an experiment. Such a person can be invaluable in picking up clues to problems that the inexperienced researcher might miss. Such willingness also shows an understanding of the need to be close to one's data and an appreciation of the potential problems if one is not.
- Find someone who wants a pilot study--you learn a lot cheaply. That knowledge gets taught very expensively if you wait to learn on the final run through.
- Does your writing need the help of an editor? Some committee members are particularly skillful at this and like to do it.
- Is the analysis likely to be complicated? Does someone on the committee have the skills to help you with it?
- How fast does the faculty member return chapters? You are often stymied in working further until you know previous work is acceptable. Will you have to wait long to get it back with comments and suggestions? Ask graduate students now using the person as a committee member.
- Is the faculty member secure enough to stand up to others in your defense if she thinks you are right? This is important if another faculty member, not on the committee, is working on or has expertise on your topic and might be involved in the oral examination in some way.

WORKING WITH YOUR ADVISER AND COMMITTEE

The Sudden Realization: It Is Your Study

The realization that this is your study to push as slowly or as rapidly as you wish comes quite early. Typically, you'll find that scheduling of meetings with your adviser and committee is up to you. Some advisers will set up a time for the next meeting as a way of keeping you on a schedule, but most will not. Some students find this disconcerting--they feel uncared for--but it is more a matter of respecting students' independence. Take the initiative in these situations to schedule the meetings as you wish and to develop the relationship with your adviser and committee that will be most helpful to you. It is *your* study.

Make a Record of Each Committee Meeting

Make notes immediately after each meeting with your adviser and committee. If there is any chance of a difference of opinion, submit your summary of the conference as a brief memo that says, "Here is what I understand we agreed upon. . . ." (Maybe even do so for every meeting. Even if everyone is agreed, it provides a record!) This will keep you from going off on a tangent on the assumption that you are doing what your committee wanted. Making such notes and checking them with the committee is a simple matter, but it can save you great gobs of time. If just once it saves you from going wrong, it will repay the time invested many, many fold. In addition, it helps keep relations smooth between you and those with whom you are working.

In this connection, it is worth noting that not all your committee's suggestions have to be acted upon. Such ideas are the committee members' way of contributing to your study; in many instances they need only be acknowledged as good ideas--but for another or a later study.

Set the Next Committee Meeting Date Before Adjourning

Before the committee members leave at the end of a meeting, it is desirable to set the time of the next meeting and discuss what you expect to have ready at that time. This is important for several reasons:

- It will save you untold phone calls trying to find a common free time for your busy faculty members. You can waste hours bouncing from one to another trying different times to get one that is free for all simultaneously.
- It sets a target and deadline for the accomplishment of the next tasks on your project. If you don't work well under deadlines and pressure, set the date far enough out so you will not feel pressured and can make it easily. Setting next tasks is a subtle reminder to faculty that they are working with you and are responsible for helping you stay out of serious trouble. Give them a chance to give advice on the upcoming tasks.
- It lets faculty know what to expect so they can plan their reading load--a real problem if they serve on many committees.

THE PROPOSAL

The nature of the proposal itself has been discussed at length in the previous material, but a few additional comments about the process that may be helpful.

Have a Written Proposal

Develop a written proposal even if, as is true in some institutions, one is not required. Don't forget to use the help of Chapter 7 regarding different types of studies--qualitative and so forth. The proposal has some of the characteristics of a written contract. It provides a basis for negotiation if you perceive that the committee is changing its mind about what you thought it agreed to earlier. It provides for continuity when a chair or committee member leaves and must be replaced. Your chair undoubtedly intends to see you through the process; but if for reasons beyond her control this is impossible, you don't want to have to start from the beginning renegotiating your project.

If there are disagreements within your committee about what you intend to do, get them resolved at the proposal stage and make sure the proposal captures just what that resolution is in terms that can be unequivocally translated into your actions. Have the written description agreed to by all concerned.

When cooperative dissertations are permitted, some independent work will be required. The proposal is your statement of what portion has been agreed upon as yours to develop independently.

Use the Proposal to Develop Your Ideas

Oral discussions are fine, but putting ideas in writing forces you to think them through in a more thorough way than merely talking about them. One can "finesse" too many things when the stream of ideas is presented orally. As noted in the section on writing in the previous chapter, there is a latency in writing that allows one to more carefully consider ideas and their implications.

The Proposal Gives a Head Start on the Final Product

Major sections of the proposal such as the literature review and procedure can often be inserted directly into the body of the dissertation. When change is required, it is usually a small expansion. Careful attention to these sections is not wasted time and effort; you'll be delighted to have them ready to drop into place, secure in the knowledge that they have already been approved by your committee. For this reason, some advisers ask that the proposal include drafts of the first three chapters of the conventional dissertation format: 1) introduction to the problem and its significance; 2) the literature review; and 3) a description of the research method, study design, and procedures.

But don't spend time polishing the proposal too brightly. Remember, it serves as a guide, but research rarely follows *all* your plans. For your final draft, you'll need to come back and adjust the parts of it you plan to use to fit what you actually did.

Other Suggestions

Don't act on your inspirations at once. Let your ideas cool 24 hours at least. The idea that seems "hot" in the excitement of proposal development may look different tomorrow. Be sure to give yourself time to think through the ramifications. This goes for suggestions made by your adviser and committee as well; they, too, are subject to enthusiasms.

Look for funding. The opportunity to carry out a funded project is an experience that will stand you in good stead in any number of lines of work. It teaches management as well as research skills. One purpose of a number of federal small-grant programs is to support dissertations. Regular competitions, with few exceptions, will consider them as well. (See Section IV) Funding can be used for self-support, thus allowing you to work full-time on your project. Should you mention that your project is a dissertation? In some competitions designed to support them, yes. But where it is competing with nondissertation research, let it stand on its own--don't stereotype it by calling attention to this characteristic. Have it judged on its merits.

Do a work plan and time schedule. It is the rare dissertation writer who prepares a detailed work plan. Yet, the number of dissertations that are incomplete because the workload exceeded the available time is very large. Completing a work plan in the form of a chart with each task on a time line (see "Work Plan," Chapter 4) makes you work through the project in detail so that there are fewer unknowns left to encounter, or, if there are any, you are aware of them. Given the uncertain demands of a dissertation committee (or certain kinds of projects such as searches, discovery efforts, and qualitative studies), developing such a detailed plan is not always possible. But when there is such a plan, and it is agreed to by the committee, then it, like the rest of the proposal, acts as a kind of contract.

Another advantage of the work plan is that it budgets the one commodity you can control--your time. Although it may seem ample and often unending, your time is costly, if nothing else, in earnings forgone. The work plan also helps you to see where the study overcommits whatever time is available and where there are tasks that are a poor use of your time. Prioritize use of your time and find other ways to get some things done. Efficient use of your time is one of the major secrets of getting through at all and especially of doing so in a reasonable time.

Finally, put actual calendar dates on your work plan based on the day you plan to start. It will show when work is scheduled at times that will interfere with holidays, with school vacations, or with other competing events that might in some way affect what you want to get done. Then reschedule or take other action to avoid the conflict.

Include a "definitions of terms" section? In a dissertation proposal the "definitions of terms" section defines the major concepts of the problem, especially new or unfamiliar terms, in relation to the explanation that undergirds the study. It usually follows or is embedded in the rationale for the study. Later, design of the study describes these terms operationally. Comparing these operationalizations with their conceptual definitions determines how well the former matches what was intended.

Whether such a section is required varies. Some advisers insist on it as an excellent pedagogical device that clarifies the chain of reasoning. Others, realizing such sections are rare in published material, prefer that the relation of concepts to their operationalization be made clear through the write-up. Read recent dissertations or ask advanced students about this section to see whether it is expected. If not, get practice in writing for publication by making the relations clear without it.

THE PROPOSAL DEFENSE

Many institutions require the student to present the proposal to some kind of group for criticism and suggestions. It may be only the dissertation committee, but usually it will involve other faculty, sometimes invited graduate students, in some institutions all graduate students from the major area.

The proposal defense serves many purposes. Most faculty and students see it as a chance to catch glitches; it has saved many a student a painful mistake. It also instructs graduate students who are coming along in what to expect. Attend some before your own. Occasionally a chair uses it as a forum where the weight of others' opinions is used to convince a headstrong student who has resisted suggestions that there are indeed some serious problems.

You may get many suggestions for improving the study. Faculty and students get their "jollies" by making suggestions; doing so makes points with peers and superiors. Accept the social process for what it is and make the most of it. As with suggestions from your committee, only those that make sense within the scope on which you and your committee have agreed need be considered. Save others for a later study!

Some such defenses are a "dry run" of what the candidate will face at the final oral examination. Clues to potential problems as well as which faculty have certain kinds of reservations can be gleaned from the questions asked. It may be prudent to write the dissertation and prepare for the final oral defense with these concerns in mind.

DOING THE STUDY

Once your adviser and committee are appointed and your proposal approved, it remains for you to implement it. The relationships you have established with your adviser and committee during the development of the proposal typically will carry over into the completion of the project. Some advisers will want to work closely with you; most will leave the amount of contact to you, letting you call on them as you need help.

If you have a deadline for completion, communicate this to your committee. Set dates for getting products to them and *meet those deadlines*. Negotiate ahead of time how much turnaround time they need to give you their reactions. Prepare an overall timetable and remind them of where you are in the timetable as you send them items for reaction. Your committee will respect you for this and will typically try to help you maintain your schedule.

The Reversal of "Expert" Roles

Perhaps the hardest thing for students to understand, since they are used to the faculty playing the "expert" role, is that there comes a point during the study when the student knows more about it than the faculty ever will. When you live with a problem the way you do in completing a dissertation, you learn more about it than those who are simply looking in on it from time to time and for whom it is one of many such projects. When that time comes, it is important that you begin to educate the faculty working with you. Most faculty will realize what has happened and accept it, but some may not; judge this for yourself. The student who educates his adviser and committee to the mysteries of his study has a much easier time of it. He helps them to assist him in completing the study, since they are in a better position to know what to suggest. He does the faculty a favor by letting them experience the study vicariously. A good graduate student is a good teacher!

Conflicts Among Committee Members

Even though the committee members may have agreed to the proposal, the words may mean different things when it comes down to actually doing the study. One may be faced with conflicting demands regarding the importance of certain areas or with requests to treat the data from incompatible perspectives. Some of these may come from different conceptualizations about the behavioral and social sciences (see the end of Chapter 11). Usually one can rely on one's chair to handle such problems; that is the first place to turn when such problems arise. Typically she will handle them on a colleague-to-colleague basis and quietly resolve them. That is one of the reasons for choosing a chair who is strong enough to stand up to colleagues and has good relations with them. It is another reason for checking with your chair before inviting committee members.

Supposing, however, your chair is a fence sitter or is unable to work it out on a person-to-person basis? Then it is time to convene the committee and throw the problem of resolving the conflict into their laps. After all, they approved the proposal; you pursued it in good faith; the present problem is not one that was anticipated, but it needs to be resolved. As Steinberg (1981, p. 143) notes, "By laying the entire issue out on the table . . . it is hoped that the depth and pain of the dilemma will be seen by everybody. There may well be a fight among the committee but resolution, at least for the candidate . . . should result." As Steinberg also notes, the losing member of the committee may decide that in good conscience he should not remain a member; that may be the best solution for all concerned. A new member can then be found to restore harmony around the agreed-upon course.

WRITING UP THE REPORT

Dr. Sharon Senk of Syracuse University shared a comment by Dr. Larry Hedges that helped her: "Sharon, the difference between a really superb dissertation and an average one buys you a little, but the difference between a dissertation and no dissertation buys you a lot!" A superb one might open some extra doors, but without the completed dissertation few doors will open, some not at all! Get it written!

General Structure and Form

Before you settle for the typical dissertation form and format discussed below, if you haven't already, be sure to read pages 250 and 251 on how to finish your dissertation with a publication. Note that the chapters listed below correspond to the sections of a typical published article. The big difference is one of size and detail, but that is a major difference.

The typical dissertation is composed of a sequence of chapters, each intended to answer one of the reader's questions. Here is a sample pattern:

Abstract: *What is the study all about?* The abstract is a one- or two-page summary that in a clear, simple, and interesting manner describes the problem, the importance of this study, the method of studying the problems, and the significant findings. It provides an advance organizer of what to expect and, it is to be hoped, makes everyone eager to read the study itself.

Chapter 1: *What is the problem and its significance?* A description of the problem and its importance, this chapter sets the scene, fore-shadowing what is to come, and puts the problem in the larger perspective of the field in which it is set.

Chapter 2: *Where does the study fit into the body of previous work and how will it contribute to it?* Previous work that contributes directly to the study is critically reviewed with attention to both its content and its methodology. The review of literature shows how this study stands on the shoulders of previous workers, reaches beyond them, avoids their mistakes, and improves on their methods. (Reread the section "Related Research" in Chapter 3; the principles set forth there for a proposal apply to this chapter, too.)

Chapter 3: *What did you do?* This chapter describes the methods, subjects, measures and observations, design, and procedures of the study.

Chapter 4: *What did you find?* This chapter describes the findings of the study. It may interpret them, or that may be left to a separate chapter, depending on length. Usually interpretation is kept separate from the findings in quantitative studies; that is much more difficult in qualitative ones, and they are usually intermingled. Chapter 4 may become multiple chapters in complex studies, each chapter related to a different aspect of the study--a different variable, setting, or whatever focus is to be explored.

Chapter 5: *How do the findings relate to what you expected? To previous work? How do you put it all together now?* This chapter interprets the data, if the previous chapter did not, and relates them to the previous findings in the area. In this chapter, sometimes in a sixth, one summarizes the entire study, puts the findings in perspective, states the limitations of this particular study, and suggests the next steps for further research.

Although these same divisions are found in many journal articles, the detail you will be expected to give in your dissertation will be much greater than any journal would accept. This is largely a matter of tradition, but it serves a pedagogical purpose: it assures your adviser and committee that you have done the study properly. Steps taken for granted in the typical journal article are often described in detail in dissertations. Should you try to replicate a study described in a journal, you will be amazed at the large number of decisions you will have to make for which no guidance is provided.

Although the five or six chapters just described are a fairly standard format, there is nothing but unwritten tradition that says this is the format your study has to follow. If your study better fits a different structure, *by all means change the format to permit an adequate description of your study; that is the real criterion.* Be sure to discuss with your chair the form your study is to take *before* proceeding. Your chair may wish to see and comment on chapter outlines before writing, and such precautionary checks may save you enormous effort.

Nearly all the criteria for a good proposal apply as well to the dissertation itself. Indeed, the only criteria not anticipated in the proposal are those of data interpretation, and to some extent, even these are anticipated in a good design.

Format

The format for footnotes, bibliography, page size, and so on is chosen by each campus. Most use either Kate L. Turabian, *A Manual for Writers of Term Papers, Theses, and Dissertations,* fourth edition, revised (Chicago: University of Chicago Press, 1973), or *The Chicago Manual of Style for Authors, Editors, and Copywriters,* thirteenth edition (Chicago: University of Chicago Press, 1982). Adopted or permissible at some universities is the manual followed by most behavioral science journals and by many publishers: *Publication Manual of the American Psychological Association,* third edition (Washington, D.C.: American Psychological Association, 1983).

If you have a choice, the APA Manual uses a simple style. Also valuable, depending on the research area and campus practice, is *MLA Handbook for Writers of Research Papers, Theses, and Dissertations* (New York: Modern Language Association, 1977).

Submitting Drafts to Your Committee

How complete and clean need the drafts be before you submit them for comment? How much do you submit? To whom do you submit them? How often?

Impressions can be lasting ones. You convey something about your standards and the seriousness with which you take your study by the draft you submit for comment. So don't turn in a first draft, even a clean one; rework it, preferably until you are comfortable with it. Then submit copy that is easy to read. Students usually submit a chapter at a time to their chair, beginning with the first and working through them in order. Some committee members prefer to see the chapters at the same time as they are sent to the chair. More often, however, they will prefer to see them only after the chair has approved them, and usually two or three at a time.

Since the first chapters often have to be revised to fit the analysis and conclusion chapters, it may seem these latter should be submitted first. Some chairs will handle them in this order; if so, great, it will make it easier to make all the chapters fit together and for the argument to flow consistently from beginning to end.

With word processors it is easy to make completely clean successive drafts with no trace of the changes. This is fine from the standpoint of appearance, but it means that with each new draft the faculty will have no clue to what was changed. They will be reluctant to completely reread the new draft, given their time pressures. Further, without guidance, faculty have to puzzle out your changes. Convey where you made substantive changes (not minor ones or corrections of typos); have your word processor print changes in italics, bold, or some distinctive type font. (You can usually remove such print controls with a single command for final printing, *provided that style of print is not used elsewhere* in the copy.) Alternatively, circle the sections with a colored pencil, or prepare a cover memo telling the changes, reason, and page numbers.

Schedule your oral when your chair and all committee members agree the dissertation is ready.

THE ORAL EXAMINATION

The oral examination is the last campus-based effort to determine whether you can build a consensus around your claim of new knowledge (see first pages of Chapter 11). A group consisting typically of your committee and outside readers or examiners is assembled to review what you have done and query you about it. In some universities, especially in developing countries, the readers or examiners are from another university, such as the University of London. But usually they are chosen from your own, most often from your school or college but not your department. If they pass your dissertation, then they will have arrived at a consensus about it three steps over on the fishscale model in Chapter 11 (yourself, your major adviser and your committee--see figure 17, p. 170, for an analogous example). Then it is up to the readers of *Dissertation Abstracts* and/or to anyone to whom you submit it for publication to confirm their decision. You are beginning to build the consensus that results in your conclusions being accepted as knowledge beyond your own university!

Overcoming Your Fear of the Examination

The first thing to remember about the oral examination is that, as already pointed out, you know a great deal more about your dissertation than almost anyone you will be facing. Having lived with it as long as you have, you know its weaknesses and strengths better than anyone else. So although you don't want to flaunt it, nonetheless, this fact should give you confidence and help you to relax.

The second thing to remember is that the faculty on your committee have a lot invested in you by this time; they don't want you to fail. They may put you to a lively test, but they would like nothing better than for you to come out of it successfully. Remember that although it may not always seem like it at all times, when the chips are down, they want you to succeed! So relax and do the very best that you can to enjoy it.

Perhaps the major fear of the oral comes from fear of the unknown; indeed, quite possibly one may never have experienced an oral examination before. Knowing your committee members, knowing the format, knowing the room in which it will take place--all these things take some of the strangeness away and therefore relieve the tension. Do what you can to familiarize yourself with what is to come if you are anxious about this hurdle. Oral dissertation examinations are nearly always open to graduate students; indeed, they are often announced in the official university calendar. Ask your chair which of those coming up would be typical of what you might expect. Some students find it helps to attend one, possibly several--familiarity breeds contempt! If you do, note the format of the examination, the extent of formality, and what seems to make the examination go smoothly. Others fear attendance will add to their anxiety, so they talk to their chair or to other students who have either visited or just gone through one.

If you are still anxious, ask your chair or some friends to read your dissertation and think up questions they would ask if they were outside examiners. As Lorraine Terracina, who made this suggestion to me commented: "Even though most of the questions were not asked . . . it made me think more specifically in . . . areas I would not have considered and gave me more of a sense I could prepare for the oral" (personal comments, Aug. 6, 1985). (She handled her examination beautifully!) Then, after you have prepared, have them play examiner roles and have a rehearsal of what the examination could be like. That will give you a chance both to anticipate the kinds of questions you may face and also to think through and try out some answers.

The Examining Committee

Oral examinations usually involve five or more faculty members. The chair is usually appointed by someone in the university administration, often by the dean of the graduate school; in some universities it is the dissertation committee chair. The chair often does not participate in questioning and may confine activities to guiding the examination, passing the questioning around so all get a turn, conducting the sessions when the candidate is out of the room, and doing the administrative paperwork. In addition to the chair, who in some institutions is always from outside the area, there are usually two outside faculty variously called readers, outside examiners, or something else. Usually their first contact with the dissertation is their reading of it before the examination. Sometimes this time is too short, or they have been too busy to give the dissertation the careful attention it deserves. But this is the exception. Usually they give it a very careful reading, and since they are coming at it afresh, they see things those who have been working with it may have missed or taken for granted. The committee members are also usually part of the examining committee. You have had plenty of reasons to establish good relations with your committee members to this point--here is another one.

How are the outside readers usually chosen? In universities using their own faculty as examiners and awarding many doctorates, finding persons for this role may be difficult because of the press of responsibilities. Further, it seems all the candidates want to finish in time to make the deadline for graduation, so they bunch up as close to the deadline as possible. That adds to the difficulty of finding outside examiners. Thus, although many schools survey faculty to see who has an interest in upcoming orals, the persons assigned to your study may simply be the ones available and may have little expertise in the topic at hand. That makes you even more the specialist, but the trade-off is that you may have to be an expert teacher. You must explain your study and its niceties well enough that they will appreciate the magnitude of what you accomplished and how well you did it.

Because the orals are open, you are free to invite a spouse or friend to come and lend support. Having outside visitors tends to put everyone on his best behavior. Having a friend to talk to helps relieve the tension when visitors and candidates leave the room at the beginning and end of the examination.

Examination Procedure

Oral examinations differ somewhat from campus to campus in their formality. For some, it is a very informal affair, in others a formal ritual. One professor, for example, preferred that students call him Dr. Jones until after the oral was passed. He would then inform them they should henceforth call him "Tom." Such customs are, I believe, dying out, but you do yourself a favor and you show the faculty your respect when you follow the expectations.

A common examination pattern, once everyone is assembled and introduced, begins by asking the student and visitors to leave the room while the faculty and chair agree on the ground rules for the examination--whether the candidate will be given time to present his study, what order of questioning to use, and so on. They may also discuss problems they anticipate and how to handle them. This usually is done quickly, but don't be concerned if it takes a while. They may be telling stories or trading the latest gossip. This is a huge event in your life, but they have engaged in many of these and will in the future, so they take them more lightly.

Often the examination begins by having the candidate talk about himself and his study. This gives everyone a common framework and gives the candidate a chance to get comfortable talking about what he knows best. In some institutions the committee chair begins the questioning in order to put the candidate at ease; sometimes it is the outside questioner, sometimes they just go around the table in whatever order they happen to sit. Each faculty member usually has a turn as the lead questioner. Questions range widely: What is the significance of the study? Its contribution? Who, in your specialty, would agree with your findings? Who disagrees? What have you learned from it? What would you do differently? Where is it leading you? How would you build on it? Other faculty members may wait for the questioner to finish having her turn and not interrupt, or they may join in the fray and add their own questions on the topic just initiated.

Be sure you understand the question; if you aren't sure, ask for it to be rephrased or restated. Possibly rephrase it yourself for confirmation and then answer as directly and to the point as possible. Asking for the question to be repeated or rephrasing it yourself may give you time to think. Your phrasing may fit the question better to your memory patterns so the answer is jarred loose.

Don't be concerned if you "fluff" some of the questions. That does *not* necessarily mean you will be flunked. After all, the faculty have been at this business a lot longer than you have, and they ought to be able to find some holes in your knowledge. Remember the subtle rivalry among faculty. It may show here too in efforts to stump the candidate or show erudition by asking abstruse questions. Roll with the punches and try to understand what is happening. Sometimes you can turn it to your advantage with a chuckle and then: "I've been waiting for you to unload!" said with a big smile. It is the rare candidate who doesn't have trouble with some of the questions. Along these same lines, don't be afraid to say you don't know when you don't. You can make things worse by trying to bluff and be wrong; they'll think you don't recognize your problems.

The lead questioner, with the help of the chair, controls the pace of questioning. He asks questions until he is finished or the chair indicates it is time for another to take over and the next person's questioning begins. This continues until she is finished and passes the responsibility on to the next. The examination usually proceeds in this manner until all have had their turn, until they have all asked what they wish, or until a conventional time limit, such as two hours, is reached. Then they will again ask you to leave the room while they deliberate your fate.

After the Examination Is Completed

The minutes you spend waiting for their decision will be some of the longest in your life. It may be some comfort for you to know that it is extremely rare that individuals completely fail the oral. If there are problems with the dissertation, the candidate is usually passed with minor, occasionally major, corrections. The latter may require a second examination, but that is extremely rare. It is not at all uncommon, however, for there to be some rewriting and for candidates to pass with minor corrections. In fact, at most institutions, that is the norm. In some instances, even major changes can be done without a second examination. On occasion some member of the examining committee may reserve approval until changes are made to her satisfaction.

Usually, if you have been asked to make changes, your dissertation committee chair, or your chair plus one or more of the committee members with the required expertise, will be asked to see that the changes are satisfactorily made. Whichever it is, negotiate immediately the nature of changes to be made, and put your understanding in writing so that there are clear expectations on both sides. Since there is rarely any recorder for the examination, you and the responsible persons will have to reconstruct what is to be done. You may have little memory of it, since you were too busy answering questions. Often your chair takes responsibility for making notes of changes to be made as the examination progresses. If not, have a friend attend and do so for you. As in the other phases, negotiate to ensure that these changes are within the context of your study and that you are not taking on a whole new aspect. *Then get them done just as quickly as you can while the study is still fresh in your mind!!*

* * * * *

I hope that this material has made it easier to succeed, has freed you of some misperceptions, and, most of all, has given you the necessary perspective to maximize the value of the dissertation experience. You probably don't believe this, but you'll never again have as much free time to read and learn the things that interest you. Take advantage of it! Good luck![1]

* * * *

Success = (Ability) x (Motivation)[2]

---

[1]Students wishing more help with the dissertation and doctoral process will find references at the end of Appendix A.

Appendix A
Additional Reading

SAMPLE PROPOSALS

Brodsky, Jean. *The Proposal Writer's Swipe File.* Taft Corporation, 5125 MacArthur Blvd., Washington, DC 20016.

> Professionally written proposals to foundations only a few of which deal with research topics. Brodsky describes the contents as "thought joggers." They are! Note especially the first paragraphs of the proposals. Many succeed beautifully in grabbing the reader's attention, in opening new vistas, and in pulling the reader into the proposal. There are now three volumes: *File I*, 1973 (12 proposals), *File II*, 1976 (14 proposals), *File III*, 1981 (edited by Susan Ezell, 15 proposals).

Caplovitz, David. (1983) *The Stages of Social Research.* New York: Wiley.

> Chapter 2 reprints four winning research proposals. Chapter 3's research proposal appears with *Grants Magazine* staff's comments and background on the proposal's development. Chapter 5 reproduces a losing proposal with comments by the reviewers and author. Highly recommended reading. The author is a bit defensive but realistic.

Coleman, William et al. (Eds.). (1982) *A Casebook of Grant Proposals in the Humanities.* Neal Schuman, 23 Cornelia St., New York, NY 10014, 284 p.

> It is always helpful to see what has succeeded.

Grants Magazine. Published by Plenum Press, 233 Spring St., New York, NY 10013.

> Begun in 1977 for writers of any kind of grant; each issue contains suggestions and information covering a wide spectrum. A particular valuable feature column has been "The Grants Clinic," which until recently always reprinted with comments on a proposal that had been submitted for funding.

Locke, Lawrence F., Wyrick Spirduso, Waneen, and Silverman, Stephen J. (1987) *Proposals That Work: A Guide for Dissertations and Grant Proposals*, 2nd Ed. Newbury Park, CA: Sage Publications.

> In process of publication, said to contain four annotated proposals of widely varying types.

Sinclair, James P. (1982) *How to Write Successful Corporate Appeals-- with Full Examples.* Public Service Materials Center, 111 N. Central Ave., Hartsdale, NY 10530, 110 p.

> Includes sample appointment letters, covering letters, general-purpose proposals, postsubmission letters, and renewal letters.

White, Virginia P. (Ed.). (1983) *Grant Proposals That Succeeded*. Plenum Press, 233 Spring St., New York, NY 10013, 240 p.
>   Includes the texts of proposals followed by useful comment; helpful in providing models. Three research grants, three training grants, four arts proposals, and one humanities education request make up the entries. There are also sections on the federal RFP and on foundations and corporations.

ON PROPOSALS, GRANTS, AND FUNDING

Bauer, David G. (1984) *The "How To" Grants Manual*. New York: Macmillan, 229 p.
>   Excellent source; very complete and detailed directions for getting information on federal as well as foundation and private funding. Good samples of information sources and numerous checklists for aspects of the proposal process. The book comprises three sections: getting ready to seek support, government funding sources, and private funding sources. The author makes a living consulting in this area, and this very useful book tells the methods he teaches.

Cavin, Janis I. (1984) *Understanding the Federal Proposal Review Process*. American Association of State Colleges and Universities, One Dupont Circle, Suite 700, Washington, DC 20036-1193.
>   Except for articles, this is one of the few sources that discuss the federal review process. It is approached both from the point of view of the common elements in the review process across agencies and in describing the individual procedures of five agencies.

CFAE Corporate Handbook. (1983) Council for Financial Aid to Education (CFAE), 680 Fifth Ave., Dept. IS, New York, NY 10019.
>   Describes the programs of over 200 of America's leading corporations, about a third of corporate giving. Tells program goals, who makes decisions, types of programs and educational institutions supported, and size of grants. Includes a categories-of-giving index. Very useful for those seeking support from businesses.

Cook, Desmond L. (1979) *Program Evaluation and Review Techniques: Applications in Education.* Lanham, MD: University Press of America, 112 p.
>   Useful material on PERT, critical path method, and similar work-planning techniques. Helpful analysis of alternatives when project time is tight. An earlier book by Cook, now out of print but possibly in your library, discusses control and management of complex projects as well. It was published as *Educational Project Management* (Columbus, OH: Charles E. Merrill, 1971, 243 p.).

Dermer, Joseph. (1977) *How to Write Successful Foundation Presentations.* Public Service Materials Center, 415 Lexington Ave., New York, NY 10017, 80 p.
>   A collection of sample letters to foundations, largely for social action

projects, but there are some useful ideas here.

Engelbret, David. (1972) "Storyboarding--A Better Way of Planning and Writing Proposals." *IEEE Transactions on Professional Communication,* 15, Dec., pp. 115-118.
> Applies TV's storyboarding technique to proposal writing. Story-boarding provides a modularized specification for each topic in the proposal. Requires, first, outlining to select topics, second, expansion of topics into thesis sentences, and third, developing both the key thoughts and the illustrations to support each thesis. Note extension of storyboard's modular concept to the completed proposal: two-page modules with text on the left and illustrations, charts, and diagrams on the right; topic heading and thesis sentence underlined at top left. Excellent example of the nonverbal gestures that clarify a proposal, invite reading, and facilitate understanding it.

Grantsmanship Center News, The Grantsmanship Center, 1015 W. Olympic Blvd., Los Angeles, CA 90015. Kiritz, Norton J. (1980) *Program Planning and Proposal Writing.* Shakely , Jack. (1974) *"The Annual Register of Grant Support,"* 1(5); Saasta, Timothy. (1976) *"The Catalog of Federal Domestic Assistance,"* 2 (6), pp. 33-48, available separately as a reprint. Baker, Keith. (1976) "The New Contractsmanship," 2(7), pp. 21-27, available separately as a reprint that also includes "How to Use *Business Commerce Daily"* and "An Inside Look at How HEW Evaluates Proposals" from the same issue.
> These are selected titles from a reprint series published by the center. Many others are also valuable. Kiritz, an expanded version of an early article, is excellent. Helpful and detailed directions on the use of the *Register, Catalog,* and *Daily* go beyond those given elsewhere. "Contractsmanship" discusses RFPs and was originally published by its author in *American Sociologist,* Vol. 9 (1975), pp. 206-218, under the title "The New Grantsmanship." The original article, aimed at university professors, shows the declining share of research dollars they are receiving because of the rise of RFPs, and tells why. Professors should read this version. The *News* article has changed this orientation to a more general focus. "An Inside Look" is reprinted in this book, pages 208-209.
> The *News* is currently oriented more toward the nonprofit community service organization, and many of the other reprints and the journal itself would be helpful to such organizations.

Hall, Mary. (1977) *Developing Skills in Proposal Writing.* Continuing Education Publications, 1633 S.W. Park, P.O. Box 1491, Portland, OR 97207, 339 p.
> Excellent resource! Clear and very well written for a variety of educational grants. Includes sample forms.

Lindvall, Carl M. (1959) "The Review of Related Research." *Phi Delta Kappan.* 40 , p. 179.
> Helpful and detailed discussion of this important part of the proposal.

Margolin, Judith B.   (1983) *The Individual's Guide to Grants.* Plenum Press, 233 Spring St., New York, NY 10013, 295 p.
> This book is essential for its intended audience, the individual seeking a grant with no institutional affiliation. But in addition, it was written by a former director of the Foundation Center Library in New York City, and the hand of experience shows! An excellent resource on grant seeking in general, especially from foundations. Contains much wise counsel.

Plotkin, Harris M. (1972) "Preparing a Proposal, Step by Step." *Journal of Systems Management, 23* pp. 36-38.
> A description of a commercial company's plan for answering an RFP, including a flow chart of the steps. The advance planning, use of technical writers, and division of labor may be an eye opener for university professors, for whom the old saw becomes "If you're going to lick 'em, join 'em!" Adapt and adopt some of the commercial methods, especially the simulated proposal evaluation team. But set the proposal evaluation earlier in the flow chart. Where it is placed in the article, the team's reaction is too late to be of much help if anything major turns up.

Wessell, Nils Y. (1975) "Foundation-University Relations." *SRA Journal,* 6(Spring), 17-23.
> The foundation officer's point of view. Mostly obvious points, but the fact that he felt he needed to make them indicates obvious errors are being made. Also may serve to introduce the reader to the *Journal of the Society of Research Administrators.* It is largely concerned with research management, but sometimes with the grant-getting process.

White, Virginia P. (1975) *Grants: How to Find Out About Them and What to Do Next.* Plenum Press, 223 Spring St., New York, NY 10013, 354 p.
> One of the best books on the grant process. Excellent coverage of information sources for both federal and foundation grants. Includes a chapter on business and industry grants. Full discussion of budgets. Very helpful discussion of the variety of federal constraints (protection of human subjects, animals, affirmative action, and so on). A general volume for all fields of work.

White, Virginia P. (1980) *Grants for the Arts.* Plenum Press, 233 Spring St., New York, NY 10013, 360 p.
> Identifies sources of support as well as information about how to approach them and prepare proposals.

ON WRITING

Barzun, Jacques. (1985) *Simple and Direct: A Rhetoric for Writers* (rev. ed.). New York: Harper & Row.
> Widely used; an excellent reference, very readable.

Becker, Howard S.   (1986)   *Writing for Social Scientists.* Chicago:

University of Chicago Press, 180 p.
  Very helpful insights on writing: from the author's personal experience as an expert qualitative methods researcher and also from teaching a course in academic writing.

Day, Robert A. (1983) *How to Write and Publish a Scientific Paper*, (2nd ed.). ISI Press, 3501 Market St., Philadelphia, PA 19104, 181 p.
  Mainly natural science illustrations about some very useful material; don't miss Appendix 4, "Words and Expressions to Avoid," and Chapter 26, "Use and Misuse of English."

Dugdale, Kathleen. (1967) *A Manual on Writing Research* (2nd ed.). Indiana University Bookstore, Bloomington, IN 47401, 48 p.
  526 suggestions on preparing a research study. Especially useful for graduate students. Good listings of suggestions for clear and effective writing plus 11 pages of troublesome words and constructions and what to do about them.

FOR DOCTORAL STUDENTS

Balian, Edward S. (1982) *How to Design, Analyze, and Write Doctoral Research.* Lanham, MD: University Press of America.

Blanton, Judith S. (1983) "Midwifing the Dissertation." *Teaching of Psychology, 10 , 74-76.*
  This is an especially useful reference for faculty.

Long, Thomas J., Convey, John J., and Chwalek, Adele R. (1985) *Completing Dissertations in the Behavioral Sciences and Education: A Systematic Guide for Graduate Students*. San Francisco: Jossey-Bass, 210 p.
  A very thorough book with useful advice, a good section on library research.

Madsen, David. (1983) *Successful Dissertations and Theses: A Guide to Graduate Student Research from Proposal to Completion.* San Francisco: Jossey-Bass.

Scheppele, Kim L., and others. (1986) "Writing a Dissertation: Advice from Five Award Winners." *PS, 19 ,* 61-70.
  Five graduate students who have just finished and been given awards by the American Political Science Association give advice to those who will follow them. Straight from the heart and worded in ways that will strike home. Highly recommended.

Steinberg, David. (1981) *How to Complete and Survive a Doctoral Dissertation*. New York: St. Martin's Press, 231 pp.
  Chatty, informal, and very, very helpful, as one can judge from the number of times it is cited in this book.

Appendix B: Additional Sources of Information on Federal Funding

As indicated in the text, some sources of information have been around for quite a while, and one can expect they will continue to be; such are the sources listed here. But the service field changes rapidly and new sources develop in response to perceived needs. The *American Psychological Association's Guide to Research Support* has a section devoted to these sources and will, as new editions of the *Guide* are issued, provide an up-to-date listing of reliable sources. Similarly, the Consortium of Social Science Associations's *Guide to Federal Funding for Social Scientists* will keep you up to date.

Newspapers

The Chronicle of Higher Education, a weekly tabloid, regularly covers the federal scene as it applies to higher education through listings of new funding, deadlines, program activities, and policy changes. It also lists large grants, both foundation and federal. Address: 1255 23rd St. NW, Washington, D.C. 20037.

Education Week, also a weekly tabloid, is oriented more to the elementary and secondary scene. Its regular Washington section has a column "Federal File" that lists activities, and the column "In Federal Agencies" gives a brief paragraph summary of programs and changes announced in the *Federal Register* of interest to schools, including research programs. Neither newspaper does much with requests for proposals. For subscriptions, the address is P.O. Box 1939, Marion, Ohio 43305. Editorial offices are in Suite 775, 1255 23rd St. NW, Washington, D.C. 20037.

Newsletters and Periodicals

Academic Research Information System publishes three *ARIS Funding Messenger* periodicals: *Medical; Social and Natural Sciences;* and *Creative Arts and Humanities.* These give funding data for their respective fields. For information and sample issues write: Academic Research Information Systems, Inc., 2940 16th St., Suite 314, San Francisco, Calif. 94103.

Capitol Publications publishes newsletters in various education fields and includes information on agencies and programs relevant to a range of behavioral sciences. *Federal Grants and Contracts Weekly* deals with grants and non-defense-related contracts. It includes a Grants Alert section on new grants, a listing of requests for proposals (RFPs) available, and grants and RFP calendars as well as the usual general information about agencies. There is a parallel *Health Grants and Contracts Weekly.* In addition, Capitol publishes a number of biweekly newsletters--e.g. *Report on Educational Research, Report on Education of the Disadvantaged, Education of the Handicapped*--which are a mixture of reprinted articles from its daily newsletter *Education Daily* and new material. These contain information about the field and about research programs.

For information and a sample copy write: Education News Services Div., Capitol Publications, Inc., 1300 N. 17th St., Arlington, Va. 22209.

Federal Grants Management Handbook is concerned with grants management more than attaining a grant. It consists of two looseleaf volumes for ease of updating. Volume 1 is a basic grants management guide with sections on obtaining grants, organizing for receipt of grants, their financial administration, complying with "strings attached," and disputes, appeals, and remedies. Volume 2 is a monthly newsletter of current developments. They are published by Grants Management Advisory Service, 1725 K St., NW, Suite 200, Washington, D.C. 20006.

Federal Notes are for grant and contract seekers in educational, biomedical, and scientific fields and are issued twice monthly. They include new programs and legislation. For information and a sample copy write: Federal Notes, P.O. Box 986, Saratoga, Calif. 95070.

Federal Research Report gives information on research-oriented programs issuing grants and contracts. For information and a sample copy write: Federal Research Report, P.O. Box 1067, Blair Station, Silver Spring, Md. 20910.

Grantsmanship Center News is increasingly oriented toward the small nonprofit community agency rather than research. But it retains sections dealing with research programs in the *Federal Register*, as well as listing research application deadlines. Contains other useful information, especially about foundations. Published bimonthly. Many of the center's reprints are highly relevant to the proposal development and grant-getting process and are excellent: "Basic Grantsmanship Library," "Congressional Resources for the Grant Seeker" "How to Use the *Catalog of Domestic Federal Assistance*," "Researching Foundations" (in two parts), "Exploring the World of Corporate Giving." For information, a sample copy, and a price list of reprints, write: The Grantsmanship Center, 1031 S. Grand Ave., Los Angeles, Calif. 90015.

Oryx Press's *Grant Information System* covers grants, both public and private, broken into a broad range of subject areas. Its monthly Faculty Alert Bulletins are divided into six broad subject fields, and it also publishes fund sources in health and allied fields. For information and a sample copy, write: Oryx Press, 3930 E. Camelback Rd., Phoenix, Ariz. 85018.

Appendix C: Sources of Information on Foundation Funding

The Foundation Center
79 Fifth Avenue
New York, NY 10003
212-620-4230

The Foundation Center
Kent H. Smith Library
1442 Hanna Building
1422 Euclid Avenue
Cleveland, OH 44115
216-861-1933

The Foundation Center
1001 Connecticut Avenue NW
Washington, DC 20036
202-331-1400

The Foundation Center
312 Sutter Street
San Francisco, CA 94108
415-397-0902

COOPERATING COLLECTIONS

ALABAMA

Birmingham Public Library
2020 Park Place
Birmingham 35203
205-226-3600

Huntsville-Madison County Public
Library
108 Fountain Circle
P. O. Box 443
Huntsville 35804
205-536-0021

Auburn University at Montgomery
Library
Montgomery 36193-0401
205-271-9649

ALASKA

University of Alaska, Anchorage
Library
3211 Providence Drive
Anchorage 99504
907-786-1848

ARIZONA

Phoenix Public Library
Business and Sciences Department
12 East McDowell Road
Phoenix 85004
602-262-4782

Tucson Public Library
Main Library
200 South Sixth Avenue
Tucson 85701
602-791-4393

ARKANSAS

Westark Community College Library
Grand Avenue at Waldron Road
Fort Smith 72913
501-785-4241

Little Rock Public Library
Reference Department
700 Louisiana Street
Little Rock 72201
501-370-5950

CALIFORNIA

Inyo County Library-Bishop Branch
210 Academy Street
Bishop 93514
619-872-8091

California Community Foundation
Funding Information Center
3580 Wilshire Blvd., Suite 1660
Los Angeles 90010
213-413-4042

Community Foundation for
Monterey County
420 Pacific Street
Monterey 93942
408-375-9712

California Community Foundation
4050 Metropolitan Drive
Orange 92668
714-937-9077

Riverside Public Library
3581 7th Street
Riverside 92501
714-787-7201

California State Library
Reference Services, Rm. 309
914 Capital Mall
Sacramento 95814
916-322-0369

San Diego Community Foundation
625 Broadway, Suite 1015
San Diego 92101
619-239-8815

Orange County Community
Developmental Council
1440 East First Street, 4th Floor
Santa Ana 92701
714-547-6801

Penisula Community Foundation
1204 Burlingame Avenue
Burlingame 94011-0627
415-342-2505

Santa Barbara Public Library
Reference Section
40 East Anapamu
P. O. Box 1019
Santa Barbara 93102
805-962-7653

Santa Monica Public Library
1343 Sixth Street
Santa Monica 90401-1603
213-458-8603

Tuolumne County Library
465 S. Washington Street
Sonora 95370
209-533-5707

North Coast Opportunities, Inc.
101 West Church Street
Ukiah 95482
707-462-1954

COLORADO

Pikes Peak Library District
20 North Cascade Avenue
Colorado Springs 80901
303-473-2080

Denver Public Library
Sociology Division
1357 Broadway
Denver 80203
303-571-2190

CONNECTICUT

Hartford Public Library
Reference Department
500 Main Street
Hartford 06103
203-525-9121

D.A.T.A.
880 Asylum Avenue
Hartford 06105
203-278-2477

D.A.T.A.
25 Science Park
Suite 502
New Haven 06513

Information taken from Read (1986), Appendix G

DELAWARE

Hugh Morris Library
University of Delaware
Newark 19717-5267
302-451-2965

FLORIDA

Volusia County Public Library
  City Island
Daytona Beach 32014
904-252-8374

Jacksonville Public Library
Business, Science and Industry
  Department
122 North Ocean Street
Jacksonville 32202
904-633-3926

Miami-Dade Public Library
  Florida Collection
One Biscayne Boulevard
Miami 33132
305-579-5001

Orlando Public Library
10 North Rosalind
Orlando 32801
305-425-4694

University of West Florida
  John C. Pace Library
Pensacola 32514
904-474-2412

Selby Public Library
1001 Boulevard of the Arts
Sarasota 33577
813-366-7303

Leon County Public Library
Community Funding Resources Center
1940 North Monroe Street
Tallahassee 32303
904-478-2665

Palm Beach County Community
  Foundation
324 Datura Street, Suite 311
West Palm Beach 33401
305-659-6800

GEORGIA

Atlanta-Fulton Public Library
  Ivan Allen Department
1 Margaret Mitchell Square
Atlanta 30303
404-688-4636

HAWAII

Thomas Hale Hamilton Library
  General Reference
University of Hawaii
2550 The Mall
Honolulu 96822
808-948-7214

Community Resource Center
The Hawaiian Foundation
Financial Plaza of the Pacific
111 South King Street
Honolulu 96813
808-525-8548

IDAHO

Caldwell Public Library
1010 Dearborn Street
Caldwell 83605
208-459-3242

ILLINOIS

Belleville Public Library
121 East Washington Street
Belleville 62220
618-234-0441

DuPage Township
300 Briarcliff Road
Bolingbrook 60439
312-759-1317

Donors Forum of Chicago
208 South LaSalle Street
Chicago 60604
312-726-4882

Evanston Public Library
1703 Orrington Avenue
Evanston 60201
312-866-0305

Sangamon State University Library
Shepherd Road
Springfield 62708
217-786-6633

INDIANA

Allen County Public Library
900 Webster Street
Fort Wayne 46802
219-424-7241

Indiana University Northwest Library
3400 Broadway
Gary 46408
219-980-6580

Indianapolis-Marion County Public
  Library
40 East St. Clair Street
Indianapolis 46204
317-269-1733

IOWA

Public Library of Des Moines
100 Locust Street
Des Moines 50308
515-283-4259

KANSAS

Topeka Public Library
  Adult Services Department
1515 West Tenth Street
Topeka 66604
913-233-2040

Wichita Public Library
223 South Main
Wichita 67202
316-262-0611

KENTUCKY

Western Kentucky University
  Division of Library Services
Helm-Cravens Library
Bowling Green 42101
502-745-3951

Louisville Free Public Library
Fourth and York Streets
Louisville 40203
503-223-7201

LOUISIANA

East Baton Rouge Parish Library
  Centroplex Library
120 St. Louis Street
Baton Rouge 70821
504-389-4960

New Orleans Public Library
  Business and Science Division
219 Loyola Avenue
New Orleans 70140
504-596-2583

Shreve Memorial Library
424 Texas Street
Shreveport 71101
318-226-5894

MAINE

University of Southern Maine
Center for Research and
  Advanced Study
246 Deering Avenue
Portland 04102
207-780-4411

MARYLAND

Enoch Pratt Free Library
Special Science and History
  Department
400 Cathedral Street
Baltimore 21201
301-396-5320

MASSACHUSETTS

Associated Grantmakers of Mass.
294 Washington Street
Suite 501
Boston 02108
617-426-2608

Boston Public Library
Copley Square
Boston 02117
617-536-5400

Walpole Public Library
Common Street
Walpole 02081
617-668-5497 ext. 340

Western Massachusetts Funding
Resource Center
Campaign for Human Development
Chancery Annex
73 Chestnut Street
Springfield 01103
413-732-3175 ext. 67

Grants Resource Center
Worcester Public Library
Salem Square
Worcester 01608
617-799-1655

MICHIGAN

Alpena County Library
211 North First Avenue
Alpena 49707
517-356-6188

University of Michigan-Ann Arbor
Reference Department
209 Hatcher Graduate Library
Ann Arbor 48109-1205
313-764-1149

Henry Ford Centennial Library
16301 Michigan Avenue
Dearborn 48126
313-943-2337

Purdy Library
Wayne State University
Detroit 48202
313-577-4040

Michigan State University Libraries
Reference Library
East Lansing 48824
517-353-9184

Farmington Community Library
32737 West 12 Mile Road
Farmington Hills 48018
313-553-0300

University of Michigan-Flint Library
Reference Department
Flint 48503
313-762-3408

Grand Rapids Pubic Library
Sociology & Education Department
Library Plaza
Grand Rapids 49502
616-456-4411

Michigan Technological University
Library
Highway U.S. 41
Houghton 49931
906-487-2507

MINNESOTA

Duluth Public Library
520 Superior Street
Duluth 55802
218-723-3802

Southwest State University Library
Marshall 56258
507-537-7278

Minneapolis Public Library
Sociology Department
300 Nicollet Mall
Minneapolis 55401
612-372-6555

Rochester Public Library
Broadway at First Street, SE
Rochester 55901
507-285-8002

Saint Paul Public Library
90 West Fourth Street
Saint Paul 55102
612-292-6311

MISSISSIPPI

Jackson Metropolitan Library
301 North State Street
Jackson 39201
601-944-1120

MISSOURI

Clearinghouse for Midcontinent
Foundations
University of Missouri, Kansas City
Law School, Suite 1-300
52nd Street and Oak
Kansas City 64113
816-276-1176

Kansas City Public Library
311 East 12th Street
Kansas City 64106
816-221-2685

Metropolitan Association for
Philanthropy, Inc.
5585 Pershing Avenue
Suite 150
St. Louis 63112
314-361-3900

Springfield-Greene County Library
397 East Central Street
Springfield 65801
417-866-4636

MONTANA

Eastern Montana College Library
Reference Department
1500 N. 30th Street
Billings 59101-0298
406-657-2262

Montana State Library
Reference Department
1515 E. 6th Avenue
Helena 59620
406-444-3004

NEBRASKA

University of Nebraska, Lincoln
106 Love Library
Lincoln 68588-0410
402-472-2526

W. Dale Clark Library
Social Sciences Department
215 South 15th Street
Omaha 68102

NEVADA

Las Vegas-Clark County Library
District
1401 East Flamingo Road
Las Vegas 89109
702-733-7810

Washoe County Library
301 South Center Street
Reno 89505
702-785-4190

NEW HAMPSHIRE

The New Hampshire Charitable
Fund
One South Street
Concord 03301
603-225-6641

Littleton Public Library
109 Main Street
Littleton 03561
603-444-5741

NEW JERSEY

Cumberland County Library
800 E. Commerce Street
Bridgeton 08302
609-455-0080

The Support Center
17 Academy Street, Suite 1101
Newark 07102
201-643-5774

County College of Morris Masten
Learning
Resource Center
Route 10 and Center Grove Road
Randolph 07869
201-361-5000 ext. 470

New Jersey State Library
Governmental Reference
185 West State Street
Trenton 08625
609-292-6220

NEW MEXICO

Albuquerque Community Foundation
6400 Uptown Boulevard N.E.
Suite 500-W
Albuquerque 87110
505-883-6240

New Mexico State Library
325 Don Gaspar Street
Santa Fe 87503
505-827-3824

NEW YORK

New York State Library
Cultural Education Center
Humanities Section
Empire State Plaza
Albany 12230
518-474-7645

Bronx Reference Center
New York Public Library
2556 Bainbridge Avenue
Bronx 10458
212-220-6575

Brooklyn in Touch
101 Willoughby Street
Room 1508
Brooklyn 11201
718-237-9300

Buffalo and Erie County Public
  Library
Lafayette Square
Buffalo 14203
716-856-7525

Huntington Public Library
338 Main Street
Huntington 11743
516-427-5165

Levittown Public Library
  Reference Department
One Bluegrass Lane
Levittown 11756
516-731-5728

SUNY/College at Old Westbury
  Library
223 Store Hill Road
Old Westbury 11568
516-876-3201

Plattsburgh Public Library
  Reference Department
15 Oak Street
Plattsburgh 12901
518-563-0921

Adriance Memorial Library
93 Market Street
Poughkeepsie 12601
915-485-4790

Queens Borough Public Library
89-11 Merrick Boulevard
Jamaica 11432
718-990-0700

Rochester Public Library
Business and Social Sciences Division
115 South Avenue
Rochester 14604
716-428-7328

Onondaga County Public Library
335 Montgomery Street
Syracuse 13202
315-473-4491

White Plains Public Library
100 Martine Avenue
White Plains 10601
914-682-4488

NORTH CAROLINA

The Duke Endowment
200 S. Tryon Street, Ste. 1100
Charlotte 28202
704-376-0291

Durham County Library
300 N. Roxboro Street
Durham 27701
919-683-2626

North Carolina State Library
109 East Jones Street
Raleigh 27611
919-733-3270

The Winston-Salem Foundation
229 First Union National Bank Bldg.
Winston-Salem 27101
919-725-2382

NORTH DAKOTA

Western Dakota Grants Resource
  Center
Bismarck Junior College Library
Bismarck 58501
701-224-5450

The Library
North Dakota State University
Fargo 58105
701-237-8876

OHIO

Public Library of Cincinnati and
  Hamilton County
Education Department
800 Vine Street
Cincinnati 45202
513-369-6940

CALLVAC Services, Inc.
370 South Fifth Street
Suite 1
Columbus 43215
614-221-6766

Lima-Allen County Regional
  Planning Commission
212 N. Elizabeth Street
Lima 45801
419-228-1836

Toledo-Lucas County Public Library
Social Science Department
325 Michigan Street
Toledo 43624
419-255-7055 ext. 221

Ohio University-Zanesville
Community Education and
  Development
1425 Newark Road
Zanesville 43701
614-453-0762

OKLAHOMA

Oklahoma City University Library
NW 23rd at North Blackwelder
Oklahoma City 73106
405-521-5072

The Support Center
525 NW Thirteenth Street
Oklahoma City 73106
405-236-8133

Tulsa City-County Library System
400 Civic Center
Tulsa 74103
918-592-7944

OREGON

Library Association of Portland
  Government Documents Room
801 S.W. Tenth Avenue
Portland 97205
503-223-7201

Oregon State Library
State Library Building
Salem 97310
503-378-4243

PENNSYLVANIA

Northampton County Area
  Community College
Learning Resources Center
3835 Green Pond Road
Bethlehem 18017
215-865-5358

Erie County Public Library
3 South Perry Square
Erie 16501
814-452-2333 ext. 54

Dauphin County Library System
  Central Library
101 Walnut Street
Harrisburg 17101
717-234-4961

Lancaster County Public Library
15 North Duke Street
Lancaster 17602
717-394-2651

The Free Library of Philadelphia
Logan Square
Philadelphia 19103
215-686-5423

Hillman Library
University of Pittsburgh
Pittsburgh 15260
412-624-4423

Economic Development Council of
  Northeastern Pennsylvania
1151 Oak Street
Pittston 18640
717-655-5581

James V. Brown Library
12 E. 4th Street
Williamsport 17701
717-326-0536

RHODE ISLAND

Providence Public Library
  Reference Department
150 Empire Street
Providence 02903
401-521-7722

SOUTH CAROLINA

Charleston County Public Library
404 King Street
Charleston 29403
803-723-1645

South Carolina State Library
  Reader Services Department
1500 Senate Street
Columbia 29201
803-758-3138

SOUTH DAKOTA

South Dakota State Library
State Library Building
800 North Illinois Street
Pierre 57501
605-773-3131

Sioux Falls Area Foundation
404 Boyce Greeley Building
321 South Phillips Avenue
Sioux Falls 57102-0781
605-336-7055

TENNESSEE

Knoxville-Knox County Public Library
500 West Church Avenue
Knoxville 37902
615-523-0781

Memphis Shelby County Public Library
1850 Peabody Avenue
Memphis 38104
901-725-8876

Public Library of Nashville and
  Davidson County
8th Avenue and Union Street
Nashville 37203
615-244-4700

TEXAS

Amarillo Area Foundation
1000 Polk
P. O. Box 25569
Amarillo 79105-2569
806-376-4521

The Hogg Foundation for Mental Health
The University of Texas
Austin 78712
512-471-5041

Corpus Christi State University
  Library
6300 Ocean Drive
Corpus Christi 78412
512-991-6810

Dallas Public Library
  Grants Information Service
1515 Young Street
Dallas 75201
214-749-4100

Pan American University
  Learning Resource Center
1201 W. University Drive
Edinburg 78539
512-381-3304

El Paso Community Foundation
El Paso National Bank Building
Suite 1616
El Paso 79901
915-533-4020

Funding Information Center
Texas Christian University Library
Ft. Worth 76129
817-921-7664

Houston Public Library
Bibliographic & Information Center
500 McKinney Avenue
Houston 77002
713-224-5441 ext. 265

Funding Information Library
507 Brooklyn
San Antonio 78215
512-227-4333

UTAH

Salt Lake City Public Library
Business and Science Department
209 East Fifth South
Salt Lake City 84111
801-363-5733

VERMONT

State of Vermont Department
  of Libraries
Reference Services Unit
111 State Street
Montpelier 05602
802-828-3261

VIRGINIA

Grants Resources Library
Hampton City Hall
22 Lincoln Street, Ninth Floor
Hampton 23669
804-727-6496

Richmond Public Library
Business, Science, & Technology
  Department
101 East Franklin Street
Richmond 23219
804-780-8223

WASHINGTON

Seattle Public Library
1000 Fourth Avenue
Seattle 98104
206-625-4881

Spokane Public Library
  Funding Information Center
West 906 Main Avenue
Spokane 99201
509-838-3361

WEST VIRGINIA

Kanawha County Public Library
123 Capitol Street
Charleston 25301
304-343-4646

WISCONSIN

Marquette University Memorial
  Library
1415 West Wisconsin Avenue
Milwaukee 53233
414-224-1515

University of Wisconsin-Madison
  Memorial Library
728 State Street
Madison 53706
608-262-3647

Society for Nonprofit
  Organizations
6314 Odana Road
Suite One
Madison 53719
608-274-9777

WYOMING

Laramie County Community
  College Library
1400 East College Drive
Cheyenne 82007
307-634-5853

PUERTO RICO

Universidad del Sagrado Corazon
M.M.T. Guevarra Library
Correo Calle Loiza
Santurce 00914
809-728-1515 ext. 274

VIRGIN ISLANDS

College of the Virgin Islands Library
Saint Thomas
U. S. Virgin Islands 00801
809-774-9200 ext. 487

CANADA

Canadian Center for Philanthropy
3080 Yonge Street
Suite 4080
Toronto, Ontario M4N3N1
416-484-4118

ENGLAND

Charities Aid Foundation
14 Bloomsbury Square
London WCIA 2LP
01-430-1798

Glossary

This glossary will introduce a few new terms, but most are covered in the previous material.

The glossary can also serve as a good learning device in that a quick skimming of the terms will show you ones you may have missed in the first reading or did not retain.

Allocation: That part of the appropriation designated for a particular activity or program in an agency.

Appropriation: When funds previously authorized are approved by Congress for spending by the agency for a fiscal year, the agency has its year's appropriation. ˙ppropriations may be equal to, but usually are less than, the maximum set in the authorizing legislation for a given fiscal year. The 1986 appropriation would be the funds to be spent between 10/1/85 and 9/30/86.

Approved but not funded: The project was approved for funding by reviewers, but funds ran out before it was reached on the priority list. See **priority score.**

Authorization: Congress must pass authorizing legislation before it can approve an appropriation for a program. The authorizing legislation describes the program, what it will do, who can apply, what agency will be responsible for the program, and the maximum appropriation for each fiscal year during the authorization period.

Bidders' list: The list of researchers and/or organizations to be contacted for research in certain areas which is maintained by some federal agencies. Getting on certain lists requires particular experience or expertise; for others, one need only request inclusion.

Continuation project: A multiyear project for which funds have been committed only for the current fiscal year. Find out the costs of continuation projects for a program and subtract them from the current year's allocation to find the money available for new commitments.

Continuing resolution: Congress does not always pass the appropriation legislation before the end of the fiscal year. In order to provide funds for an agency after the beginning of the new fiscal year, it passes a continuing resolution, which typically allows the agency to spend funds to the *lower* of the appropriation levels approved by either House or Senate.

Contract: An agreement to provide a service or a product for the stipulated remuneration. Fixed-price contracts stipulate a firm price for which the product or service must be provided even if it costs more. Cost-plus contracts allow the charging of costs plus a fee or profit. Contract funds availability is announced in *Commerce Business Daily* or an RFP.

Cooperative agreement: An arrangement whereby a project is conducted in cooperation with federal agency staff who agree to undertake certain responsibilities in the project.

Cost sharing: You or your organization agrees to pay a share of the project costs.

Demonstration grant: Funds allocated to develop a prototype service or product that is intended to serve as an example for others.

Development grant: Funds to use an already proven method to create a product or service.

Differential overhead: The difference between the institution's approved indirect cost rate and that actually charged. These indirect costs are not charged to the government even though the organization is legally entitled to do so and may be used for cost sharing.

Directed research: Research that is to address priorities specified by the funder. Contrasts with unsolicited research, which may be on any topic relevant to the program. Congress tends to prefer funding directed research on the assumption that there will be more results if efforts are targeted rather than random.

Discretionary funds: Funds that may be spent at the discretion of an administrator. Usually used to provide a special emphasis to a program deemed important by that person.

Entitlement programs: Programs that dispense funds to any qualified person in accordance with set criteria--e.g. Medicare, veteran's benefits. Their significance for research is that once eligibility requirements are established, they cannot be controlled by the appropriation process. This open-ended characteristic may result in their becoming so large that discretionary funds must be cut, and that is always bad news for research funding.

Evaluation: Determination of the effectiveness or usefulness of a service or product for intended purposes. Usually also involves means of improving it and the discovery of unintended effects.

Extension: Allows additional time to complete the original scope of work and to continue drawing on the original allotment of funds. No-cost extensions provide no additional funds and are generally granted provided there are good reasons for failure to meet the original termination date and the request for extension is made early enough to be processed before the original grant period ends.

Extramural research: Research conducted by other than federal personnel.

Field-initiated research: See **unsolicited proposals.**

Fiscal year (FY): The business year, in contrast to the calendar year. The federal fiscal year begins 10/1 and ends 9/30. Years are designated by the ending date: FY 88 ends 9/30/88.

Forward funding: Funds are provided for a multiyear project in their entirety from the outset, in contrast to the usual process of being refunded each year. It eliminates continuation costs but means fewer projects can be funded the first few years forward funding is practiced.

Funding cycle: The cycle in which proposals are considered for funding, in which deadlines at certain times of the year are followed by review meetings, and so on. Projects received too late for one funding cycle are held over until the next one.

Grant: Funds provided by an agency to help an organization or individual to carry out an activity that the recipient has proposed. Contrasts with a contract, where the activity is proposed by the agency. With a grant, the agency may carry all or part of the costs. Unused funds return to the agency.

Guidelines: The part of a program description that describes how the program will be administered and the basis on which applications will be considered. They should be followed carefully if a proposal is to be seriously considered.

Impoundment: Refusal of the administration to spend appropriated funds. This may be for purposes of delay until something can be clarified, or to provide time for Congress to approve a request for rescission.

Indirect costs: Costs for services, equipment, facilities, and so forth that are not charged to a project directly, but as a percentage of the grant or contract funds.

In-kind contribution: Contributed services, equipment or facility use, and so on for which no charge is made to the project. These are usually contributions from indirect costs.

Intramural research: Research done by federal employees. Contrasts with **extramural research.**

Overhead: Another name for indirect costs.

anel: A group of peer reviewers assembled for purposes of judging roposals. ¯nel members are usually chosen to represent different kinds of expertise. They usually meet to discuss the proposals before assigning final ratings.

Peer review: Judging of proposals by individuals who are nonfederal researchers.

Person-year: The cost of a professional person working full-time on a project for a year, including all indirect and support costs (secretarial, supplies, and so on).

Preliminary proposal: Either a draft of a proposal used to determine an agency's interest in your idea and to get suggestions or the first application in a two-stage judging process. The latter is a brief presentation of what the full proposal would look like. Enables the agency to pick those proposals it would like to see in fully developed form in the second stage of judging.

Principal investigator (PI), project director: The individual who will direct the project and who is designated by the institution as responsible for completing it as agreed to.

Prior approval: The researcher must obtain approval from the funding agency in advance for issuing large subcontracts, for moving funds from one category to another in amounts larger than those previously agreed to, for an extension of time, for charging funds spent prior to formal receipt of the contract or grant, and so on.

Priority score: A score that determines the ranking of the proposal for funding. Projects are usually funded according to their rank until funds are exhausted. The score is derived from the reviewers' ratings.

Regulation: Published rules by which an agency agrees to implement a program authorized by Congress. Usually published in preliminary form for comment in the *Federal Register*. After comments are received, regulations are revised as deemed appropriate and published in final form in the same publication.

Rescission: A request to Congress to cancel a previous appropriation; follows an impoundment. Initiated by the administration, it must be approved by Congress within 45 days to be effective.

RFA, Request for Applications: Announces a new grant program or the current funding cycle in an old one and requests submission of applications. Usually used to announce availability of funds on a particular topic.

RFP, Request for Proposal: Announces the intent to award a contract and specifies the service or product to be delivered, the criteria to be used, applicant qualifications, person-years anticipated, and deadline. Published in *Commerce Business Daily.*

Small-grant program: Typically a program for new researchers or doctoral students that has a maximum grant size and length.

Sole-source contract: When an agency decides that the service or product can be obtained only from a certain contractor, it gets the contracting office to agree to a sole-source contract, which is not sent out for bids. Obviously it usually requires considerable justification to circumvent the bidding process.

Targeted research: Same as **directed research.**

Unsolicited proposals: Proposals submitted to an agency that are not in response to a particular program or contract announcement but are research projects the proposers believe the agency ought to be interested in funding. Usually responsive to a funding announcement in a broad subject area.

References

Allen, Ernest M. (1960) "Why Are Research Grant Applications Disapproved?" *Science, 132,* 1532-1534.

Allison, G. T. (1971) *Essence of Decision: Explaining the Cuban Missile Crisis.* Boston: Little, Brown.

Backer, Thomas. (1977) *A Directory of Information on Tests.* ERIC TM Report 62-1977. Princeton, NJ: ERIC Clearinghouse on Tests, Measurement and Evaluation, Educational Testing Service.

Bauer, David G. (1984) *The "How To" Grants Manual.* New York: Macmillan.

Becker, Howard S. (1986) *Writing for Social Scientists.* Chicago: University of Chicago Press.

Blanton, Judith S. (1983) "Midwifing the Dissertation." *Teaching of Psychology, 10,* 74-76.

Bogdan, Robert. (1971) *A Forgotten Organizational Type.* Unpublished doctoral dissertation, Syracuse University.

Bogdan, Robert. (1985) "The Principal's Role in Mainstreaming." In Douglas Biklen (Ed.), *The Complete School.* New York: Teachers College Press.

Bronfenbrenner, Urie. (1977) "Toward an Experimental Ecology of Human Development." *American Psychologist, 32,* 513-531.

Burke, Marti (Ed.). (1986) *Addendum to APA's Guide to Research Support, 2nd Edition.* Washington, DC: American Psychological Association.

Campbell, Donald T. (1977) "Descriptive Epistemology: Psychological, Sociological and Evolutionary." Preliminary draft of the William James Lectures, Harvard University.

Campbell, Donald T., and Stanley, Julian C. (1963) "Experimental Designs for Research on Teaching." In N. L. Gage (Ed.), *Handbook of Research on Teaching.* Chicago: Rand McNally. (Also available from the publisher as a monograph under the chapter title.)

Cavin, Janis I. (1984) *Understanding the Federal Proposal Review Process.* Washington, DC: American Association of State Colleges and Universities.

Chalfant, James C., and Nitzman, Margaret. (1965) "Shortcomings of Grant Applications to the Handicapped Children Research Program." *Exceptional Children, 32,* 180-185.

Chisholm, Donald. (1986) "On Writing a Dissertation." *PS, 19* (Winter), 65-69.

Cohen, J. (1977) *Statistical Power Analysis for the Behavioral Sciences* (rev. ed.). New York: Academic Press.

Cook, Desmond L. (1979) *Program Evaluation and Review Technique.* Lanham, MD: University Press of America.

Cook, Tom, and Campbell, Donald T. (1979) *Quasi-Experimentation.* Chicago: Rand McNally.

Cooper, Harris, and Rosenthal, Robert. (1980) "Statistical Versus Traditional Procedures for Summarizing Research Findings." *Psychological Bulletin, 87,* 442-449.

Crano, William D. (1986) "Research Methodology: The Interaction of Substance with Investigative Form." In Vivian Parker Makosky (Ed.), *The G. Stanley Hall Lecture Series* (vol. 6). Washington, DC: American Psychological Association.

Cronbach, Lee J. (1982) *Designing Evaluations of Educational and Social Programs.* San Francisco: Jossey-Bass.

Cronbach, Lee J. (1984) *Essentials of Psychological Testing* (4th ed.). New York: Harper & Row.

Cuca, Janet M. (1986) "The National Institutes of Health: Extramural Funding and the Peer Review Process." In Susan Quarles (Ed.), *Guide to Federal Funding for Social Scientists*. New York: Russell Sage Foundation.

Day, Robert A. (1983) *How to Write and Publish a Scientific Paper.* Philadelphia: ISI Press.

Derboort, John. (1987) *Social Support and the Renal Patient: A Quantitative and Qualitative Exploration of a Life Transition.* Unpublished doctoral dissertation, Syracuse University.

Dusek, E. Ralph, et al. (Eds.). (1984) *American Psychological Association's Guide to Research Support* (2nd ed.). Washington, DC: American Psychological Association.

Dycus, Robert M. (1975) "Relative Effectiveness of Proposal Approaches--An Experimental Study." *Technical Communications,* 22 (1), 9-10.

Ebel, Robert L., and Frisbie, David A. (1986) *Essentials of Educational Measurement* (4th ed.). Englewood Cliffs, NJ: Prentice-Hall.

Einstein, A., and Infeld, L. (1938) *The Evolution of Physics.* New York: Simon & Schuster.

Eisenberg, N., and Lennon, R. (1983) "Sex Differences in Empathy and Related Capacities." *Psychological Bulletin*, 94, 100-131.

Ezell, Susan (Ed.). (1981) *Proposal Writer's Swipe File III.* Washington, DC: Taft Corporation. See also Brodsky, Jean in Appendix A.

Feyerabend, P. (1975) *Against Method.* London: Verso.

Getzels, J. W. (1982) "The Problem of the Problem." In R. M. Hogarth (Ed.), *Question Framing and Response Consistency.* New Directions for Methodology of Social and Behavioral Science, No. 11. San Francisco: Jossey-Bass.

Glass, Gene V. (1976) "Primary, Secondary and Meta-Analysis." *Educational Researcher*, 5, 3-8.

Glass, Gene V., McGaw, Barry, and Smith, Mary Lee. (1981) *Meta-Analysis in Social Research.* Beverly Hills, CA: Sage Publications.

Grant, Ruth. (1986) "Advice to Dissertation Writers." *PS*, 19 (Winter), 64-65.

Guy, W., Gross, M., and Dennis, H. (1967) "An Alternative to Double Blind Procedure." *American Journal of Psychiatry*, 123, 1505-1512.

Harris, Kathleen. (1985) "Effect of Prior Experience on Decisions to Submit Proposals." *SRA Journal*, 16, 29-35.

Hauser-Cram, Penny. (1983) "Some Cautions in Synthesizing Research Studies." *Educational Evaluation and Policy Analysis*, 5, 155-162.

Hays, William. (1981) *Statistics for the Social Sciences* (3rd ed.). New York: Holt, Rinehart and Winston.

Hedges, Larry W., and Olkin, Ingram. (1985) *Statistical Methods for Meta-Analysis.* Orlando, FL: Academic Press.

Horst, Donald T., Tallmadge, Kasten, and Wood, Christine. (1975) *A Practical Guide to Measuring Project Impact on Student Achievement.* Los Altos, CA: RMC Research Corporation. (ERIC Document No. ED 106 376)

Howarth, Cynthia Ilana. (1980) "Factors Which Discriminate Between Technically Acceptable and Technically Unacceptable Research Proposals." *Dissertation Abstracts International*, Order No. 8025456.

Hunter, J. E., Schmidt, F. L., and Jackson, G. B. (1982) *Meta-Analysis: Cumulating Research Findings Across Studies.* Beverly Hills, CA: Sage Publications.

Joint Committee on Standards for Educational Evaluation. (1981) *Standards for Evaluations of Educational Programs, Projects, and Materials. New York: McGraw-Hill.*

Kaufman, Roger A. (1979) *Needs Assessment: A Concept and Application.* Englewood Cliffs, NJ: Educational Technology Publications.

Kounin, Jacob, S. (1970) *Discipline and Group Management in Classrooms.* New York: Holt, Rinehart and Winston.

Kounin, Jacob S., Friesen, Wallace V., and Norton, A. Evangeline. (1966) "Managing Emotionally Disturbed Children in Regular Classrooms." *Journal of Educational Psychology, 57,* 1-13.

Kounin, Jacob S., and Obradovic, Sylvia. (1968) "Managing Emotionally Disturbed Children in Regular Classrooms: A Replication and Extension." *Journal of Special Education, 2,* 129-135.

Krathwohl, David R. (1985) *Social and Behavioral Science Research: A New Framework for Conceptualizing, Implementing, and Evaluating Research Studies.* San Francisco: Jossey-Bass.

Levine, Felice J. (1986) "Social and Behavioral Science Support at NSF." In Susan Quarles (Ed.), *Guide to Federal Funding for Social Scientists* · New York: Russell Sage Foundation.

Light, Richard J. (1979) "Capitalizing on Variation: How Conflicting Research Findings Can Be Helpful for Policy." *Educational Researcher, 8* (8), 3-8.

Light, Richard J., and Pillemer, David. (1984) *Summing Up: The Science of Reviewing Research* . Cambridge, MA: Harvard University Press.

Long, Thomas J., Convey, John J., and Chwalek, Adele R. (1985) *Completing Dissertations in the Behavioral Sciences and Education: A Systematic Guide for Graduate Students.* San Francisco: Jossey-Bass.

Lowman, Robert P. and Dusek, E. Ralph (1984) "Federal Research Support: A Primer for Proposal Writers." In E. Ralph Dusek et al. (Eds.), *The American Psychological Association's Guide to Research Support* (2nd ed.). Washington, DC: American Psychological Association.

Margolin, Judith B. (1983) *The Individual's Guide to Grants.* New York: Plenum Press.

Mitchell, James V., Jr. (1985) *The Ninth Mental Measurements Yearbook.* Lincoln: University of Nebraska Press.

Morrill, William and Duby, Martin. (1986) "Academics and Contract Research." In Susan Quarles (Ed.), *Guide to Federal Funding for Social Scientists* . New York: Russell Sage Foundation.

Mullen, Brian, and Rosenthal, Robert. (1985) *BASIC Meta-Analysis: Procedures and Programs.* Hillsdale, NJ: Lawrence Erlbaum Associates.

Quarles, Susan (Ed.). (1986) *Guide to Federal Funding for Social Scientists.* New York: Russell Sage Foundation.

Quarles, Susan, and Cianci, Salvatore. (1986) "The ADAMHA Grant Review Process." In Susan Quarles (Ed.), *Guide to Federal Funding for Social Scientists*. New York: Russell Sage Foundation.

Read, Patricia E. (Ed.) (1986) *Foundation Fundamentals: A Research Guide for Grantseekers* (3rd ed.). New York: Foundation Center.

Rogers, Theresa F., et al. (1970) *Small Grant Projects of the Regional Research Program: Final Report*. New York: Bureau of Applied Social Research, Columbia University. (ERIC Document No. ED 054 074)

Romiszowski, A. J. (1981) *Designing Instructional Systems.* London: Kogan Page; New York: Nicholas Publishing.

Rosenthal, Robert. (1969) "Interpersonal Expectations: Effect on Experimenters' Hypothesis." In R. Rosenthal and R. Rosnow (Eds.), *Artifact in Behavioral Research*. New York: Academic Press.

Rosenthal, Robert. (1978) "Combining Results of Independent Studies." *Psychological Bulletin, 85,* 185-193.

Rosenthal, Robert. (1979) "The 'File Drawer' Problem and Tolerance for Negative Results." *Psychological Bulletin, 86,* 638-641.

Rosenthal, Robert. (1984) *Meta-Analytic Procedures for Social Research.* Beverly Hills, CA: Sage Publications.

Rosenthal, Robert, and Rubin, D. (1980) "Summarizing 345 Studies of Interpersonal Expectancy Effects." In Robert Rosenthal (Ed.), *Quantitative Assessment of Research Domains.* New Directions for Methodology of Behavioral Science, No. 5. San Francisco: Jossey-Bass.

Rosner, Stanley, and Abt, Lawrence. (1970) *The Creative Experience*. New York: Grossman Publishers.

Rossi, P. H., and Lyall, K. C. (1976) *Reforming Public Welfare: A Critique of the Negative Income Tax Experiment.* New York: Russell Sage Foundation.

Rowe, Mary B. (1974) "Relation of Wait-Time and Rewards to the Development of Language, Logic and Fate Control. Part I: Wait-Time." *Journal of Research in Science Teaching, 11,* 81-94.

Shelly, Anne, and Sibert, Ernest. (1985) *The QUALOG User's Manual (DEC-10 Version).* Technical Report No. CIS-85-2. Syracuse, NY: School of Computer and Information Science, Syracuse University.

Skinner, B. F. (1954) "The Science of Learning and the Art of Teaching." *Harvard Educational Review*, 24, 86-97.

Skinner, B. F. (1957) *Verbal Behavior.* New York: Appleton-Century-Crofts.

Slovic, P., Fischhoff, B., and Lichtenstein, S. (1982) "Response Mode, Framing, and Information-Processing Effects in Risk Assessment." In Robin M. Hogarth (Ed.), *Question Framing and Response Consistency.* New Directions for Methodology of Social and Behavioral Science, No. 11. San Francisco: Jossey-Bass.

Smith, Gerald R. (1965) "How to Write a Project Proposal." *Nation's Schools*, 76, 33-35, 57.

Smith, Mary Lee, and Glass, Gene V. (1977) "Meta-Analysis of Psychotherapy Outcome Studies." *American Psychologist*, 32, 752-760.

Smith, Mary Lee, Glass, Gene V., and Miller, T. I. (1980) *Benefits of Psychotherapy.* Baltimore, MD: Johns Hopkins University Press.

Steinberg, David. (1981) *How to Complete and Survive a Doctoral Dissertation.* New York: St. Martin's Press.

Tversky, A., and Kahneman, D. (1982) "The Framing of Decisions and the Psychology of Choice." In Robin M. Hogarth (Ed.), *Question Framing and Response Consistency.* New Directions for Methodology of Social and Behavioral Science, No. 11. San Francisco: Jossey-Bass.

Wax, Murray L., and Wax, Rosalie H. (1980) "Fieldwork and the Research Process." *Anthropology and Education Quarterly*, 9, 29-37. St. Louis, MO: Washington University.

Webb, E. J., Campbell, D. T., Schwartz, R. D., and Sechrest, L. (1966) Unobtrusive Measures. Chicago: Rand McNally.

Wessell, Nils. (1975) "Foundation-University Relations." *SRA Journal*, 6, 17-23.

Woodbury, Marda L. (1982) *A Guide to Sources of Educational Information* (2nd ed.). Arlington, VA: Information Resources Press.

Zimbardo, Philip, Andersen, S. M., and Kabat, L. G. (1981) "Induced Hearing Deficit Generates Experimental Paranoia." *Science, 212*, 1529-1531.

Index